# The Pleasures of Exile

*by*

George Lamming

Foreword by Sandra Pouchet Paquet

*Ann Arbor Paperbacks*

THE UNIVERSITY OF MICHIGAN PRESS

First edition as an Ann Arbor Paperback 1992
Foreword copyright © by the University of Michigan 1992
Text copyright © 1960 by George Lamming
All rights reserved
Published in the United States of America by
The University of Michigan Press
Manufactured in the United States of America

2004  2003  2002  2001    8  7  6  5

*A CIP record for this book is available from the British Library.*

**Library of Congress Cataloging-in-Publication Data**

Lamming, George, 1927–
    The pleasures of exile / by George Lamming.
        p.   cm. — (Ann Arbor paperbacks)
    ISBN 0-472-09466-1 (alk. paper). — ISBN 0-472-06466-5 (pbk. :
    alk. paper)
        1. Lamming, George, 1927–  .  2. Novelists, Barbadian—20th
    century—Biography.  3. Caribbean Area—Intellectual life—20th
    century.  4. Caribbean Area in literature.  5. Colonies in
    literature.  6. Exiles in literature.  I. Title.
    PR9230.9.L25Z466  1992
    813—dc20
    [B]                                                    92-27443
                                                              CIP

# The Pleasures of Exile

*Also by George Lamming*

FOR

THE CHILDREN

*Gordon and Natasha*

AND FOR

*Biddy Crozier, C. L. R. James*

AND

*Ethel de Keyser*

WHOSE FRIENDSHIP WILL NEVER BE

MEASURED OR FORGOTTEN

# FOREWORD

•

The American edition of George Lamming's first novel, *In the Castle of My Skin* (1953), was introduced by Richard Wright. Wright's introduction was eloquent and passionate in its exhortation:

> One feels not so much alone when, from a distant witness, supporting evidence comes to buttress one's own testimony. And the voice I now bid you hear is sounding in Lamming's *In the Castle of My Skin*. (vi)

The novel was very well received and has held its own as a classic of modern Black writing. In the years that followed, Lamming published five novels and *The Pleasures of Exile* (1960), a seminal work of self-inquiry and cultural assessment in the context of Caribbean life.[1] These notes of a native son engage powerfully and directly with the contrary legacies affecting the social, political, and artistic dimensions of Black writing in our time. Their geography ranges from the Caribbean to Europe, West Africa, and the United States. They have relevance for students of Caribbean literature and Black cultural studies everywhere and illuminate contemporary literary and philosophical debates around minority discourse and postcolonial writing.

*The Pleasures of Exile* is a series of interrelated essays on cultural politics incorporating Lamming's memoirs of his life as a writer in self-imposed exile in England and of his travels in the Caribbean, West Africa, and the United States. It includes extended dialogues with Shakespeare's *The Tempest*, C. L. R. James's *The Black Jacobins*, and Lamming's own fiction and poetry. This text-based discourse locates the author and the reader in a specific intellectual and cultural domain, but Lamming's frame of reference includes alternative cultural contexts. Like Said's traveler on a ceaseless quest for knowledge and freedom, Lamming occupies different geographical and cultural spaces, uses different idioms, assumes a variety of disguises, masks, and rhetorics ("Identity" 18) in a shifting combination of playfulness and seriousness, irony and commitment. *The Pleasures of Exile* anticipates the postcolonial critic's preoccupation with the politics of migration, cultural hybridity, and the prerogatives of minority discourse. Beyond this, the politicized, self-celebrating subjectivity of the author as traveling writer and resistant colonial subject clarifies issues around the mediation of literary production as a national enterprise in postcolonial discourse. In *The Pleasures of Exile*, Lamming conjures up a specific subjectivity—his own—as evidence and example of a wide range of physical, intellectual, psychological, and cultural responses to colonialism. The text is self-consciously rendered as an alternative discourse with an ideological bias specific to the author's experience as colonial subject. And it calls attention to its own artfully rendered ideological bias as a part of the dynamic process of cultural production and consumption in a period of decolonization.[2]

As intellectual history, *The Pleasures of Exile* is specific to the colonial Caribbean; it also illuminates the coercive, transgressive processes of meaning production in colonial societies everywhere. Underlying the text is a theory of language, discourse, and representation that transforms the author as colonial subject and consumer of British intellectual and cultural history into a self-conscious producer of alternative discourses. Lamming calls attention to the performative function of the text, to its autobiographical framework and its dialogic intent. His goal is "the dismantling of a colonial structure of awareness" (*Pleasures*, 36). To this end, he enters into dialogue with the cultural assumptions of classic texts of imperialism and decolonization and, in the process, creates a counterdiscourse of his own around his lived experience as a migrating writer in the country that colonized his history. With the assumed authority of a transgressive cultural presence, he critiques British cultural institutions from Shakespeare to the Institute of Contemporary Arts, the British Broadcasting Corporation (BBC), the *Times Literary Supplement*, and the *Spectator*. He names an alternative hierarchy of values that is rooted in the Caribbean of the Haitian ceremony of the Souls, C. L. R. James's *The Black Jacobins*, his own childhood, and a community of writers from the colonial Caribbean.

Anticipating challenges to his alternative discourse, Lamming makes play with assumptions of cultural authority as an artifice to which he, and others like him, are also entitled.

It will not help to say that I am wrong in the parallels which I have set out to interpret; for I shall reply that my mistake, lived and deeply felt by millions of men like me—proves the positive value of error. It is a value which you must learn. (13)

His dissenting voice is personal and collective.[3] As colonial subject, Lamming offers himself as a representative text to be read and as a privileged interpreter of his own historical moment. The form and value of his organizing and legitimizing presence in the text lies in the relationship between self-reflection and the performance of critical reading. He is observer of his own experience and of a wide range of experience within his cultural domain as colonial subject. Self acquires meaning and value as part of a pattern of Caribbean migration, Caribbean writing, colonial servitude, and a tradition of resistance and revolt. The controlling "I" of this multivoiced text is a plurality of texts, generating a multiplicity of meanings that determines the text's shifting value in and out of time as method and document of cultural and intellectual history.

The very title of the text, *The Pleasures of Exile*, suggests the paradox and ambiguity of spatial and psychic disjunction wrought by the whole etiology of the Caribbean as a colonial enterprise that took on a life of its own as a distinct cultural entity, while still subordinate to, and dependent on, the discourses of empire for self-definition. The pleasure of the text lies in its play on the paradoxical and unorthodox.[4] Exile is a site of both alienation and reconnection.[5]

This may be the dilemma of the West Indian writer abroad; that he hungers for nourishment from a soil which he (as an ordinary citizen) could not at present endure. The pleasure and the paradox of my own exile is that I belong wherever I am. My role, it seems, has rather to do with time and change than with the geography of circumstances; and yet there is always an acre of ground in the New World which keeps growing echoes in my head. I can only hope that these echoes do not die before my work comes to an end. (50)

The writer in exile is the subject and vehicle of Caribbean cultural and intellectual history here; the value of his individual life is embedded in a productive, transformational relationship to the Caribbean persona as imperial fiction. Cultural ambiguity is evidence of both cultural resistance and synthesis.[6] The writer as traveler and expatriate links his destiny to the circumstances of his birth and his history as a necessary beginning. The ideological "I," distinctly committed to the new world of the Caribbean as a decolonized space, takes precedence as the foundation of self and discourse.

> . . . I do believe that what a person thinks is very much determined by the way that person sees. This book is really no more than a report of one man's way of seeing, using certain facts of experience as evidence and a guide. (56)

Perspective is expressive of resistance, commitment, and self-celebrating creativity. It emphasizes the substance and method of the writer's calculated decentering of colonial discourse as the exclusive privilege of British intellectuals and institutions. In "What the Twilight Says: An Overture," Derek Walcott writes about "the learning of looking" that restores the subject colonial writer to the original space of his birth and his personal history as a necessary beginning.

> My generation had looked at life with black skins and blue eyes, but only our own painful, strenuous looking, the learning of looking, could find meaning in the life around us, only our own strenuous hearing, could make sense of the sounds we made. (9)

In Richard Wright's "Blueprint for Negro Writing," perspective is a theory about the meaning, structure, and direction of the modern world, a theory the writer fashions for himself when he has looked and brooded hard and long at the circumstances of his race in relation to subject peoples everywhere: "It is that fixed point in intellectal space where a writer stands to view the struggles, hopes, and sufferings of his people" (400).

In *The Pleasures of Exile*, perspective is demystified as an intellectual process that resituates the colonial writer as an active agent of decolonization. Part of the text's message is its form. Lamming makes his way of seeing the subject and method of the text. He reconstitutes the idiosyncrasies of his writerly disposition, chance encounters, and unusual events as representative of the sociocultural processes of colonialism in his own time. Each fragment, each shift in the dialogic mode of discourse, each new combination of description, reflection, and analysis, reveals or confirms some facet of the author's personal experience as evidence and example of the cultural conditioning of British colonialism and his commitment to dismantling "the colonial structure of awareness which has determined West Indian values" (36). The discursive space of the text is a self-authorizing, self-interrogating space that rejects the cultural authority of the Institute of Contemporary Arts, the BBC, the *Times Literary Supplement*, or the *Spectator* over the apportionment of value in the Caribbean and in the world.

Autobiography might seem incidental in such a politically charged text, yet it is fundamental to the occasional nature of the text and to the task of dismantling a "colonial structure of awareness" as Lamming conceptualizes it. There is no troubling delay between the moment of critique and the activity of political resistance. Lamming calls attention to the autobiographical framework of the text in the titles of chapters, such as "The Occasion for Speaking," "Evidence and Example," and "A Way of Seeing." He represents himself as both witness to and participant in a great collective movement. He constructs the prototypical paradigm of the colonial exile around his own high degree of historical awareness and resistant consciousness as a Caribbean writer. The author as narrator and subject of the text is a highly visible and audible presence. The narrating "I" is authoritative, combative, and judgmental and is identified with the author quite explicitly. Self-imaging is skewed purposefully to personal reminiscences as method and substance of a self-authorizing Caribbean intellectual history: "In order to take you on the inside of what I know, I shall have to draw on what an older man would justly call his reminiscences" (24). Self-focus enhances rather than diminishes authority; it serves to establish the author's credibility in an original cultural space of his own creation.

The autobiographical framework of *The Pleasures of Exile*, with its calculated historical specificity, anticipates C. L. R. James's use of autobiography as an intellectual and cultural framework in *Beyond a Boundary* (1963). "The autobiographical framework shows the ideas more or less in the sequence that they developed in relation to the events, the facts and the personalities which prompted them" (*Beyond*, Preface). In both *The Pleasures of Exile* and *Beyond a Boundary*, the autobiographical framework grounds intellectual and cultural history in an experience that is lived passionately. Self is problematized, but the performative function of the text remains stable. Deeply interactive with the anti-imperialist imperative of Caribbean nationhood, the author as colonial subject turns self-analysis into a method of observation, representation, and cultural assessment. His writerly disposition becomes an index of the defects and possibilities of his historical moment.

In *The Pleasures of Exile*, Lamming locates himself in autobiographical time and space as a Caribbean writer in self-imposed
exile in London at the age of thirty-two (50) without committing
himself to an account of his life in England. The discursive space of
the text shifts continually from multiple sites of marginality—London, Africa, the Caribbean, and North America—contesting old no-
tions of self and story and destabilizing generic margins (Smith 21).
Yet Lamming struggles to stay rooted in his original space, as the
activating dynamic of his writerly resistance. His voluntary exile is
not the alienation of "the neurotic intellectual," alone and rudderless (*Pleasures*, 152). He identifies with a historically aware resistant community of creative writers, scholars, and activists from the
Caribbean and the greater Americas, "that started as an alternative to the old and privileged Prospero, too old and too privileged to
pay attention to the needs of his own native Calibans" (152). His
dialogue with C. L. R. James, identified as an inspirational fellow-
traveler, models his ideal of intellectual community.

> There was neither master nor slave, but two West Indians
> sprung from two different islands of the Caribbean, separated by
> some twenty-five years, talking from two different generations,
> talking always about their world, and talking, therefore, about a
> world infinitely wider than their islands; for the new world of the
> Caribbean is, in the time sense of the world, the Twentieth Cen-
> tury. (152)

The two share a perspective but see differently. The colonizing imperative of the teacher as master is superseded by conversation
among equals.

Throughout his extended dialogue with James's *The Black
Jacobins*, Lamming's persona identifies himself with a tradition of
resistance and lays claim to the Haitian revolution as a facet of his
New-World-African-Caribbean identity on behalf of the whole Caribbean. In West Africa and in the United States, the authorial
persona is the traveling colonial who measures the meaning of his
condition in alternative contexts for self-definition. Whether he is
covering the funeral of King George VI for the BBC, driving from
Kumasi to Zaria, or exploring Harlem, there is a pronounced sense
of contributing to a Caribbean destiny (50). Autobiographical values are determined by the narrator's acute and pervasive sense of
participating in a great historical moment. His valuable life surrenders its meaning in a gesture of collectivity.

In the shifting symbolic codes Lamming employs in his introduction, he is prosecutor, defense counsel, witness for the defense and for the prosecution, and hangman (10–12). In addition to these interpretive cues for reading the self's place and importance in the world, Lamming sketches in an interactive theoretical framework that roots the ideological position of the author in his exemplary flawed status as Caribbean colonial. The dominant contexts for ideological positioning are the Haitian ceremony of the Souls, *The Tempest*, and *The Black Jacobins*. They are used to situate personal experience as evidence and example of colonial alienation and exile transformed into a site of liberation from "his original knowledge, the knowledge of his original fact" (11) as colonial subject. The shifting frames of identity in *The Pleasures of Exile*, from "the field of vision to the space of writing," from personal experience to public debate, is a disputed colonial space that spans Africa, the Americas, and Europe, geographically and culturally, and anticipates many of the arguments regarding the Barthian Deep Me, The Written Me, The Subaltern and Postcolonial Subject in contemporary postcolonial discourse (Bhabha 6).

The Haitian ceremony of the Souls, as Lamming describes it, is an indigenous Vodun religious ritual of redemptive dialogue between the living and the dead (9–10). The ceremony has symbolic significance for Lamming as a Caribbean cultural model for negotiating the nightmare of colonial history.

It is not important to believe in the actual details of the ceremony. What is important is its symbolic drama, the drama of redemption, the drama of returning, the drama of cleansing for a commitment towards the future. ("West Indian People," 64–65)

The ceremony validates and authorizes this Caribbean writer's commitment to a dialogistic mode of discourse that privileges a Caribbean way of seeing. Dialogue is prelude to awareness, and awareness is "a minimum condition for attaining freedom" (*Pleasures*, 12). Lamming repeatedly calls attention to the dialogic nature of the text; to the "I" that writes out of the oppositional space of otherness as a way of dismantling the monologic imperative of colonial history.

This book is based upon facts of experience, and it is intended as an introduction to a dialogue between you and me. I am the whole world of my accumulated emotional experience, vast areas of which remain unexplored. You are the other, according to your way of seeing me in relation to yourself. (12)

Lamming's emphasis on dialogue contextualizes the aggressive intent of the text, in which dialogistic and conversational overtures periodically assume the contentiousness of a public trial. In a discursive shift from one cultural context to another, Lamming uses *The Tempest* to schematize the terms of dialogue: "It is my intention to make use of *The Tempest* as a way of presenting a certain state of feeling which is the heritage of the exiled and colonial writer from the British Caribbean" (9). Though the narrator identifies himself as a descendant of both Prospero and Caliban, his sympathetic identification is with Caliban in the oppositional discourse that follows. Lamming wraps himself in the plural symbolic, cultural codes of Caliban "as a landscape and human situation" (119), and tailors his self-image as cultural historian and critic to a Caliban who never loses "the spirit of freedom" or "his original sense of rootedness" (101), who "keeps answering back" and refuses to be silent (102). Transformed into a twentieth-century cultural icon, Lamming's Caliban recognizes and uses his enslavement by Prospero as a transformative juncture.

> Caliban had got hold of Prospero's weapons and decided that he would never again seek his master's permission. That is also my theme: a theme which embraces both literature and politics in our time. (63)

Caliban's wide-awake resistance is a calculated response to oppression, evil, and mystification. Caliban as symbol of ignorance and savagery in Shakespeare's imperialist discourse is refashioned in Lamming's liberationist discourse as symbol of heroic resistance. In the nineteenth-century Caribbean, Caliban is Toussaint. In 1939, he is C. L. R. James celebrating Toussaint's military victory as a Caribbean epic in *The Black Jacobins*.[7] In 1960, he is the historically aware resistant colonial writer from the British Caribbean.

The verbal aggressiveness of Lamming as latter-day Caliban carries something of an apocalyptic threat. "The time is ripe—but may go rotten—when masters must learn to read the meaning contained in the signatures of their former slaves. There may be more murders; but Caliban is here to stay" (63). The stridency of tone that characterizes the book as a whole and the invective that Lamming reserves for the "colour-baiters" and "culture-vultures" of the Institute of Contemporary Arts (83) and for the reviewers of the *Times Literary Supplement* and *The Spectator* (28–29) illuminate another facet of exemplary flawed self-imaging in the text. The authorial persona, as Caliban, creates multiple spaces for the frank expres-

sion of personal bitterness, distrust, cynicism, irony, defiance, and
jubilation, in the text's characterization of self as colonial Other
writing himself and his Caribbean reality into existence at the
heart of empire.[8]
Lamming's appropriation of Caliban as exemplary flawed revolutionary hero who models the ambiguities of the resistant,
liberationist spirit of his time and place initiates a text-based
counterdiscourse around *The Tempest* in the modern Caribbean
that incorporates complex issues of identity, authority, and freedom.[9] Lamming makes a singular contribution to the discourse
around O. Mannoni's use of *The Tempest* to legitimize his theory of
the psychology of colonialism in *Prospero and Caliban: the Psychology of Colonialism* and the spirited responses to Mannoni's theory
in Frantz Fanon's *Black Skin, White Masks* and Aimé Césaire's
*Discourse on Colonialism.* Lamming uses the facts of his own migration to London as part of a larger migrating labor force from the
Caribbean after World War II to investigate issues of cultural and
psychological dependence that Mannoni and Fanon had explored in
regard to Madagascans and to Antilleans at home, respectively. In
contrast to Mannoni's use of Caliban to demonstrate his theory of
the dependency complex of colonized peoples, Lamming creates a
different set of values around Shakespeare's fictive Caliban and
stakes out his own position on Caribbean language and culture in
the process.

> The old blackmail of Language simply won't work any longer. For
> the language of modern politics is no longer Prospero's exclusive
> vocabulary. It is Caliban's as well; and since there is no absolute
> from which a moral prescription may come, Caliban is at liberty
> to choose the meaning of this moment. (158)

While Lamming's observations on cultural dependency in the
British colonies of the Caribbean complement Fanon's in *Black
Skin, White Masks*, Lamming stresses the difference between Lan-
guage as an agent of colonization and that Language rechristened
as the product of Caribbean endeavor; between the Language of
Shakespeare and the Language of C. L. R. James.

> This gift of Language is the deepest and most delicate bond of
> involvement. It has a certain finality. Caliban will never be the
> same again. This gift of Language meant not English, in particu-
> lar, but speech and a concept as a way, a method, a necessary
> avenue towards areas of the self which could not be reached in

any other way. Caliban's future . . . the very name for possibilities—must derive from Prospero's experiment. (109)

In *The Pleasures of Exile*, this gift of Language is an ambiguous space that can fertilize and extend the resources of human vision beyond the colonizing process. Though intended as a prison of service and measure of superiority, Language is created anew in the Caribbean (110–11, 119). If Language as education is "the first important achievement of the colonising process" (109), a colonial "education" paradoxically nurtures historical awareness and a spirit of resistance in the case of Toussaint L'Ouverture, architect of the Haitian Revolution, and C. L. R. James, Lamming, and a community of named Caribbean writers. *The Pleasures of Exile* is designed as evidence and example of this paradox at work.

In "Caribbean and African Appropriations of *The Tempest*," Rob Nixon notes the double incongruity of Caribbean and African intellectuals' use of a canonical European text like *The Tempest*, "given Shakespeare's distinctive position as a measure of the relative achievements of European and non-European civilizations" (560). Roberto Fernández Retamar calls it "an alien elaboration, although in this case based on our concrete realities" (Retamar 16). The perceived incongruity of the Caribbean intellectual's use of the play models the process of assimilation and transformation James describes in *Beyond a Boundary* as the genesis of a Caribbean-based regional identity. In James's classic text, a passion for Thackeray nurtures a spirit of liberation, a model British public school education in Trinidad produces a Pan-Africanist and nationalist, Caribbean mastery of English cricket transforms a ritual of colonial dominance into a ritual of resistance and national pride.[10] Within the contradictory legacies of colonialism, genius subverts and transforms the structures that were meant to confine it. The perceived incongruity in fact models an ideological and aesthetic resolution of the historical and cultural contradictions of the multiethnic, multiracial, polyglot Caribbean. Lamming's ideological and aesthetic commitment is to the production of the culture of a new society after centuries of colonial rule; the migration of themes from one era to another is dialectical. As Trotsky observes, "Artistic creation is always a complicated turning inside out of old forms, under the influence of new stimuli which lie outside of art" (37). This is the essence of Walcott's aesthetic and ideological resolution of the Manichaean conflicts engendered by slavery and colonialism, the writer's "creative use of his schizophrenia, an electric fusion of the old and the new" (17).

Lamming's selective reading of *The Tempest*, followed by an equally selective reading of *The Black Jacobins*, illuminates this creative process at work in the colonial and postcolonial Caribbean. The emerging discourse invests specific cultural authority in the written word as agent of colonization and also of decolonization. Richard Hakluyt's *The Principal Navigations, Voyages, Traffiques and Discoveries of the English Nation* (1598–1600) and Shakespeare's *The Tempest* are identified by Lamming as complementary pre-texts that reveal the centuries-old process by which Europe laid the foundations of its colonizing mission on the fictions of explorers, travelers, and adventurers. Lamming calls attention to the misrepresentation of Caribbean reality in the reprehensible renaming of the Carib as Cannibal and, alternatively, as Caliban (*Pleasures*, 12–13). The fabrications of Sir Walter Raleigh and Sir John Hawkins inspired and justified European annexation of the Americas, even as they circumscribed the Manichaean aesthetics of Shakespeare's Prospero and Caliban in *The Tempest*. Lamming elaborates a comprehensive argument about the specifically ideological content of the European book as purveyor of cognitive codes of cultural superiority and a civilizing mission. The complicated relationship between literature and history in sustaining the apparatus of empire and, conversely, in dismantling that apparatus and constructing alternatives permeates the self-conscious design of this multifaceted text.

In *The Tempest*, Prospero's power and authority derive from magical books, which are his exclusive property. In *The Signifying Monkey*, Henry Louis Gates examines the trope of the magical Talking Book in the narratives of James Gronniosaw, John Marrant, John Jea, Ottobah Cuguoano, and Olaudah Equiano (127–69). The authority of the book as insignia of authority in the colonization of the New World has even wider significance, as Nathan Wachtel demonstrates in *The Vision of the Vanquished*. Atahuallpa's failure to recognize the significance of the Bible that Pizarro hands him as a test of fealty leads to his prompt arrest and execution, and the collapse of the Incan empire (Wachtel 14–15). The significance of this historic event is heightened further once it is understood that Pizarro is himself illiterate.[11] The book as fetish and insignia of authority problematizes the relationship between the written word as cultural artifact and the conquest of the New World. The substance of the book and its use are distinct spheres of value that are nonetheless intimately related.

In *The Pleasures of Exile*, Lamming targets the myth-making value of the book as a literary and political phenomenon that links

Hakluyt and Shakespeare to the destiny of the modern Caribbean. The reading and writing of books are no longer Prospero's exclusive property. Lamming, as traveler to the native land of Hakluyt, Hawkins, and Raleigh, reverses the journey and the intention of their travel narratives. The dialogic intention of his text not only reverses the colonizing intention of the imperial monologue, but also takes as its first casualty the mythical character of European constructions of alterity. The book as fetish and insignia of authority is reconstituted as a site of transgressive appropriation.[12] If Prospero's magic resides in his books, then they hold the key to his undoing. Prospero's books become a necessary site of contention in the struggle to redefine and reorder colonial reality.[13]

Lamming challenges the privilege of the English text by offering his own unorthodox evaluation of the thought systems, values, and ideals in *The Tempest* as evidence of a pervasive decadence and corruption in colonialism from its inception. Using *The Tempest* to clarify his ideological position, Lamming directly challenges Shakespeare's authority over Caliban's cultural space as a misrepresentation of Caliban's reality. He uses James's *The Black Jacobins* to name an alternative reality, "Caliban as Prospero had never known him" (119). His use of Caliban as emblematic of creative and persistent resistance rather than a brutish child of Nature iterates both the arbitrariness of critical theory as an intellectual exercise and its usefulness in the creation of alternative liberationist cultural codes.

"West Indians first became aware of themselves as a people in the Haitian Revolution," observes James in his appendix to the 1963 edition of *The Black Jacobins* (391). The gap between Shakespeare's Caliban and the resistant spirit of the African slave in James's *The Black Jacobins* marks the difference between a European and a Caribbean mythology. Rob Nixon concludes that the value of *The Tempest* for Caribbean and African intellectuals "faded once the plot ran out. The play lacks a sixth act which might have been enlisted for representing relations among Caliban, Ariel, and Prospero once they entered the post-colonial era" (Nixon 576). That remains to be seen in the Caribbean, where Caliban has been reinvented as a spirit of revolt, as a landscape and a human situation with creative resources unenvisioned in Shakespeare's play. Unlike Jean Rhys's fictional reconstruction of Charlotte Bronte's *Jane Eyre* in *Wide Sargasso Sea*, Lamming's use of *The Tempest* in *The Pleasures of Exile* and in *Water with Berries* is unconstrained by the play's plot. Lamming's use of the play, like Césaire's *Une tempête,* Brathwaite's "Caliban," and Retamar's "Caliban: Notes To-

wards a Discussion of Our America," gives Caliban a mythical life
of his own as "a possibility of spirit" (*Pleasures*, 107) whose future
is unrealized in Shakespeare's play.

When Lamming made James's text a focal point of his literary
and political discourse in *The Pleasures of Exile*, James's pioneer-
ing Caribbean-centered history was out of print and neglected.
Lamming might have celebrated Toussaint L'Ouverture's singular achievement without reference to *The Black Jacobins*, but he
chose to identify a culture of resistance already in place in the
Caribbean that binds the literary endeavors of James the historian to Toussaint the soldier and revolutionary (*Pleasures*, 148).
Lamming's tone is celebratory as he illuminates cultural connections that nurture a regional culture of resistance and nationalism.

And it is wonderful that this epic of Toussaint's glory and his
dying should have been rendered by C. L. R. James, one of the
most energetic minds of our time, a neighbour of Toussaint's island, a heart and a desire entirely within the tradition of
Toussaint himself, a spirit that came to life in the rich and
humble soil of a British colony in the Caribbean. (150)

Furthermore, it is "James more than any man I know" who rouses
Lamming to a similar sense of responsibility as a writer and intellectual (*Pleasures*, 15–52).[14] In the interest of an evolving Caribbean-centered, text-based discourse, Lamming self-consciously
models literary production based on formal lines of continuity
among Caribbean texts beyond the continuity of "internal repul-
sions and breaks" (Trotsky 37). He reads, repeats, and revises
James's text and, in the process, links his own text to James's as a
necessary beginning.

The cultural authority of the written word as an instrument of
decolonization is at the heart of *The Pleasures of Exile*. Lamming
invokes the Haitian ceremony of the Souls as a symbolic drama
with authoritative magical properties of its own, but Lamming's
medium is the book. Under the sign of its internal contradictions
and the alienations of its colonial history, Lamming provides a
theoretical base for reading the meaning and direction of the new
literature of the Caribbean in regional and political terms. He provides an alternative to the marginalization of the new Caribbean
writing by uncomprehending English and Caribbean reviewers that
grounds the discourse in a Caribbean social, political, economic,
and emotional reality. The issues he raises continue to be part of
the postcolonial debate around art as regional and national in ex-

pression, and around totalizing poststructuralist theories of language, discourse, and representation that trivialize the conditions in which art is produced.

In *The Pleasures of Exile*, the emergence of a dozen or so novelists in the British Caribbean with some fifty books to their credit between 1948 and 1958 is a major historical event, not because of "what the West Indian writer has brought to the English language," but because of "what the West Indian novelist has brought to the West Indies" (36). Lamming's emphasis is on the "West Indian contribution to English reading" as opposed to "English writing" (44). He models a self-conscious self-criticism of the tendencies of the new writing as a Caribbean cultural enterprise: "As it should be, the novelist was the first to relate the West Indian experience from the inside. He was the first to chart the West Indian memory as far back as he could go" (38). Lamming's blueprint for imaginative writing in the Caribbean privileges sympathetic identification with peasant themes and the distinctive rhythms of peasant speech.[15] In this context, the performative function of literary production in decolonization is self-possession through self-definition; the meaning and value of the new writing is explicitly national and political. Nor is this an isolationist, closed cultural enterprise, for Lamming announces his affiliation with Wright, Baldwin, Melville, Whitman, and Mark Twain as a way of registering and celebrating the Caribbean's New World difference (29).

*The Pleasures of Exile* charts the events of a ten-year period beginning with Lamming's arrival in London in 1950, but it is only in "The African Presence" that Lamming includes notes ostensibly written while traveling in West Africa and visiting friends in New York. The text is usefully compared with Claude McKay's *A Long Way from Home* as a self-study of the Caribbean writer as traveler and expatriate. Unlike McKay, however, Lamming remains heavily invested in defining the parameters of the Caribbean experience. The center of the expatriate's world remains the colonial Caribbean and the writer's mission of ideological demystification. The lives of Caribbean expatriates in West Africa and in the United States are more important than any objective account of the place and the people. The Caribbean as cultural cradle remains the text's organizing center for seeing and depicting the world.

Africa is not the same quality of beginning for Lamming in *The Pleasures of Exile* as it is for Brathwaite writing in 1970, after eight years of living and working in Ghana.

> Slowly, slowly, ever so slowly, I came to a sense of identification of myself with these people, my living diviners. I came to connect

my history with theirs, the bridge of my mind now linking Atlantic and ancestor, homeland and heartland. When I turned to leave, I was no longer a lonely individual talent; there was something wider, more subtle, more tentative; the self without ego, without I, without arrogance. (Brathwaite, "Timehri," 33–34)

Lamming's reclamation of Africa for all the Caribbean is part of the text's program of ideological demystification, part of a necessary rounding out of the New World African writer's perspective. West Africa, like Black America, is both familiar and strange to the Caribbean writer. In both he discovers a colonial relation that strengthens his original perception of a colonizing European presence and of a shared relationship to that presence. In a startling replay of Claude McKay's encounter with the colonial Jamaica of his childhood in Casablanca and Marrakesh,[16] Lamming sees himself in a troop of Boy Scouts assembled at the airport in Ghana to welcome a colonial dignitary.

It was a profound experience, for I was seeing myself in every detail which they lived. . . . This experience was deeper and more resonant than the impression left by the phrase: 'we used to be like that.' It was not just a question of me and my village when I was the age of these boys. Like the funeral ceremony of the King, it was an example of habits and history reincarnated in this moment. (161–62)

In the United States, the supremacy of the white standards is measured against a similar structure of values in the Caribbean: "To be accepted on merit as a worshipper in that great Cathedral [the *New York Times*] where taste is supposed to be no respecter of complexions, is not unlike the West Indian's delight with the prim-lipped approval of the *London Times*" (202). "The African Presence" is a formal act of reconnection after the violent dispossession of slavery and colonialism, but the writer's destiny is linked to the elaboration of a Caribbean reality. According to Brathwaite, *The Pleasures of Exile* belongs to the age of the emigrant: "The West Indies could be written about and explored. But only from a vantage point outside the West Indies" ("Timehri," 32–33). In fact, *The Pleasures of Exile* provides a culture-specific context for understanding the relationship between exile and the narrative imagination, from Mary Prince to Jamaica Kincaid, and a better understanding of the nature of creativity itself.

Despite the complexity of the text, resistance and liberation are an exclusively male enterprise in *The Pleasures of Exile*. The autobiographical framework generates a self-conscious, self-celebrating male paradigm that goes unchallenged in the text. In *The Pleasures of Exile*, Caliban, like Melville's Ishmael, is left alone; creation is a male enterprise. Miranda shares Caliban's creative potential to the degree to which she shares his innocence and ignorance of Prospero's magic, though their difference in status turns their common experience into an oppositional space.

> In some real, though extraordinary way, Caliban and Miranda are seen side by side: opposite and contiguous at the same time. They share an ignorance that is also the source of some vision. It is, as it were, a kind of creative blindness. (*Pleasures*, 115)

Sycorax, as symbol of a landscape and a changing human situation, is a memory, an absence, and a silence. In *The Pleasures of Exile*, Lamming consciously postpones consideration of Sycorax and Miranda's mother as contributing subjects of Caribbean cultural history (116).

In "Beyond Miranda's Meanings," Sylvia Wynter makes a strong case for the insufficiency of *The Tempest* as a theoretical interpretive model that silences and erases the "native" woman in liberationist discourse. In Lamming's corpus, it takes a shift in genre to alter the male paradigm of resistance and liberation. In Lamming's *Season of Adventure*, a novel published in the same year as *The Pleasures of Exile*, the central character is a woman who is given a pivotal role in the revolutionary restructuring of corrupt neocolonial rule in a fictive Caribbean republic. But Lamming's emphasis is on the transformation of a male-directed society, not on the liberation of women as an isolated social category. In *Water with Berries* (1971) and in *Natives of My Person* (1972), the existence of an obsessive-compulsive male paradigm of achievement is itself the subject of investigation, and "Miranda's mother" assumes the contours of victim and oppressor in colonial history.

In his introduction to the 1984 edition of *The Pleasures of Exile*, Lamming emphasizes the value of the text as a document of intellectual and cultural history, even as he distances himself from it in time and tone.

> Much has changed in the fate and names of places; but the central issues have remained the same. Some of the judgements on people and events may have seemed extravagant and provocative, but these may also serve as reliable evidence of a particular

way of seeing. There was a great temptation to revise and update, but that would have led to a different kind of book at a later stage of development. (Introduction)

Lamming mediates the value of his own text as evidence of a specific consciousness and practice. Twenty-four years after it was first published, he stresses the sincerity, the authenticity, and the truthfulness of the text as evidence of its singular value. He reminds the reader of the time and place of the text's creation to locate its value for the reader in 1984; the self-conscious self-criticism of the author in 1960 has value as a social text in the decades that follow.

Despite the distance the author places between himself and the text in his role as mediator of its value, the dynamics of the original text are restated. It stands as a record and reminder of his personal development as a Caribbean writer and of the sociocultural dynamics of the colonial and postcolonial Caribbean:

The Pleasures of Exile was intended to be read as a writer's extended notes on the themes which had appeared and would persist in a body of novels. The voice was not only personal in tone. It registered a collective experience of the period, and sought to reflect and interpret the anxieties and aspirations of a Caribbean sensibility at home and abroad. (Introduction)

The codes of value established in the text of 1960 are reaffirmed as representative of a specific consciousness and practice that is fundamentally celebratory of the writer's productive, transformative relationship to his society in a period of revolutionary social change.

In the 1984 retrospective, Lamming invites a historical reading of the text. He calls attention to a past reality that is directly reflected in the text, to its value as a subtext to his fiction and as a frame of reference for readers, in and out of the Caribbean, "who were born after 1960." The experiences reflected in The Pleasures of Exile are identified as part of an ongoing process of literary production that illuminates the endeavors of new generations of Black British who "are closer in feeling and language to their equivalent in New York than they are to the same generation in any Caribbean island." In its cultural specificity, The Pleasures of Exile is a precursor to Paul Gilroy's There Ain't No Black in the Union Jack as well as C. L. R. James's Beyond a Boundary. It mediates a historically determinate system of meaning that illuminates the

Caribbean and the Black British texts. *The Pleasures of Exile* contains ideas and insights about the thematic obsessions of modern Caribbean writing—colonialism and nationalism, departure and return, emigration and exile, identity and ethnicity, language, history, myth and legend, the interdependence of oral and written traditions, and the role of the writer in a time of revolutionary social change. It also provides an interpretive model that illuminates and contextualizes issues around the production of literature as a national enterprise in relation to postcolonial formations of identity, race, ethnicity, and cultural hybridity.

Sandra Pouchet Paquet
University of Pennsylvania

NOTES

1. The five novels are *The Emigrants* (1954), *Of Age and Innocence* (1958), *Season of Adventure* (1960), *Water with Berries* (1971), and *Natives of My Person* (1972).

2. Approaching intellectual history from a semiological perspective, Hayden White observes that the complexity of the intellectual historical artifact "has to do with the extent to which the classic text reveals, indeed actively draws attention to, its own processes of meaning production and makes of these processes its own subject matter, its own 'content'" (211).

3. Rob Nixon stresses the importance of Lamming's use of collectivity in "Caribbean and African Appropriations of *The Tempest*":

Lamming's assertion that his unorthodoxy is collectively grounded is crucial: those who defend a text's universal value can easily discount a solitary dissenting voice as uncultured or quirky, but it is more difficult to ignore entirely a cluster of allied counterjudgments, even if the group can still be stigmatized. (558)

4. In some respects, the title anticipates the pleasure/bliss principle of Roland Barthes's *The Pleasure of the Text* (1975).

5. In *Exile and the Narrative Imagination*, Michael Seidel notes: "The task for the exile, especially the exiled artist, is to transform the figure of rupture back into a figure of connection" (x).

6. In a 1983 interview with Philippe Decraene, the Martiniquan poet and playwright, Aimé Césaire takes the position that the wealth and originality of the West Indies are the fruit of synthesis (*Discourse*, 64).

7. In his Preface to *Beyond a Boundary*, James appears to accept the designation Caliban but substitutes Caesar for Prospero: "To establish his own identity, Caliban, after three centuries, must himself pioneer into regions Caesar never knew."

8. Bakhtin calculates the impact of theomachy and anthromachy on au-

tobiographical self-accounting in *Art and Answerability*:

> An element of theomachy and anthromachy is possible in confessional self-accounting, that is, the refusal to accept a possible judgment by God or by man, and as a result tones of resentment, distrust, cynicism, irony, defiance appear. (146)

9. For example: Aimé Césaire's adaptation of Shakespeare's play, *Une tempête*; Roberto Fernández Retamar's *Caliban and Other Essays*; Edward Kamau Brathwaite's "Caliban" in *The Arrivants* and his "Caliban, Ariel, and Unprospero in the Conflict of Creolization"; George Lamming's novel *Water with Berries*; and Sylvia Wynter's "Beyond Miranda's Meanings: Un/silencing the 'Demonic Ground' of Caliban's 'Woman.'"

10. According to Manthia Diawara, *Beyond a Boundary* "shows that West Indian cricket represents the taking-away and the appropriation of the game from Englishness" (41).

11. The taking of the Amazon from Amerindian people through land titles is a recent example of the preeminence of paper over fact. The moral definition of land ownership, through hundreds of years of planting nut and fruit trees and harvesting the forest, is supplanted by the legal definition of land claim and possession for purposes of deforestation.

12. The collusion of colonization and textual constructions of alterity is richly explored in Peter Hulme's *Colonial Encounters: Europe and the Native Caribbean 1492–1797* and Eric Cheyfitz's *The Poetics of Imperialism*.

13. Helen Tiffin identifies *The Pleasures of Exile* as a resistance autobiography, along with Jean Rhys's *Smile, Please* and V. S. Naipaul's *The Enigma of Arrival*:

> In these three resistance autobiographies, then, the unmasking of imperial fictions is important, not just in terms of specific texts, but through examination of the book as fetish, dream, and insignia of authority. (31)

14. In an interview with Reinhard Sander and Ian Munro, Lamming clarifies his position:

> So although I would make a distinction about *functions*, I do not make a distinction about *responsibilities*. I do not think that the responsibility of the professional politician is greater than the responsibility of an artist to his society. (Munro and Sander, 13)

15. In *History of the Voice* Edward Kamau Brathwaite describes an evolving Caribbean aesthetic around the use of "nation language" or the vernacular in Anglophone poetry.

16. "Marrakesh moved me. It was like a big West Indian picnic, with flags waving and a multitude of barefoot black children dancing to the flourish of drum, fiddle and fife" (McKay, 304);

> . . . some Guinea sorcerers (or Gueanoua, as they are called in Morocco) were performing a magic rite. The first shock I registered was the realization that they looked and acted exactly like certain peasants of Jamaica who give themselves up to the celebrating of a religious singdance orgy which is known as Myalism. The only difference was in their clothing. (297)

REFERENCES

Bakhtin, M. M. *Art and Answerability*. Trans. Vadim Liapunov and Kenneth Brostrom. Austin: University of Texas Press, 1990.

Barthes, Roland. *The Pleasure of the Text*. Trans. R. Miller. New York: Hill and Wang, 1975.

Bhabha, Homi. "Interrogating Identity." *ICA Documents* 6 (1989): 5–11.

Brathwaite, Edward Kamau. *The Arrivants*. London: Oxford University Press, 1973.

———. "Timehri." In *Is Massa Day Dead?*, ed. Orde Coombs, 28–44. New York: Anchor, 1974.

———. "Caliban, Ariel, and Unprospero in the Conflict of Creolization: A Study of the Slave Revolt in Jamaica in 1831–32." In *Comparative Perspectives on Slavery in New World Plantation Societies*, ed. Vera Rubin and Arthur Tuden, 41–62. New York: New York Academy of Sciences, 1977.

———. *History of the Voice: The Development of Nation Language in Anglophone Poetry*. London: New Beacon Books, 1984.

Césaire, Aimé. *Discourse on Colonialism* (1955). Trans. Joan Pinkham. New York: Monthly Review Press, 1972.

———. *Une tempête*. Paris: Editions du Seuil, 1969.

Cheyfitz, Eric. *The Poetics of Imperialism*. New York: Oxford University Press, 1991.

Diawara, Manthia. "Black British Cinema: Spectatorship and Identity Formation in *Territories*." *Public Culture* 3, no. 1 (Fall 1990): 33–48.

Fanon, Frantz. *Black Skin, White Masks* (1952). Trans. Charles Lam Markmann. New York: Grove, 1967.

Gates, Henry Louis, Jr. *The Signifying Monkey: A Theory of Afro-American Literary Criticism*. New York: Oxford University Press, 1988.

Hulme, Peter. *Colonial Encounters: Europe and the Native Caribbean 1492–1797*. London: Methuen, 1986.

James, C. L. R. *The Black Jacobins*. 1938. Reprint. New York: Vintage, 1963.

———. *Beyond a Boundary*. London: Hutchinson, 1963.

Lamming, George. *In the Castle of My Skin*. 1953. Reprint. Ann Arbor: University of Michigan Press, 1991.

———. Introduction to *The Pleasures of Exile*. London: Allison and Busby, 1984.

———. *Season of Adventure*. 1960. Reprint. London: Allison and Busby, 1979.

———. *Water with Berries*. London: Longman Caribbean, 1971.

———. *Natives of My Person*. London: Longman Caribbean, 1972.

———. "The West Indian People." *New World Quarterly* 2, no. 2 (1966): 63–74.

McKay, Claude. *A Long Way from Home*. 1937. Reprint. New York: Harcourt Brace, 1970.

Mannoni, O. *Prospero and Caliban: The Psychology of Colonization* (1950). Trans. Pamela Powesland. 1964. Reprint. Ann Arbor: University of Michigan Press, 1990.

Munro, Ian, and Reinhard Sander, eds. *Kas-Kas*. Austin: African and Afro-American Research Institute, University of Texas, 1972.

Naipaul, V. S. *The Enigma of Arrival*. New York: Knopf, 1987.

Nixon, Rob. "Caribbean and African Appropriations of *The Tempest*." *Critical Inquiry* 13 (Spring 1987): 557–78.

Retamar, Roberto Fernández. *Caliban and Other Essays*. Trans. Edward Baker. Minneapolis: University of Minnesota Press, 1989.

Rhys, Jean. *Smile, Please: An Unfinished Autobiography*. New York: Harper, 1979.

———— *Wide Sargasso Sea*. 1966. Reprint. New York: Popular Library, 1975.

Said, Edward W. "Identity, Authority and Freedom: The Potentate and the Traveler." *Transition* 54:4–18.

Seidel, Michael. *Exile and the Narrative Imagination*. New Haven: Yale University Press, 1986.

Smith, Sidonie. "Self, Subject, and Resistance: Marginalities and Twentieth-Century Autobiographical Practice." *Tulsa Studies in Women's Literature* 9, no. 1 (1990): 11–24.

Tiffin, Helen. "Rites of Resistance: Counter-Discourse and West Indian Autobiography." *Journal of West Indian Literature* 3, no. 1 (January 1989): 28–46.

Trotsky, Leon. *Trotsky on Literature and Art*. Ed. Paul N. Siegel. New York: Pathfinder, 1970.

Wachtel, Nathan. *The Vision of the Vanquished: The Spanish Exploration of Peru through Indian Eyes*. 1971. Reprint. New York: Harper and Row, 1977.

Walcott, Derek. "What the Twilight Says: An Overture." *Dream on Monkey Mountain and Other Plays*. New York: Farrar Straus Giroux, 1970.

White, Hayden. *The Content of the Form: Narrative Discourse and Historical Representation*. Baltimore: Johns Hopkins University Press, 1987.

Wright, Richard. Introduction to *In the Castle of My Skin* by George Lamming. New York: McGraw Hill, 1954.

————. "Blueprint for Negro Writing." In *Voices from the Harlem Rennaissance,* ed. Nathan I. Huggins, 394–402. New York: Oxford University Press, 1976.

Wynter, Sylvia. "Beyond Miranda's Meanings: Un/silencing the 'Demonic Ground' of Caliban's 'Woman.'" Afterword to *Out of the Kumbla,* ed. Carole Boyce Davies and Elaine Savory Fido, 355–72. Trenton, N. J.: Africa World Press, 1990.

# CONTENTS

# INTRODUCTION

●

History is a nightmare from which I am trying to awaken.
JAMES JOYCE.

IN THE republic of Haiti—one corner of the Caribbean cradle—a native religion sometimes forces the official Law to negotiate with peasants who have retained a racial, and historic, desire to worship their original gods. We do not have to share their faith in order to see the universal significance of certain themes implicit in the particular ceremony of the Souls which I witnessed four years ago in the suburbs of Port-au-Prince.

The details of this ceremony are very elaborate; but the outline, the conscious style of intention, is quite simple. In our time it is even familiar. This drama between religion and the Law is important to my purpose; for it suggests parallels with William Shakespeare's play, *The Tempest;* and it is my intention to make use of *The Tempest* as a way of presenting a certain state of feeling which is the heritage of the exiled and colonial writer from the British Caribbean.

Naturally, I anticipate from various quarters the obvious charge of blasphemy; yet there are occasions when blasphemy must be seen as one privilege of the excluded Caliban. Such is this occasion, and I am determined to tell you why.

This ceremony of the Souls is regarded by the Haitian peasant as a solemn communion; for he hears, at first hand, the secrets of the Dead. The celebrants are mainly relatives of the deceased who, ever since their death, have been locked in Water. It is the duty of the Dead to return and offer, on this momentous night, a full and honest report on their past relations with the living. A wife may have to say why she refused love to her husband; a husband may have to say why he deprived his wife of their children's affection. It is the duty of the Dead to speak, since their release from that purgatory of Water cannot be realised until they have fulfilled the contract which this ceremony symbolises. The Dead need to speak if they are going to enter that eternity which will be their last and permanent Future. The living demand to hear whether there is any need for forgiveness,

9

for redemption; whether, in fact, there may be any guide which may help them towards reforming their present condition. Different as they may be in their present state of existence, those alive and those now Dead—their ambitions point to a similar end. They are interested in their Future.

Through the medium of the Priest, the Dead speak of matters which it must have been difficult to raise before; and through the same medium, the living learn and understand what the Dead tongues have uttered. Revenge, guilt, redemption, and some future expectation make for an involvement which binds the Dead and the living together. The ceremony takes its course according to custom, and the result is, probably, always the same except in details. But it is precisely the details which may determine each future.

The official Law which, it seems, is never more than a temporary arrangement for our safety, has difficulty in applying its rules. This particular ceremony had been 'allowed.' But there are times when the Law decrees that there should be no Vodum rites. The peasants find it difficult to obey. Fearful of being found in their wooden *tonelles*, they will perform their rites in the street. The ceremony is simple. You make certain *ververs* in the dust, and wherever two or three are gathered together by the sign of the *ververs*, the gods are there. It is that sign, like a cross, which reminds them of their need. Then the Law arrives. The police arrive without warning; but no charge can be made. For the worshippers stand to welcome their protectors, the police, and in the same moment their feet have erased the signs of invocation which they had made in the dust. The god is not there, for his cross has gone. But the moment the police depart, the signatures will be made again; the god will return, and prayer will assume whatever needs those peasants whisper.

The Law can bring a charge of loitering, which is the privilege of Beggars and Kings, a way of life for both idle and unemployed. Like Prospero identified with his privilege, the Haitian peasant exercises a magic that vanishes and returns according to the contingencies of the moment.

But let's assume that a charge, other than loitering, is brought. Let's assume that there is a trial; that you are on trial for the very evidence which you have given; or worse still, for withholding the evidence which it is within your power to give. How can we proceed? In the widest and narrowest terms of reference? I shall state them.

We accept the fact of a trial. We realise that the Judge is late, and may, in fact, not even arrive before the accused escapes. The accused is there, but like an agent with his magic, he appears and disappears, and with each stage of evidence, he appears to change his role. We know that there must be a trial; for we have all offered to give evidence, some from rumour and others from facts. Among us there is a witness who says that he cannot distinguish between rumour and fact. Sometimes he recognises fact, accepts it, exploits it, lives it until he discovers that its original author was cheating. Another time he confronts a rumour, investigates it, memorises it, stores it away as a reservation which must not be used against fact until his awareness changes, until he sees that the rumour was not altogether invalid; for it has given birth to new facts which demand that he liberate himself from his original knowledge, the knowledge of his original fact.

The case remains open. Each in his own way is conspiring with the other to postpone the hearing. But the trial goes on. It cannot be suspended while they are alive, for they are the trial, changing the roles of Judge and Jury, demanding to be prosecutor as well as chief witness for the defence.

Another witness arrives claiming extraordinary privileges. He wants to assume Prospero's privilege of magic, while arguing in his evidence that no man has a right to use magic in his dealings with another. On the other hand he sees himself as Caliban while he argues that he is not the Caliban whom Prospero had in mind. This witness claims a double privilege. He thinks he is, in some way, a descendant of Prospero. He knows he is a direct descendant of Caliban. He claims to be the key witness in the trial; but his evidence will only be valid if the others can accept the context in which he will give it. For it is only by accepting this special context that his evidence can reveal its truth. What is the context which he proposes?

He says: I am chief witness for the prosecution, but I shall also enter the role of Prosecutor. I shall defend the accused in the light of my own evidence. I reserve the right to choose my own Jury to whom I shall interpret my own evidence since I know that evidence more intimately than any man alive. Who then is most qualified to be the Judge? For the Law itself, like the men involved, is in some doubt about the nature of this charge. The result may be capital punishment, and I shall be hangman, provided I do not have to use the apparatus that will put the accused to death. It is likely that the accused, when he is found and convicted and forgotten, may turn out to be Innocent. That is unfortunate, for I am working on the fundamental belief that there are no degrees of innocence.

Involvement in crime, whether as witness, or an accomplice, makes innocence impossible. To be innocent is to be eternally dead. And this trial embraces only the living. Some may be corpses, but their evidence is the evidence of a corpse who has returned to make the unforgivable apology: 'Gentlemen I did not realise. Although I was there, although I took part, believe me, I did not realise! I was not aware!' The confession of unawareness is a confession of guilt. This corpse, dead as he may be, cannot be allowed to go free; for unawareness is the basic characteristic of the slave. Awareness is a minimum condition for attaining freedom.

'He is asking the impossible,' you say. Agreed. But it is the privilege of his imagination to do so.

'Is he God or What?' You ask the question in a way which implies a chosen denial of his answer. It is not the right spirit for just enquiry; so the question must remain open.

This book is based upon facts of experience, and it is intended as an introduction to a dialogue between you and me. I am the whole world of my accumulated emotional experience, vast areas of which probably remain unexplored. You are the other, according to your way of seeing me in relation to yourself. There will be no chairman. Magic is permissible. Indeed, any method of presentation may be used. There is one exception. Don't tell lies. From time to time, the truth may go into hiding; but don't tell lies.

We have met before. Four centuries separate our first meeting when Prospero was graced with the role of thief, merchant and man of God. Our hero was 'the right worshipfull and valiant knight sir John Haukins, sometimes treasurer of her Majesties navie Roial'; and it is his first Voyage in search of human merchandise.

'With this companie he put off and departed from the coast of England in the moneth of October 1562 and in his course touched first at Teneriffe, where he received friendly entertainment. From thence he passed to Sierra Leona, upon the coast of Guinea, which place by the people of the countrey is called Tagarin, where he stayed some good time, and got into his possession, *partly by the sworde, and partly by other meanes, to the number of 300 Negros at the least, besides other merchandises which that countrey yieldeth. With this praye he sayled over the Ocean sea unto the Iland of Hispaniola and arrived first at the port of Isabella.'*

The narrative is Hakluyt, but the italics are my way of pointing the triangular course of that tremendous Voyage which swept Caliban from his soil and introduced him to Heaven through the long wet hell of the Middle Passage.

'The 29 of this same moneth we departed with all our shippes from Sierra Leona, towardes the West Indies, and for the space of eighteen dayes, we were becalmed, having nowe and then contrary windes, and some Ternados, amongst the same calme, which happened to us very ill, beeing but reasonably watered, for so great a companie of Negros, and our selves, which pinched us all, and that which was worst, put us in such feare that many never thought to have reached to the Indies, without great death of Negros, and of themselves: *but the Almightie God, who never suffereth his elect to perish*, sent us the sixteenth of Februarie, the ordinary Brise, which is the Northwest winde, which never left us, till wee came to an Island of the Canybals, called Dominica.'

Now we know—although we cannot locate—the seeds of Prospero's eternal confidence. The slave whose skin suggests the savaged deformity of his nature becomes identical with the Carib Indian who feeds on human flesh. Carib Indian and African slave, both seen as the wild fruits of Nature, share equally that spirit of revolt which Prospero by sword or Language is determined to conquer.

'The Canybals of that Island, and also others adjacent are the most desperate warriers that are in the Indies, by the Spaniardes report, who are never able to conquer them, and they are molested by them not a little, when they are driven to water there in any of those Islands: of very late, not two moneths past, in the said Island, a Caravel being driven to water, was in the night sette upon by the inhabitants, who cutte their cable in the halser, whereby they were driven ashore, and so taken by them, and eaten.'

I cannot read *The Tempest* without recalling the adventure of those voyages reported by Hakluyt; and when I remember the voyages and the particular period in African history, I see *The Tempest* against the background of England's experiment in colonisation. Considering the range of Shakespeare's curiosity, and the fact that these matters were being feverishly discussed in England at the time, they would most certainly have been present in his mind. Indeed, they must have been part of the conscious stuff of his thinking. And it is Shakespeare's capacity for experience which leads me to feel that *The Tempest* was also prophetic of a political future which is our present. Moreover, the circumstances of my life, both as a colonial and exiled descendant of Caliban in the twentieth century, is an example of that prophecy.

It will not help to say that I am wrong in the parallels which I have set out to interpret; for I shall reply that my mistake, lived and deeply felt by millions of men like me—proves the positive value of error. It is a value which you must learn.

My subject is the migration of the West Indian writer, as colonial and exile, from his native kingdom, once inhabited by Caliban, to the tempestuous island of Prospero's and his language.

This book is a report on one man's way of seeing.

# IN THE BEGINNING

•

Be not afeard; the isle is full of noises,
Sounds and sweet airs, that give delight, and hurt not
Sometimes a thousand twangling instruments
Will hum about mine ears; and sometimes voices,
That, if I then had wak'd after long sleep,
Will make me sleep again: and then, in dreaming,
The clouds methought would open, and show riches
Ready to drop upon me; that, when I wak'd
I cried to dream again.

*Tempest*, Act III, Scene II

I

IT IS a tribal habit in certain reserves of the B.B.C. to pay for the resurrection of the Dead. The ritual is expensive; but it is an important part of contemporary culture. The result describes a need. It relaxes our hearing. It keeps us in touch with the past, and provides us with subjects for future conversation. Through the perfected necrophily of the living, we are allowed to tune in on the forgotten secrets of the Dead. The Dead are now honoured by their absence; preserved in our memories, summoned by engineers to inhabit the little magic box of sound. Prospero may have thrown away his Book; but the art of radio will rescue his weariness from despair; immortalise his absence; remind us that poetry is a way of listening. The art of radio may be too mortal for belief, but sound has its echoes whose future is eternal.

In the meantime, the divers loiter, bribing the sea to release its Dead for an interview with the living.

Studio Engineer: 'Stand by, stand by, we will go ahead in ten seconds from . . .' Now which the immortality of the Dead will not allow.

Announcer: 'Tomorrow, at nine-thirty, you can hear again . . .'

The hour may change for reasons which we on the other side of Radio should not investigate. It is enough to know that Tomorrow will not desert us; that Tomorrow cannot refuse our habitual waiting; for Prospero may have thrown away his Book; but the art of Radio will rescue his voice from the purgatory of the Ocean which is and may always be a neighbour to eternity.

Time, Magic and Man are the inseparable trinity of *The Tempest*. It is the ocean which made Prospero aware of Now; it is the supernatural privilege of his magic which made him feel that he might climb to the sky. But it was Man, the condition, which recalled him to his sense of decency: Man in the form of Miranda, his own creation, the measure of his probable mismanagement; Man in the terrible apparel of Caliban: his slave, his long and barely liveable purgatory. For Caliban is Man and other than Man. Caliban is his convert, colonised by language, and excluded by language. It is precisely this gift of language, this attempt at transformation which has brought about the pleasure and paradox of Caliban's exile. Exiled from his gods, exiled from his nature, exiled from his own name! Yet Prospero is afraid of Caliban. He is afraid because he knows that his encounter with Caliban is, largely, his encounter with himself.

The gift is a contract from which neither participant is allowed to withdraw. Caliban plots murder against Prospero, not in hatred, and not in fear, but out of a deep sense of betrayal. Prospero threatens Caliban with pain; but he never mentions murder; for he knows that the death of Caliban is the death of an occasion which he needs in order to escape the purgatory which has been crystallised by their encounter. Miranda is the innocent half of Caliban; Caliban is the possible deformity which Miranda, at the age of experiment, might become.

But Prospero is always there, dangerously poised between his doing and his doubt. He is not beyond Caliban's pardon; but he dare not ask it. To ask a favour of Caliban is to enter too fully into what is not known: for Caliban is a child of Nature and a slave. These are not synonymous. A child of Nature is an innocence which is enslaved by a particular way of learning, a particular way of receiving. But a slave is not a child. Nor is a slave in a state of Nature. A slave is a project, a source of energy, organised in order to exploit Nature.

All this Prospero knows; and so do I. For I am a direct descendant of slaves, too near to the actual enterprise to believe that its echoes are over with the reign of emancipation. Moreover, I am a direct descendant of Prospero worshipping in the same temple of endeavour, using his legacy of language—not to curse our meeting—but to push it further, reminding the descendants of both sides that what's done is done, and can only be seen as a soil from which other gifts, or the same gift endowed with different meanings, may grow towards a future which is colonised by our acts in this moment, but which must always remain open.

2

Some years ago I was a guest in the house of an English family. Their son was asked to entertain me with conversation until his mother arrived. His first question was: 'Where are you from?' I replied, 'The Caribbean'; and proceeded to talk about my particular island in relation to the others.

Suddenly he said: 'Excuse me.'

I thought he had gone to the lavatory. But when he returned, he set about spreading a great carpet of paper over the floor. Without explanation or apology, he simply said: 'Now let's see where we are talking about.' He had brought his map.

That boy was no more than nine years old. If he can preserve that spirit of curiosity and concreteness, his generation will save West Indians and others the torture of adult indifference. It is to the spirit of that boy that we shall address our discourse, and since I shall call on West Indian children to reply to that spirit, I must ask you to accept the use of legend. How and where is the Caribbean?

First the facts as stated by an American citizen of the New World:

'In the great arc of colonial territories that stretches from the Bahamas on the north to French Guinea on the south, more than 2,000 miles, there are almost six million people, living under the flags of four great powers; about 3,000,000 under the rule of Great Britain, 2,000,000 under the United States, 600,000 under France and 300,000 under the Netherlands.'

Now let us fertilise these figures by an image of their appearance in a particular landscape.

Islands of the Caribbean are evidence of some ancient mountain range that rode once without a flaw between the extreme points of North and South America. None but geologists can now conceive the years, lost by the millions, before that huge, continuous family of mountains broke and fell beneath the sea. Long submerged, it has left an archipelago of peaks like a swarm of green children patiently awaiting its return.

These islands are scattered in a curve of dots and distances continuing for nearly two thousand miles from the coast of Florida to the northern tip of South America. Coaxed by wind and water, these volcanic peaks display strange and familiar shapes: a camel's turbulent hump, the sleek, swollen arches of the snail, crabs' claws, a turtle fast asleep.

Many have seen now and again the terrible eye of the hurricane, from Haiti in the North, where valleys yawn to receive the feeble signatures of small houses that lose their legs and their way in the wind, to Barbados more than a thousand miles south, a flat disc of coral shivering in the still turning claws of the sea.

Their history has been similar, a sad and hopeful epic of discovery and migration. First Columbus, coaxing and bullying his crew to find India by a western route, choosing that name from his mistake and a legend of his time; for that land, known as Antiglia or the Antilles, which ancient charts show in the region of the Azores, was still a legend. Next the full European descent, urged both by adventure and greed; Spain, France, England, Holland as well as the Danes and Swedes, and a tiny, almost forgotten rock-pool of Germans! All arrived in this Caribbean sea like an epidemic ignorant of its specific target: human heroes and victims of an imagination and a quest shot through with gold. And all have remained in the complexions of their descendants who now inhabit these lands.

The indigenous Carib and Arawak Indians, living by their own lights long before the European adventure, gradually disappear in a blind, wild forest of blood. That mischievous gift, the sugar cane, is introduced, and a fantastic human migration moves to the New World of the Caribbean; deported crooks and criminals, defeated soldiers and Royalist gentlemen fleeing from Europe, slaves from the West Coast of Africa, East Indians, Chinese, Corsicans, and Portuguese. The list is always incomplete, but they all move and meet on an unfamiliar soil, in a violent rhythm of race and religion. Today their descendants exist in an unpredictable and infinite range of custom and endeavour, people in the most haphazard combinations, surrounded by memories of splendour and misery, the sad and dying kingdom of Sugar, a future full of promises. And always the sea!

What a strange view this flight, at low altitude, offers from Haiti and the Dominican Republic, past Puerto Rico and over the American Virgin islands to the quiet of Antigua!

The sea is cobalt, changing frivolously to green, bright semicircles of foam along the coast that stretches and contracts like arms in a gymnasium. The tide seems to encourage those exiled pieces of land to turn into islands. They prolong themselves in a squad of green surfaces; they narrow into brief mounds of vegetation, entirely silenced by the ocean. Then they reappear, tiny islands in a heroic effort to resist the total embrace of the sea, gaining length and eloquence as they form new rings of foam that lash into the curve of the land which continues its extraordinary shape; an illogical geometry on the blue-bright screen of the morning, appearing almost suspended between sea and sky, an enchanting exchange of blues turning to green and back again.

At last, exhausted, they halt, as though rearranging themselves into new and sudden formations of flotsam, maintaining, as it were, a faith in the immortality of the land; and knowing, for certain, that their efforts will be renewed with the appearance of St Thomas. Islands multiply everywhere.

### 3

'But what happened before all those different people went sailing that way? Who were there before Christopher Columbus lost his way?'

Folding up his map, this little English boy wants to have an answer. Nothing is certain in this region of time. Legend is our only guide; and since legend is the natural language of children, it is better to let children reply; and the children should be of the Caribbean. Three boys: Singh, Lee and Bob!

Imagine them in the open air, approaching or approached by an English visitor who might, after all, be a remote descendant of Columbus himself. The first thing the Lady will notice is their diversity of complexions. They might have come from three different parts of the world. Yet they speak the same idiom, live the same history, and are obviously agreed on making a little money out of her.

What are their names? How did they come by their names? And why does one boy's name perplex her?

Singh seems a perfectly suitable name for the boy with the Indian face. Lee is obviously a gift from China.

And Bob? The visitor recognises the original Robert. It is a white name which this exuberant black boy uses as though he had invented it himself. 'Bob what?' the Lady asks. But he wants to get on with the story, so he replies: 'Bob whatever you like.'

It's a strange way to treat names, but it's his way. In the age of religious expansion, this Lady would have given him a second name on the spot. But it is too late to bother about names, for the question about the Caribs remains.

'Who are these Tribe Boys,' the Lady asks.

' 'Tis some history 'bout San Cristobal,' says Bob. 'We learn it from early.'

'An' if any strangers around,' said Singh, 'sometimes we tell it as a work. 'Cause not everybody know how to tell it.'

The Lady takes a seat and the face of China like the face of India glances a boy's message to the face of Africa. They are not going to miss this chance. A moment's hesitation, an interval of nervous stammering, and then they are off.

' 'Twas like in that time when the world know only nature an' noise.'

'Bird noise and wind,' said Singh.

'An' plain animal talk,' Bob continued. 'An' the fish dancin' wild an' makin' faces at the bottom o' the ocean, an' only the sun get permission to say the time, an' the moon only makin' plans to decide the size o' the sea, or makin' fun at some mountains which couldn't climb no more, an' sometimes collapse if a new tide turn upside down, and shake up the sand. Like such a time it was for San Cristobel, long, long before human interference.'

'Like in Genesis,' Lee said.

'As in the beginnin',' said Bob, 'before sense start to make separation betwixt some things an' some things.'

'An' food was free,' said Singh, ' 'cause there was no han' to hide what it take.'

'Except for the animals who fight an' fail,' said Lee.

'Except for them,' said Bob, 'but lan' didn't belong to nobody, an' the law, you feel, was only nature authorisin'.'

'Or refusin' to interfere,' said Lee.

'So why we say,' Bob continued, 'that San Cristobal set up a good example like the world before men make arrangements.'

'You better take over from here,' said Bob. Singh nodded quickly.

'Well just so it was,' said Singh. 'Exactly the state o' the island when the Tribe Boys arrive. Right here on San Cristobal. Nobody know where they sail from or how they favour here from home. But just so. They set foot on San Cristobal, see it was empty, and say there an' then that it belong to them.'

'Exact,' said Lee, 'exact. It may not satisfy simple sense nowadays, but that time was when a man could set a foot first anywhere, an' decide where his foot rest an' could further ramble belong to him.'

'So the Tribe Boys take possession,' said Singh, 'an' they settle in behavin' as their nature teach them. Their wife cook and make bed, an' the land begin to take a human shape, turnin' soft, an' sheddin' new food wherever the Boys put down their fingers, tendin' seed an' tiny plant for what we call harvest. An' it work like a miracle in the sky, the way things seem to respect them. An' it seem that what we refer to as family was not a mere man an' woman with the result thereof, but animals too. The land play human too, learnin' to obey, an' they had some peace.'

'A lot o' peace,' said Bob, 'plenty peace. The Tribe Boys had peace.'

'Just so,' said Singh, 'as you say, they had peace. The day was for doin', when their hand hold the land, an' the night was for knowin' what happen in the day. That is peace, real peace.'

'No trainin' with alphabet,' said Bob, 'temptin' the brain to turn soft, an' confuse everything or go extreme.'

'Exact,' said Singh, 'as you say. Peace. But a peace which touch more than ordinary sense. The peace which touch the Tribe Boys at night take them in a trance to the top o' the world an' to the beginnin' an' end o' the ocean. An' that peace last for a time no man feel it necessary to count. An' then without any warnin' at all, like a next kind o' miracle, peace disappear. Some Kings come on the scene. Things get tight for the Tribe Boys, an' 'twas only then we see what they never show before. The Tribe Boys had a human will complete. That is to die before takin' any kind o' defeat in disgrace. An' so the fighting start.'

'Where a man work,' said Lee, 'you can't always tell what turn his reward will take. So with the Tribe Boys. They put a seed in the ground expectin' nature to raise it up an' train it with time to make a certain taste, and sudden so, like when the Kings come, something say that taste is one thing, but what now sweeten the tongue must turn to a kind o' terror. An' the Tribe Boys use simple food to fight with.'

' 'Cause they didn't know the secret o' the gun,' said Singh, 'an' the Kings went to work with guns. An' a man ain't worth much in the eyes of the gun. Strength or no strength, when bullets begin to talk, there's only one tune to expect. A man must say "amen".'

' 'Tis true what you say 'bout the guns,' said Lee, 'an' the Tribe Boys understand. But what they understand better was the sweet talk of the Kings. The Kings talk like angels, ever so gentle like a beggar in his bags. So the Kings say they claim San Cristobal, claim was the word they use, they claim San Cristobal, but the Tribe Boys could stay an' help. Help mean serve, and serve mean, you know what? So the Tribe Boys make their intention clear. They won't serve. So they take to the hills where they had their pepper trees plant like a forest for hidin'. An' the guns follow them, and the Kings who know the strength in a man, wait for the bullets to make a silence in the hills, an' then follow after.'

'An' that fightin' stop and start again,' said Singh, 'an' last till only God knows how long. An' the Bandit Kings would turn back for a time an' then come again with a next surprise o' battle.   But whenever the Kings make a little retreat, an' leave the islan' for a time, the Tribe Boys work like their hands gone mad. They was makin' a hole right 'cross the ground under San Cristobal.'

'More than one way to kill a mouse,' said Bob.

'Bet your life,' said Singh, 'an' the same turn out true for Kings who carry guns. 'Cause when they reach in the forest which once use' to flavour food, the Tribe Boys had a new home that reach right 'cross San Cristobal under the earth. A hole that just open an' close at one end an' a next, holdin' nothing but a total darkness that turn left and right. The Tribe Boys went crawling like worms through the belly o' the lan'. An' San Cristobal, on top, where the hills use' to swim whenever wind come, poor San Cristobal was nothing but fire and smoke. The pepper trees just burn and the Kings crawl like cripples who can't find their crutch, 'cause when that smoke wrap round them, it put the fire o' hell in every eye.'

'Ever bite a pepper in the centre?' said Bob, 'just where the seeds waitin' to touch your tongue?'

'You got to remember that,' said Singh, 'then maybe you feel for a secon' or so what it mean when smokin' pepper sit in a poor human eye. It is time an' a half before nature show itself again in a proper vision. An' by then the Tribe Boys come up to the surface o' the lan' like sharks playing hide-and-seek, an' they knife every King who couldn't make his way to the shore. Those who escape take to sea. An' the Tribe Boys creep out on to the lan' again, an' San Cristobal stay quiet for some time. But not with the peace as before.'

'Never that same peace,' said Singh, 'from then to now, preparation for food had to mean also preparation for fightin'.'

' 'Cause the Kings set their ambition on San Cristobal,' said Lee, ' 'an every Tribe Boy know they would come back.'

'An' when they reach back,' said Bob, 'what a time it was.'

'They come back with a terrible cargo,' said Lee. 'They bring some ants. The warrior Ants.'

'You can't fight ants,' said Singh, 'not the warrior Ants.'

'The Tribe Boys had bow and arrow ready to do battle with the guns they remember,' said Lee, 'but ants don't understand, an' you can't fight an enemy who don't understand . . .'

'Those Kings forget they had guns,' said Bob, 'they just let the ants inhabit the hole which the Tribe Boys make home.'

'An' that was the end of the Tribe Boys,' said Lee. 'While they keep looking out for the Kings, they didn't notice those warrior Ants multiplyin', making a camp in the belly o' San Cristobal, an' when sense surprise them, it was too late. The ants went all over the hole. They take to every corner an' the hole the Tribe Boys make under the island soon overflow with the warrior Ants. Men alone can't do nothing with creatures o' the kind, an' the Tribe Boys just drop like numbers from five to three, or nineteen to ten.'

'A terrible thing for the eye to see,' said Singh.

'Maybe we understand,' said Bob, 'if we remember some dead chicken which the owner forget to put away. So the Tribe Boys some mornings see their brother or sister, nothing but the shape of a human, only ants, ants in the eyes an' ants in the ears, ants inside an' ants outside the three-days corpse, an' their numbers just keep dropping for them to see. An' soon as they creep out one by one, the guns cut them down till they was but a handful left. An' then they make a decision.'

' 'Twas that human will you talk 'bout,' said Singh.

'Nothin' else,' said Lee, 'the Tribe Boys who remain walk out like they surrender, an' the Kings wait for them to kneel an' beg, 'cause they was goin' to let them serve if they only kneel in surrender.'

'But they won't,' said Bob, 'they swear in whisper one to the next never to take defeat from the Kings, never to be victim complete. An' they walk without stoppin', and the Kings only watch them walk like they join a trance, right to the top o' Mount Misery. An' there they kiss on the cliff for ever, an' then lean their heads down in a last minute dive to their own funeral.'

'They all drown,' said Lee.

'An' those ants take possession.' said Singh, 'complete, terrible possession in the belly o' San Cristobal till the island went under water.'

'That is it,' said Bob, ' 'tis how it happen with the Tribe Boys an' the Bandit Kings.'

Then the Lady asks: 'This really happened?'

And the island of India replies: 'Right here in San Cristobal.'

And the island of Africa replies: 'An' may happen again.'

And the island of China replies: 'Only in a different way.'

These are the islands of the Tempest colonised by the language of Prospero's once absolute wisdom. These are the islands from which the voices of Caliban's descendants have fled with their song.

The theme of this book is the migration of the writer from the Caribbean to the dubious refuge of a metropolitan culture. The metropolis is London.

# THE OCCASION FOR SPEAKING

•

Fashions in proud Italy,
Whose manners still our tardy apish nation
Limps after in base imitation.
*Richard II*, Act II, Scene I

While you here do snoring lie,
Open ey'd conspiracy
His time doth take.
If of life you keep a care,
Shake off slumber, and beware:
Awake, Awake!
*Tempest*, Act II, Scene I

IN ANY country, during this century, it seems that the young will remain too numerous and too strong to fear being alone. It is from this premise that I want to consider the circumstances as well as the significance of certain writers' migration from the British Caribbean to the London metropolis. I shall regard these writers as the product of a new situation—new in the historic sense of time—and I want to regard this situation as one example of a new force in the modern world.

How has it come about that a small group of men, different in years and temperament and social origins, should leave the respective islands they know best, even exchange life there for circumstances which are almost wholly foreign to them? Soldiers have often had to do it as a job, but foreign occupation is not altogether without its attractions. Some civilians have been forced by economic necessity to undertake this risk of migration. But what about the West Indian writers who are now resident in Britain? Why have they migrated? And what, if any, are the peculiar pleasures of exile? Is their journey part of a hunger for recognition? Do they see such recognition as a confirmation of the fact that they are writers? What is the source of their insecurity in the world of letters? And what, on the evidence of their work, is the range of their ambition as writers whose nourishment is now elsewhere, whose absence is likely to drag into a state of permanent separation from their roots?

Like writers from any other country, each West Indian may have made his decision for very personal reasons. But this is a case where all these writers—often regarded both in England and the West Indies as a phenomenon in contemporary literature—all have made the same decision, independent of discussion among themselves, in some cases ignorant of each other except by name. The problem is to examine how this group, as far as my memory serves, is related to that decision.

In order to take you on the inside of what I know, I shall have to draw on what an older man would justly call his reminiscences. I would like to suggest the psychological origins of such a migration so that we may be able to reflect on how this journey towards each writer's expectation may have been responsible for his development both as a man and a writer. I shall use, as evidence, the names and remembered conversations of writers whom I have known and in some cases quarrelled with. For quarrelling may be a necessary error among all men, but it is a distinguishing feature in exiles; and among exiles whose ambitions and predicaments are similar, the quarrel becomes a normal way of being together.

But one characteristic of the West Indian is the tendency to forget; and the most bitter denunciations are often used at a later stage as an opportunity for coming together in order to agree. Jealousy may be present among us; but I think that malice is rare.

The exile is a universal figure. The proximity of our lives to the major issues of our time has demanded of us all some kind of involvement. Some may remain neutral; but all have, at least, to pay attention to what is going on. On the political level, we are often without the right kind of information to make argument effective; on the moral level we have to feel our way through problems for which we have no adequate reference of traditional conduct as a guide. Chaos is often, therefore, the result of our thinking and our doing. We are made to feel a sense of exile by our inadequacy and our irrelevance of function in a society whose past we can't alter, and whose future is always beyond us. Idleness can easily guide us into accepting this as a condition. Sooner or later, in silence or with rhetoric, we sign a contract whose epitaph reads: To be an exile is to be alive.

When the exile is a man of colonial orientation, and his chosen residence is the country which colonised his own history, then there are certain complications. For each exile has not only got to prove his worth to the other, he has to win the approval of Headquarters, meaning in the case of the West Indian writer, England. If the West Indian writer had taken up residence in America—as Claud Mac-Kay did—his development would probably be of a different, indeed, of an opposed order to that of a man who matured in England. One reason is that although the new circumstances are quite different, and even more favourable than those he left in the West Indies, his reservations, his psychology, his whole sense of cultural expectation have not greatly changed. He arrives and travels with the memory, the habitual weight of a colonial relation. On more than one occasion I have seen a West Indian writer *pleased* by compliments which should have been recognised and accepted as simple truths about himself and his work.

I have lately tried to argue, in another connection, that the West Indian student, for example, should not be sent to study in England. Not because England is a bad place for studying, but because the student's whole development as a person is thwarted by the memory, the accumulated stuff of a childhood and adolescence which has been maintained and fertilised by England's historic ties with the West Indies. It would have been better, perhaps, if he had gone to study in France or Germany, to mention countries with a different language; any place where his adjustments would have to take the form of understanding the inhabitants from scratch. He would have to learn to read the German face, the French way of seeing, and so on. In England he does not feel the need to try to understand an Englishman, since all relationships begin with an assumption of previous knowledge, a knowledge acquired in the absence of the people known. This relationship with the English is only another aspect of the West Indian's relation to the *idea* of England.

As an example of this, I would recall an episode on a ship which had brought a number of West Indians to Britain. I was talking to a Trinidadian Civil Servant who had come to take some kind of course in the ways of bureaucracy. A man about forty to forty-five, intelligent enough to be in the senior grade of the Trinidad Civil Service which is by no means backward, a man of some substance among his own class of people. We were talking in a general way about life among the emigrants. The ship was now steady; the tugs were coming alongside. Suddenly there was consternation in the Trinidadian's expression.

'But . . . but,' he said, 'look down there.'

I looked, and since I had lived six years in England, I failed to see anything of particular significance. I asked him what he had seen; and then I realised what was happening.

'*They* do that kind of work, *too*?' he asked.

He meant the white hands and faces on the tug. In spite of films, in spite of reading Dickens—for he would have had to at the school which trained him for the Civil Service—in spite of all this received information, this man had never really felt, as a possibility and a fact, the existence of the English worker. This sudden bewilderment had sprung from his *idea* of England; and one element in that *idea* was that he was not used to seeing an Englishman working with his hands in the streets of Port-of-Spain.

This is a seed of his colonisation which has been subtly and richly infused with myth. We can change laws overnight; we may reshape images of our feeling. But this myth is most difficult to dislodge. It may be modified by circumstances, exploited or concealed by the behaviour each chooses for particular situations; but it is there, a part of the actual texture of behaviour itself. Sometimes it will take the form of a calculated aggressiveness; at other times it may take the form of sulking. At its worst, it is the soil from which the perfect lackey is born.

It has a great effect upon the culture of a community; for it contains—and can even succeed in establishing as permanent—important judgments of value. I remember how pleased I was to learn that my first book, *In the Castle of My Skin*, had been bought by an American publisher. They were very enthusiastic, and they had asked the famous Negro novelist, Richard Wright, to write an introduction. I was going to be launched, so to speak. I started to make the most modest calculations about its sale. My naïve enthusiasm and assurance had set me thinking, with conviction, that my first book was going to capture at least a third of Richard Wright's buying public. The Negro reading class in America might not buy it—I had heard something similar about Wright—but that was not important since I had no objection to white money.

It was the money I was thinking of to the exclusion of the book's critical reputation in America. The book had had an important critical press in England; its reputation here was substantial; so it could make no difference what America thought. My sole wish was that it might be reviewed by someone like Edmund Wilson whose critical intelligence I respected and admired. The point I am making is that American judgment, on the whole, could not IMPRESS me. I didn't even question that premiss. In this sense, my attitude was no different from that of the average English middle-class intellectual who opens and closes the case with the weight of a privileged ignorance: 'You know what the Americans are like . . .' Which is precisely what we don't know.

This is what I mean by the *myth*. It has little to do with lack of intelligence. It has nothing to do with one's origins in class. It is deeper and more natural. It is akin to the nutritive function of milk which all sorts of men receive at birth. It is *myth* as the source of spiritual foods absorbed, and learnt for exercise in the future. This *myth* begins in the West Indian from the earliest stages of his education. But it is not yet turned against America. In a sense, America does not even exist. It begins with the fact of England's supremacy in taste and judgment: a fact which can only have meaning and weight by a calculated cutting down to size of all non-England. The first to be cut down is the colonial himself.

This is one of the seeds which much later bear such strange fruit as the West Indian writers' departure from the very landscape which is the raw material of all their books. These men had to leave if they were going to function as writers since books, in that particular colonial conception of literature, were not—meaning, too, are not supposed to be—written by natives. Those among the natives who read also believed that; for all the books they had read, their whole introduction to something called culture, all of it, in the form of words, came from outside: Dickens, Jane Austen, Kipling and that sacred gang.

The West Indian's education was imported in much the same way that flour and butter are imported from Canada. Since the cultural negotiation was strictly between England and the natives, and England had acquired, somehow, the divine right to organise the native's reading, it is to be expected that England's export of literature would be English. Deliberately and exclusively English. And the further back in time England went for these treasures, the safer was the English commodity. So the examinations, which would determine that Trinidadian's future in the Civil Service, imposed Shakespeare, and Wordsworth, and Jane Austen and George Eliot and the whole tabernacle of dead names, now come alive at the world's greatest summit of literary expression.

How in the name of Heavens could a colonial native taught by an English native within a strict curriculum diligently guarded by yet another English native who functioned as a reliable watch-dog, the favourite clerk of a foreign administration: how could he ever get out from under this ancient mausoleum of historic achievement?

Some people keep asking why the West Indian writers should leave the vitality and freshness (frankly I don't believe in the vitality talk, as I shall explain) for the middle age resignation of England. It seems a mystery to them. The greater mystery is that there should be West Indian writers at all. For a writer cannot function; and, indeed, he has no function as writer if those who read and teach reading in his society have started their education by questioning his very right to write.

I returned to the West Indies in 1956 and took the opportunity of speaking to the sixth forms in the different grammar schools. I was now something of a name in these circles. They had started to read West Indian books. At the end of one of these lectures in British Guiana, a girl got up to put what was generally regarded as the key question.

'Mr Lamming,' she said, 'would you say that the praise for your books, and all the things the English critics say about them are only due to the novelty of what you are writing about?'

It would have taken too long to explain to her the history of the IDEA behind that question. It was asked in all honesty, and without the slightest trace of disrespect. What can one do, within an hour, but answer, hoping that one's voice offers the right tone of ambiguity and rebuke: 'Perhaps, perhaps it may be so.'

Not long after that I returned to England. And here is an English critic, Mr Kingsley Amis, discussing West Indian novelists in the *Spectator*, ruminating from the ambivalent wisdom of don-novelist and week-end reviewer.

'The idea about experiment being the life-blood of the English novel is one that dies hard. "Experiment," in this context, boils down pretty regularly to "obtruded oddity," whether in construction—multiple viewpoints and such—or in style; it is not felt that adventurousness in subject-matter or attitude or tone really counts. Shift from one scene to the next in mid-sentence, cut down on verbs or definite articles, and you are putting yourself right up in the forefront, at any rate in the eyes of those who were reared on Joyce and Virginia Woolf and take a jaundiced view of more recent developments. (Victims of this malady are also likely to suffer from a craving for uplift, manifested in bouts of transitory enthusiasm for digests of the Kierkegaard-Nietzsche-Shaw line-up and a hysterical aversion to contemporary British philosophy.) In such a situation, it becomes possible for a reviewer in the *Times Literary Supplement* to argue that the English novel now lies in the hands of the non-English, accompanying the claim with side-swipes at the incompetence of the English to write English poetry.'

Note the emphases; for later there is a tone of caution and scrupulosity which suggests that the answer has already been formed. The references to the 'Kierkegaard-Nietzsche-Shaw line-up and a hsyterical aversion to contemporary British philosophy'—this reference has absolutely nothing to do with the West Indian novel. But Kingsley Amis is here using the occasion of the West Indian novel to rebuke the critic in the *Times Literary Supplement* whom, it is not unlikely, Amis knows. I am not sure of that acquaintance; but I am sure that the Kierkegaard-Nietzsche-Shaw line-up is a direct attack on the young writers Colin Wilson and Stuart Holroyd who, I presume, have little or no use for Amis and his crowd.

In other words, the *Spectator*, an important week-end review, invites a British intellectual to consider the meaning of the West Indian novel; and he uses that opportunity to get off his chest major grievances which have nothing to do with the subject he is discussing. It is not unlikely that the critic in the *Times Literary Supplement* was using the occasion of reviewing Mr Carew's book in order to throw darts at Mr Amis and others. What maddens one is the fact that this type of mind cannot register the West Indian writer as a subject for intelligent and thoughtful consideration.

The historical fact is that the 'emergence' of a dozen or so novelists in the British Caribbean with some fifty books to their credit or disgrace, and all published between 1948 and 1958, is in the nature of a phenomenon. There has been no comparable event in culture anywhere in the British Commonwealth during the same period. What is more important than Amis and all that, is the tragedy that there is hardly a West Indian politician—Williams is the only exception to my knowledge—who knows this fact, or who would be capable of evaluating its significance.

Yet there are a few Germans who are working on this 'strange phenomenon of the British Caribbean novelist.' They are not doing it to attack anybody. They are doing it because it is another piece of evidence for some thesis they are trying to work out about the universality of regional cultures. I do not share all their views about the West Indian writers, but what really matters here is that they are serious readers and the nature of their interest is a good basis for dialogue. The review by Amis—a consideration of eight books—runs to some fifteen hundred words; but the name 'America' is never used once. And the West Indian novel, particularly in the aspect of idiom, cannot be understood unless you take a good look at the American nineteenth century, a good look at Melville, Whitman and Mark Twain. I don't believe this has ever occurred to Amis who chose the books or had them chosen as though one were picking raffle tickets from a hat. The article ends:

'All in all investigation suggests only one inclusive statement about West Indian writers: that they are far too various for any just generalisation about them to be offered. There could be no better portent for the future.'

That is what we are left with after all those sentences. Amis as a critic or novelist is of no more than topical importance; but it is not irrelevant to point out that he is also a teacher of English literature in a British University.

The girl in British Guiana was about seventeen. This critic is nearly forty. But there is, fundamentally, no difference in their relation to the myth which prompts these surmises. The girl does not yet understand what it means to be colonial. On the other hand, and as part of this historic contract, the English critic accepts—for what else can he do?—the privilege so natural and so free of being the child and product and voice of a colonising civilisation. Hence the girl's assurance in dealing with a native writer, and the English critic's leisurely objectivity in assessing a colonial literature. This critic might have been, at least, interesting if he were sufficiently active, mentally, to consider the meaning of his own predicament. I mean *consider*: a process which has nothing to do with shouting, in mockery, the adolescent privileges that are the theme of any Mr Don't-really-care-a-damn-except-to-be-as-decent-as-possible. If he were black (notice how the colour is creeping in) He might have been regarded as a simple, articulate boy. Which is, perhaps, how he regards one or two of the West Indian writers. This has nothing to do with colour prejudice, in the sense that either this critic or I might draw stilettoes when the fog comes down over Notting Hill. It has to do with the myth which colonialism, seen as a development and later as an improvement on slavery, has created.

Mr V. S. Naipaul, a West Indian who is also a regular novel reviewer for the *New Statesman*, argues in a recent article that he could not endure the West Indian community because it was philistine. Of course, it is a philistine society; but so, I'm told, are Canada and White South Africa. Therefore one can't say philistine and leave it at that. This would be to describe their present, and in doing so by the absolute judgment of philistine, condemn them permanently to a future which you have already chosen. I reject this attitude; and when it comes from a colonial who is nervous both in and away from his native country, I interpret it as a simple confession of the man's inadequacy—inadequacy which must be rationalised since the man himself has come to accept it.

I would like to draw attention to a different kind of difficulty in the case of the American Negro novelist, Mr James Baldwin. In his most perceptive and brilliantly stated essays, *Notes of a Native Son*, he tries to examine and interpret his own situation as an American Negro who is also a novelist drawing on the spiritual legacy of Western European civilisation. Baldwin, you will notice, has made the canvas wider. Not just colonial vis-à-vis England, but American and Negro up against the monolithic authority of European culture. It is, you will see in his book, a more profound and a more useful intelligence than one can reasonably expect of Mr Naipaul.

'I know, in any case, that the most crucial time in my own development came when I was forced to recognise that I was a kind of bastard of the West; when I followed the line of my past I did not find myself in Europe but in Africa. And this meant that in some subtle way, in a really profound way I brought to Shakespeare, Bach, Rembrandt, to the stones of Paris, to the cathedral at Chartres, and to the Empire State Building, a special attitude. These were not really my creations; they did not contain my history; I might search in them in vain for ever for any reflection of myself; I was an interloper. At the same time I had no other heritage which I could possibly hope to use. I had certainly been unfitted for the jungle or the tribe. I would have to appropriate these white centuries. I would have to make them mine . . .'

That is very well stated; and it gives the background to part of the West Indian situation. From the point of view of language, for example, the British West Indian had to make English his; for English was the only word tool he started with as a reader and a learner.

But Baldwin has a special difficulty here. He speaks in anger, however controlled, of the achievement which goes with Shakespeare and Bach, the cathedral at Chartres, even the Empire State Building which he saw as a child. There is, unquestionably, a feeling of inferiority, both personal and racial, when he is in the presence of these monuments. He would really have liked to be a child of the civilisation which produced these; yet when he looks back on the meaning of his racial history (hoping, no doubt, to find some alternative achievement) what does he discover?

'I might search in vain for any reflection of myself. I had certainly been unfitted for the jungle or the tribe.'

We must pause to consider the source of Mr Baldwin's timidity; for it has a most respectable ancestry. Here is the great German philosopher Hegel having the last word on Africa in his Introduction to *The Philosophy of History*:

'Africa proper, as far as History goes back, has remained—for all purposes of connection with the rest of the world—shut up; it is the Gold-land compressed within itself—the land of childhood, which lying beyond the days of self-conscious history, is enveloped in the dark mantle of Night . . .

'The negro as already observed exhibits the natural man in his completely wild and untamed state. We must lay aside all thought of reverence and morality—all that we call feeling—if we would rightly comprehend him; there is nothing harmonious with humanity to be found in this type of character.

'At this point we leave Africa never to mention it again. For it is no historical part of the world; it has no movement or development to exhibit. Historical movement in it—that is in its northern part— belong to the Asiatic or European World . . .

'What we properly understand by Africa, is the Unhistorical, Undeveloped Spirit, still involved in the *conditions of mere nature* and which had to be presented here only as on the threshold of the World's history . . . . . .

'The History of the World travels from East to West, for Europe *is absolutely the end of* History, Asia the beginning.'

It is incredible that the mind which contributed so brilliantly to our understanding of other matters could, through rumour, bigotry and arrogance, commit itself to such uncritical folly.

He never visited Africa; and when we refer to his sources which are exclusively the accounts of the early voyagers, it doesn't bother him in the least that the actual texts are in direct contradiction to his own interpretations. He speaks with immense authority on Ashanti ('Among the Ashantees the King inherits all the property left by his subjects at their death') an opinion which is not worth a moment's consideration from anyone who has read Rattray on the subject of Land Tenure and Alienation in the Customary Laws of Ashanti.

It is important to relate the psychology implied in Mr Baldwin's regret to the kind of false confidence which Hegel represents in the European consciousness. For what disqualifies African man from Hegel's World of History is his apparent incapacity to evolve with the logic of Language which is the only aid man has in capturing the Idea. African Man, for Hegel, has no part in the common pursuit of the Universal. In other words we shall have to treat the Senegalese poet, Leopold Senghor as an absolute phenomenon, a mysterious barbarian, when he writes:

'A people who refuse the rendezvous of history, which does not believe that it bears a unique message, that people is finished; you can put it in the Museum. The Negro African is not finished before he is started; above all let him act. Let him bring like a leaven his message to the World. To help in constructing the Civilisation of the Universal.'

There would have been no need to underline all this if James Baldwin were not one of the finest writers—black or white—at work on the American scene. But it is the colonising pressure of the European claim which creates an element of embarrassment in Baldwin's glance towards Africa.

The backward glance is painful for it offers him nothing but a vision of the bush, primitive, intractable, night-black in its inaccessibility. That word, bush, the symbol of Baldwin's long night of jungle and tribe, is final. It does not occur to Baldwin to pause—his position as an American Negro born to an industrial civilisation will not allow it—and reflect on what might have been happening in that bush; that there, too, might have been men whose lives, however fearsome, were an example of some very complex discovery of social organisation. It is enough for Baldwin's purpose to leave it at the bush. Any white American would have done the same; and Baldwin is, first and foremost, an American, although he is black. We know what is meant by bush. It is the tom-tom and the axe: the tom-tom always loud with noise, and the axe for ever suggestive of blood. It is here, perhaps, that the old white myth and fear of superb sexual potency in the black male may have started.

But there is a great difference between Baldwin and a comparable West Indian. No black West Indian, in his own native environment, would have this highly oppressive sense of being Negro. That may be all to the good; but there are definite reasons. It has to do with the West Indian's social and racial situation. The West Indian, however black and dispossessed, could never have felt the experience of being in a minority. For the black faces vastly outnumber the white or expatriate white. This numerical superiority has given the West Indian a certain leisure, a certain experience of relaxation among white expatriates; for the West Indian has learnt, by sheer habit, to take that white presence for granted. Which is, precisely, his trouble.

At the other extreme, Baldwin is haunted by that white face, and the historic and cultural meaning of its achievement for him as a writer. To be black, in the West Indies, is to be poor; whereas to be black (rich or poor) in an American context is to be a traditional target for specific punishments. Racism is not just an American problem. It is an element of American culture. No such thing is true of the British West Indies. Hence the real tragedy of Notting Hill!

Is Baldwin's attitude to the treasures of European civilisation a deficiency of the Negro? I think not. Let's follow for a moment the strictures of Mr Graham Hough—one of the finest critics at work in England today—on T. S. Eliot. In his introduction to the study of D. H. Lawrence, called *The Dark Sun*, Graham Hough draws our attention to the difficulties which Mr Eliot has in acknowledging Lawrence to be a writer of the first importance. Mr Eliot's difficulty springs from his contempt for Lawrence's education and social background.

'Childhood is always provincial,' Hough writes, 'and its horizon is always restricted—and particular circumstances that make it so are not important. A rather hoity-toity concept of culture has been used

B

to show that Lawrence had a hole-and-corner upbringing, and re-mained therefore an inspired barbarian, ignorant of the grand, calm expanses of properly certified European civilisation. But the only people who ever inhabit this kind of European civilisation are culti-vated Americans like Henry James and T. S. Eliot. Europeans live in Nottingham or Nancy, Paris or Piacenza, Frankfurt or Fenny Stratford, and the actual life of any of these places has always seemed a poor and disappointing affair to visitors from the Platonic New England heights.'

Eliot and Baldwin white and black, are both American. Mr Eliot's estimate of Lawrence is colonial in intention. Mr Baldwin's terror of the African bush as well as his feeling of impotence before the massive approval of Shakespeare and Rembrandt, is equally colonial, but infinitely more serious as a crisis which any writer in his circum-stances must resolve. For in Baldwin's case, it seems that the intelli-gence suffers a kind of arthritis. There is a swift and total paralysis of native pride. Whatever eloquence the voice may achieve; what we are hearing is the colonial wail; what we are seeing is the persistent shadow of the man that writer could have been.


2


Our social background in the Caribbean is, therefore, somewhat different from that of an American Negro. It is also quite different from that of the West African who has already given warning that a new contribution is about to be made to writing in English. The West Indian occupies a most unusual position in all these social and racial blocks. In relation to the African, the American Negro, and to Western culture he is, in a sense, a peripheral man. The charge that he does not know who and what he is can be regarded as irrelevant, or a universal characteristic of his time.

What the West Indian shares with the African is a common politi-cal predicament: a predicament which we call colonial; but the word colonial has a deeper meaning for the West Indian than it has for the African. The African, in spite of his modernity, has never been wholly severed from the cradle of a continuous culture and tradition. His colonialism mainly takes the form of lack of privilege in organis-ing the day to day affairs of his country. This state of affairs is almost at an end; and its end is the result of the African's persistent and effective demand for political freedom.

On the other hand, the West Indies is, perhaps, the only modern community in the world where the desire to be free, the ambition to make their own laws and regulate life according to their own impulses, is dormant. All the criteria which are demanded of a colonial territory before it can claim independence have been met in the West Indies. The Civil Service in Trinidad and Barbados and Jamaica have been run by these natives for many decades. The level of literacy is higher than in most colonial territories which have been granted independence since the last war. The West Indies occupy a strategic position between North and South America.

'These colonies have an importance far greater than their size and population would indicate. There are outposts of growing democracy in the Western Hemisphere, rearguard garrisons of European and American imperialism, and fermenting test tubes of racial relations.'

Therefore, the demands which the Colonial Office appear to make of African territories have been met by the West Indies. The famous question which is now put to places like Nyasaland and Nigeria ('If we go, who are going to run it?') that question was answered long ago in the Caribbean. Why, then, wasn't the British West Indies a free, sovereign state ten years ago? Why isn't it a sovereign state today? The answer explains the difference in the meaning of the word colonial for an African and a West Indian. The West Indian met the criteria for self-government, answered the question who will run it; and by the very perfection of his answer, he could not move any further. The African's attitude could be summed up in the reply: 'We don't care about the criteria; and although the question about backward may be true, it is not at the moment the question we are interested in. We demand our freedom, or we are going to throw you out—but for God's sake, let us try to stand up.'

The traditional cultures of African civilisation have given the African this strength. Moreover, it is impossible to be alone when two-thirds of the world's peasantry are marching. It is the brevity of the West Indian's history and the fragmentary nature of the different cultures which have fused to make something new; it is the absolute dependence on the values implicit in that language of his coloniser which has given him a special relation to the word, colonialism. It is not merely a political definition; it is not merely the result of certain economic arrangements. It started as these, and grew somewhat deeper. Colonialism is the very base and structure of the West Indian's cultural awareness. His reluctance in asking for complete, political freedom (indeed, the Colonial Office is hoping that he hurries up and takes it, since that will help them add one more achievement to their list), his reluctance is due to the fear that he has never had to stand. A foreign or absent Mother culture has always cradled his judgment. Moreover, the lack of those hostile forces which Mr Baldwin has felt in Alabama and Georgia, this freedom from physical fear has created a state of complacency in the West Indian awareness. And the higher up he moves in the social scale, the more crippled his mind and impulses become by the resultant complacency.

In order to change this way of seeing, the West Indian must change the very structure, the very basis of his values. This would be a much more enormous task, if the time for doing it did not coincide with similar changes throughout the world. What the West Indian has to do if he is going to be released from this prison of colonialism, from this dread of standing up, is precisely what the whole world is now called upon to do. The scale of the undertaking is different; but the fundamental challenge is the same. For the West Indies—African, Chinese and Indian by mixture—the boys Singh, Lee and Bob— belong to that massive peasant majority whose leap in the twentieth century has shattered all the traditional calculations of the West, of European civilisation.

I am not much interested in what the West Indian writer has brought to the English language; for English is no longer the exclusive language of the men who live in England. That stopped a long time ago; and it is today, among other things, a West Indian language. What the West Indians do with it is their own business. A more important consideration is what the West Indian novelist has brought to the West Indies. That is the real question; and its answer can be the beginning of an attempt to grapple with that colonial structure of awareness which has determined West Indian values.

There are, for me, just three important events in British Caribbean history. I am using the term, history, in an active sense. Not a succession of episodes which can easily be given some casual connection. What I mean by historical event is the creation of a situation which offers antagonistic oppositions and a challenge of survival that had to be met by all involved.

The first event is the discovery. That began, like most other discoveries, with a journey; a journey inside, or a journey out and across. This was the meaning of Columbus. The original purpose of the journey may sometimes have nothing to do with the results that attend upon it. That journey took place nearly five centuries ago; and the result has been one of the world's most fascinating communities. The next event is the abolition of slavery and the arrival of the East—India and China—in the Caribbean Sea. The world met here, and it was at every level, except administration, a peasant world. In one way or another, through one upheaval after another, these people, forced to use a common language which they did not possess on arrival, have had to make something of their surroundings. What most of the world regard today as the possibility of racial harmony has always been the background of the West Indian prospect. Racial integration will be an achievement of the American school. In the West Indies, it is the background against which learning has taken place. We in the West Indies can meet the twentieth century without fear; for we begin with colossal advantages. The West Indian, though provincial, is perhaps the most cosmopolitan man in the world. No Indian from India, no European, no African can adjust with greater ease and naturalness to new situations than the West Indian.

The English have been helped in understanding this through cricket. When the Indian team takes the field at Lords, it is a team of Indians. Some are short and some are tall; but they *look* alike. When the Australian team takes the field at Lords; it is a team of Australians. The English recognise that they look like English people. But when a West Indian team takes the field at Lords, Lords itself is bewildered; and not because they are all that ugly. For what do we see? Short and tall, yes; but Indian, Negro, Chinese, White, Portuguese mixed with Syrian. To the English eye—it would be interesting to overhear their night-time dialogue—the mixtures are as weird and promising as the rainbow. And the combination of that team is not a political gimmick. That is the West Indian team; for it is, in fact, the West Indian situation.

Just imagine for a moment, if possible, an official South African team imitating the West Indian example. Try to imagine it in 1960; and you will get some idea of where the West Indies stand in relation to the future. It was slavery and the emancipation of slaves, leading subsequently to the arrival of Indians and Chinese—which helped to bring about such a situation.

The third important event in our history is the discovery of the novel by West Indians as a way of investigating and projecting the inner experiences of the West Indian community. The second event is about a hundred and fifty years behind us. The third is hardly two decades ago. What the West Indian writer has done has nothing to do with that English critic's assessments. The West Indian writer is the first to add a new dimension to writing about the West Indian community.

We have had travel books, some of them excellent, like Patrick Leigh Fermor's *Traveller's Tree*. We have had the social and economic treatises. The anthropologists have done some exercises there. We have had Government White papers as well as the Black diaries of Governor's wives. But these worked like old-fashioned cameras, catching what they can—which wasn't very much—as best they could, which couldn't be very good, since they never got the camera near enough. As it should be, the novelist was the first to relate the West Indian experience from the inside. He was the first to chart the West Indian memory as far back as he could go. It is to the West Indian novelist—who had no existence twenty years ago—that the anthropologist and all other treatises about West Indians have to turn.

I do not want to make any chauvinistic claim for the West Indian writer. But it is necessary to draw attention to the novelty—not the exotic novelty which inferior colonials and uninformed critics will suggest—but the historic novelty of our situation. We have seen in our lifetime an activity called writing, in the form of the novel, come to fruition without any previous native tradition to draw upon. Mittelholzer and Reid and Selvon and Roger Maïs are to the new colonial reader in the West Indies precisely what Fielding and Smollett and the early English novelists would be to the readers of their own generation. These West Indian writers are the earliest pioneers in this method of investigation. They are the first builders of what will become a tradition in West Indian imaginative writing: a tradition which will be taken for granted or for the purpose of critical analysis by West Indians of a later generation.

The novel, as the English critic applies this term, is about two hundred years old, and even then it had a long example of narrative poetry to draw on. The West Indian novel, by which I mean the novel written by the West Indian about the West Indian reality is hardly twenty years old. And here is the fascination of the situation. The education of all these writers is more or less middle-class Western culture, and particularly English culture. But the substance of their books, the general motives and directions, are peasant. One of the most popular complaints made by West Indians against their novelists is the absence of novels about the West Indian Middle Class.

Why is it that Reid, Mittelholzer in his early work, Selvon, Neville Dawes, Roger Mais, Andrew Salkey, Jan Carew—why is it that their work is shot through and through with the urgency of peasant life? And how has it come about that their colonial education should not have made them pursue the general ambitions of non-provincial writers. How is it that they have not to play at being the Eliots and Henry Jameses of the West Indies? Instead, they move nearer to Mark Twain.

I shall deal with this at greater length elsewhere. It is sufficient to say that they did not. Unlike the previous governments and departments of educators, unlike the business man importing commodities, the West Indian novelist did not look out across the sea to another source. He looked in and down at what had traditionally been ignored. For the first time the West Indian peasant became other than a cheap source of labour. He became, through the novelist's eye, a living existence, living in silence and joy and fear, involved in riot and carnival. It is the West Indian novel that has restored the West Indian peasant to his true and original status of personality.

## 3

Edgar Mittelholzer was born in British Guiana in 1909. He came to Trinidad in 1941; but he was a name to me before I left Barbados to live in Trinidad. It was a long time before I met him in Trinidad, partly because I was not senior enough in the business of writing. There was a small group who met once a month under the sponsorship of Judge Hallinam, a connoisseur of the arts, at the British Council. It was a kind of inner circle made up largely of men around Mittelholzer's age. Ernest Carr, a grand old man, Farrell, a lecturer in English at the Queen's Royal College, and such people. They read each other's work, and there was discussion.

I can't say what happened there since I never went. I must have been eighteen or nineteen at the time; I had had some poems published in the literary magazine *BIM*, but I was a stranger in Trinidad. These men, partly through age, were not among my friends, and to make everything more remote, I had the feeling that they were mainly concerned with fiction. They might have written the occasional poem as, I gathered, most writers of fiction are inclined to do. But they were not poets; and poetry was my exclusive business. I was a poet with a very positive young man's attitude about things that were not poetry. It didn't matter how good their short stories were, prose always struck me as an inferior way for any serious writer to use words. My favourite novelists at the time were Joseph Conrad and Thomas Hardy. With the exception of Ernest Carr whom I admired and whom I came to regard with deep affection and gratitude, I never met these men. But I often went to Carr's house at the edge of some magnificent forest in Belmont, and those conversations were among the best things that happened to me in Trinidad.

I admired Mittelholzer for different reasons. Not because he had had a novel published, *Corentyne Thunder*, which gave him a certain seniority of prestige among people who wrote in Trinidad. It also made him the target for the envy of some middle-class boys who were educated to the point of not accepting that Mittelholzer's novel could be any good. Many of these young men were once political in the domesticated sense that they had a debating club and used to ask English visitors to give lectures in the hope of tripping the lecturer up over details in history or English literature. They wanted to show off what they had learnt to the foreigner, which explains why, when the actual stuff was being written under their noses, they could not recognise it. An English novelist was once a target for that occasion, and when I met him in England some years later, he described one of those evenings for me. We discussed it in much the same way that I am recalling my memory of Trinidad; and he was telling me how, intelligent as those young men were, their opinions of certain contemporary writers were so exasperating, that he would have to put an end to the talk by saying: 'But I happen to know personally the writers you're talking about, and they mean no such thing. You are not talking about them. You are using them as a subject for a debate about literature.'

This was the kind of atmosphere in which all of us grew up. On the one hand a mass of people who were either illiterate, or if not had no connection whatever to literature since they were too poor or too tired to read; and on the other hand a colonial middle-class educated, it seemed, for the specific purpose of sneering at anything which grew or was made on native soil.

I felt a great admiration for Mittelholzer for the simple reason that he refused to take any permanent employment in Trinidad. There was a reverse of the division of labour in the family. His wife went to an office; and he did the house work, shopping and the lot, leaving himself some seven or eight hours a day for writing. In Trinidad at the time (it's as late as 1946) a man who made Mittelholzer's commitment, and for the same reason, was regarded in much the same way I imagine that the French Church came to regard Joan of Arc. They didn't call him a witch; but they said he wasn't altogether right in the head. This is always a way in the West Indies of warning that no one will take you seriously. And then Mittelholzer would do some strange things. He took a walk every evening about five or six around the Port-of-Spain savannah. It was his exercise before going back to work, but it usually ended with him sitting on a bench opposite the large building where the Roman Catholic archbishop of Trinidad lived.

He would sit there, eyes bright with enquiry as though he wanted to stare the whole Christian myth out of existence. But he worked and worked, and it is said that he had written many novels, often rejected by publishers, before he left Trinidad for England. I remem-

ber meeting him a few days before he left. The impression I recall is
that of a man who had served a long imprisonment, hearing that the
sentence had been commuted. At last he could get out. That is how each writer felt. Not only those who had been doing
a lot of writing, but those who had spent time complaining that the
atmosphere was too oppressive to get any writing done. The latter
remained, and among them an excellent gift, Mr Cecil Herbert, of
whom one hears almost nothing these days. Did he stop altogether?

Mittelholzer is important because he represents a different generation from Selvon and myself. He had suffered the active discourage-
ment of his own community, and he had had their verdict sanctioned
by the consistent rejection of his novels by publishers abroad. And
in spite of this he made the decision, before anyone else, *to get out*.
That is the phrase which we must remember in considering this
question of why the writers are living in England. They simply
wanted *to get out* of the place where they were born. They couldn't
argue: 'you will see'; and point to similar examples of dejection in
earlier West Indian writers who were now regarded as great figures.
There were no such West Indians to summon to your aid. We had
*to get out;* and in the hope that a change of climate might bring a
change of luck. One thing alone kept us going; and that was the
literary review, *BIM*, which was published in Barbados by Frank
Collymore. This was a kind of oasis in that lonely desert of mass
indifference, and educated middle-class treachery.

This experience is true of Trinidad. The story is the same in Barbados. British Guiana would be no different. In Jamaica, with a
more virile nationalist spirit, the difference is hardly noticeable.
They murdered Roger Mais, and they know it. And when I was
there in 1956, Vic Reid, their greatest performer in the novel, was
talking to me about going to Britain. Whether for a year or for good,
Reid needed to get out. And it's an indication of his thinking and
feeling when he said to me that evening in the course of talk about
the situation of the West Indian writers: 'You know something,
George? Roger is the first of us . . .' I knew that Mais was dead, but
it had never occurred to me to think of him as the first to die, meaning the first of the lot whose work appeared in England from 1948 to
1958. For that is the period we are talking about. This is the decade
that has really witnessed the 'emergence' of the novel as an imaginative interpretation of West Indian society by West Indians. And
every one of them: Mittelholzer, Reid, Mais, Selvon, Hearne, Carew,
Naipaul, Andrew Salkey, Neville Dawes, everyone has felt the need
*to get out*. And with the exception of Reid who is now in Canada,
every one of them is now resident in England.

Yet I think the West Indian writer, like any other writer, would like to function in his own country. He would like to be accorded the simple recognition of any other professional worker; and he would like to be supported, through that recognition, by his readers native to that country. His books could then be regarded as his country's cultural exports to the world beyond the West Indies. That is how Europe and America would come to know them. That is how China and India would know them. They would be seen as the creative products of a particular community at a particular time. I think we are beginning to move in this direction. But the pace is much too slow for the time in which we live; and the circumstances may change again before we have arrived at the point and in the spirit which would make for a new, a more profound discovery of the meaning of our own society in the Caribbean.

4

If we accept that the act of writing a book is linked with an expectation, however modest, of having it read; then the situation of a West Indian writer, living and working in his own community, assumes intolerable difficulties. The West Indian of average opportunity and intelligence has not yet been converted to reading as a civilised activity, an activity which justifies itself in the exercise of his mind. Reading seriously, at any age, is still largely associated with reading for examinations. In recent times the political fever has warmed us to the newspapers with their generous and diabolical welcome to join in the correspondence column. But book reading has never been a serious business with us.

I do not want to indulge in fixing any blame, except to say that our climate with its inhospitable sun is not a good excuse. We have had to live with a large and self-delighted middle class, who have never understood their function. One cannot accuse an illiterate man of avoiding books, but one wonders what is to be done with people who regard education as something *to have*, but not *to use*. The creation of this reading public whose elements already exist is a job which remains to be done. The absence of that public, the refusal of a whole class to respond to an activity which is not honoured by money: it is this dense and grinning atmosphere that helped to murder Roger Mais. Mittelholzer survived it by fleeing the land; and Mr Vic Reid still breathes it, preparing, for all we know, to make a similar flight.

For whom, then, do we write?

The students at University College were always raising that question in their discussion. But it was clear to me that it was no more than a conversational question; for they, the students, coming on to UCWI, are usually from the grammar schools of their respective islands. They are middle class by social habits, by training, or in some cases by bribery. Many of the West Indian writers would have passed through the same cultural climate. But the West Indian writer does not write for them; nor does he write for himself. He writes always for the foreign reader. That foreign does not mean English or American exclusively. The word *foreign* means other than West Indian whatever that other may be. He believes that a reader is *there*, somewhere. He can't tell where, precisely, that reader is. His only certain knowledge is that this reader is not the West Indian middle class, taken as a whole.

I have explained why we choose England, and not America, and how, much later, we begin to see America as a source of some ready-made cash. But the West Indian does not stop there.

Some months ago, Carew, Selvon, Mittelholzer, Hearne, Salkey and myself met to discuss the possibilities of placing the British Caribbean novels, as an example of a regional literature, in the Eastern and Eastern European markets. I must point out that there were serious disagreements about the 'risks' involved. I saw no risk, nor did Carew—who took the attitude, quite rightly, that he would go ahead on his own anyway—and Selvon, the least political of us all, made the simple and fundamental point that what he needed was a little rent money, and the chance to change the monotonous half a pint of bitter for a little shot o' whisky from time to time. After all, publishers can afford it, so why not the people whose work is the very commodity without which that publishing enterprise would have neither meaning nor existence.

One among us decided he would take no part at all. Another was doubtful, which in a colonial always means wait and see how the wind is blowing, as though there was any one of us in that room who could alter the direction of the gale which had swept us from our native islands to this dubious summer afternoon in Notting Hill.

To exclude from our considerations a whole world of different people because we have been gagged by a fear, named Communist, would be as wasteful and as silly as excluding from participation in our future the same Western civilisation which was built on the colonisation of our labour and our creative endeavour. To be anti-colonial is to be crippled if it demands such exclusion of the positive benefits which Western achievement can undoubtedly offer towards a new civilisation which is now beginning to take shape on the African continent.


5


An important question, for the English critic, is not what the West Indian novel has brought to English writing. It would be more correct to ask what the West Indian novelists have contributed to English reading. For the language in which these books are written is English—which, I must repeat—is a West Indian language; and in spite of the unfamiliarity of its rhythms, it remains accessible to the readers of English anywhere in the world. The West Indian contribution to English reading has been made possible by their relation to their themes which are peasant. This is the great difference between the West Indian novelist and the contemporary English novelist.

The English novel from its beginnings to the present exercises in anger has always been middle class in taste and middle class by intention. It had to be so. They were all writing for readers who were part of their thing, so to speak. Literacy was and still is seen as a kind of social badge. Today the regiment of illiterates has decreased. More people read in England; and more of them tend to have the same intellectual references. But the badge has changed; and we have the situation where the literate are divided into classes: intellectuals and the rest.

The topography of B.B.C. programmes is a perfect example of this. You enter the back door of the Corporation via the Colonial Service. With luck, and the right kind of public relations instinct you will get promoted from the Colonial Service to the Overseas. Both, by the way, are programmes going overseas; but there is, it would seem, a first class overseas and a second class overseas. This is not the end of the steeplechase. The track gets more tricky from here on. From overseas you will slide or leap, according to your methods, into the domestic services, that is: the Light, the Home, and the Third. And I have the impression that these services are run as though they were foreign countries, each requiring a separate and certified visa. Strange as it may seem, we are not yet at the end of this mysterious delineation of frontiers.

Next you enter a trigonometry of functions when you experience the latent conflict between the Features regiment and the Talks regiment. Features will sometimes accuse Talks of trespassing on their territory; and Talks, feeling itself more privileged in the eye of the Fellows upstairs, will arrange some compromise. If it is a mystery that there should be West Indian writers at all; it is an even greater mystery how the B.B.C., in spite of this obsolete and bewildering process, can be so good. For it is a remarkable public service, by any standards. A few comments on the B.B.C. were necessary; since it is the great impersonal hand that helps to feed a few of the West Indian writers.

Writers like Selvon and Vic Reid—key novelists for understanding the literacy and social situation in the West Indies—are essentially peasant. I don't care what jobs they did before; what kind or grade of education they got in their different islands; they never really left the land that once claimed their ancestors like trees. That's a great difference between the West Indian novelist and his contemporary in England. For peasants simply don't respond and see like middle-class people. The peasant tongue has its own rhythms which are Selvon's and Reid's rhythms; and no artifice of technique, no sophisticated gimmicks leading to the mutilation of form, can achieve the specific taste and sound of Selvon's prose.

For this prose is, really, the people's speech, the organic music of the earth. Shakespeare knew that music, and lived at a time when it permeated society. But things have changed beyond belief in England. For the young English novelist, there are really no people. There are only large numbers of dwellers, vagrant or settled vaguely somewhere. Among these there will be a few pockets of individuals who are known through encounter in the same profession, or friendships arrived at through admiration and patronage. I shall try, on another occasion, to examine in some detail this peasant characteristic in Selvon and Reid. For the time being I shall only suggest that it is not at all by chance that so much of the action of West Indian novels takes place outside, in the open air. This is a long way away from the muted whisper in the living-room cell, or the intellectual stammering which reverberates through the late night coffee caves.

The West Indian who comes near to being an exception to the peasant feel is John Hearne. His key obsession is with an agricultural middle class in Jamaica. I don't want to suggest that this group of people are not a proper subject for fiction; but I've often wondered whether Hearne's theme, with the loaded concern he shows for a mythological, colonial squirearchy, is not responsible for the fact that his work is, at present, less energetic than the West Indian novels at their best. Hearne is a first-class technician, almost perfect within the limitation of conventional story-telling; but the work is weakened, for the language is not being *used*, and the Novel as a form is not really being *utilised*. His novels suggest that he has a dread of being identified with the land at peasant level. What he puts into his books is always less interesting than the *omissions* which a careful reader will notice he has forced himself to make. He is not an example of that instinct and root impulse which return the better West Indian writers back to the soil. For soil is a large part of what the West Indian novel has brought back to reading; lumps of earth: unrefined, perhaps, but good, warm, fertile earth.

So we come back to the original question of the West Indian novelists living in a state of chosen exile. Their names make temporary noise in the right West Indian circles. Their books have become handy broom-sticks which the new nationalist will wave at a foreigner who asks the rude question: 'What can your people do except doze?'

Why don't these writers return? There are more reasons than I can state now; but one is fear. They are afraid of returning, in any permanent sense, because they feel that sooner or later they will be ignored in and by a society about which they have been at once articulate and authentic. You may say that a similar thing happens to the young English writer in England. There is the important difference that you cannot enjoy anonymity in a small island where everybody points at everybody, except the Governor, to say who he is, meaning how little prestige he has. Here, for example, is a description of the Governor's aura, shared with no less authority by the lady who wifes his needs:

'As in all colonial systems, the king-pin of the Caribbean system is the appointed governor. In the British and Dutch colonies he is a considerable figure of pomp, plumes and parades. He is supposed to take himself very seriously, to impress the natives, and his official picture usually includes all the best decorative trappings familiar to Elks and Knights Templar. His wife is the colony's social arbiter and substitute queen. The governor lives in a palace or its nearest equivalent and almost never goes among the people as an ordinary human being. When he enters a public hall the people rise, and when he leaves it the people rise again. If he sits in a legislature he does not engage in public debate.'

Moreover, there is hardly a middle-class native whose dream does not include cocktails with this simple Gentleman, transformed overnight into a Roman pro-consul.

Either you would have to go back with the specific purpose of destroying the traditional meaning of prestige; or steer clear of those accusing fingers. In spite of all that has happened in the last ten years, I doubt that any one of the West Indian writers could truly say that he would be happy to go back. Some have tried; some would like to try. But no one would feel secure in his decision to return. It could be worse than arriving in England for the first time.

And at this point the whole truth must be told. The political constitutions have been improved on; standards of living may have gone up. These standards will probably get better as more emigrants leave the land, and more foreign capital takes their place. Things are getting better; the West Indies are even proud of the reception their writers get overseas; but little has really changed in the West Indies in the last ten years. The colonial structure of our thinking at home has not been touched. Nothing has really happened; although bold attempts are now being made in Trinidad.

In a recent article in *The Nation*, C. L. R. James who, in a different way and at an earlier stage, helped to build the atmosphere in which West Indian writers might have survived in their own territories, raises this question: 'It is *our* duty—meaning Government and its extension I presume—to get them back.' Fine! But *they* are not soldiers; and James has not seriously considered the question: what are you bringing them back to? They have earned the right to ask that question. And I have no evidence to show that James can answer it to the satisfaction of any one of them. For if *they* (the exiled and articulate)—have to choose between eternal dispossession, and the ignorant sneer of a Victorian colonial outpost—condemned by the ethic of the twentieth century—isn't it clear that they will choose the former; that they will prefer to avoid the degradation of a society which is just not colonial by the actual circumstances of politics, but colonial in its very conception of its destiny. 'We can bring them home . . .' Fine! But a more urgent duty lies nearer home.

We will not raise the question of James's relation to a colonial bureaucracy; for the author of *Black Jacobins* is too great a man to be dragged into such marginal disputes. We will not involve in such polemics the sharpest and most interesting mind that the British Caribbean has produced in three centuries of learning. I have chosen his classic study *Black Jacobins* for summary in a later chapter. And after re-reading this history of the Haitian Revolt it is clear to me that, level for level, generation for generation, there was no British intellectual of the 'thirties who had a finer mind than James.

When I raised this question one evening in my Hampstead circles, some of those Hampstead 'think-talkers' believed I was simply looking for a quarrel. But there was one man who had heard from his 'professor' of James, and thought that it was absolutely necessary to reply. In other words, I should not be allowed to get away with that.

'I will tell you the mind which is the answer to you and your James,' he said.

'Is he still alive?' I asked.

'Yes,' he said.

'Name him.'

'The man is Arthur Koestler,' he said with that finality which announces that a victory has been won.

I was very slow in replying; for I do not think that we should speak with authority when we are nervous. I had no doubt that James, at the time of writing *Black Jacobins*, was a fair match for Koestler; but I remembered, in this moment, that Koestler is not English; and I am inclined to be nervous whenever I am asked to consider the benefits of foreign aid, whatever form it may take.

'Koestler, Koestler,' I kept repeating in the hope that my tongue would restore the sound of that word to its original home.

These writers will never be required in the West Indies until their meaning and their contribution have been established in national and political terms. And it is not their job to establish themselves in this way. Their business is to get on with writing their books. The rest must be done by men like Eric Williams, the Chief Minister of Trinidad, and C. L. R. James. And it is not enough to show the writers off when the occasion requires some kind of cultural decoration.

In Nigeria where these particular gifts are fewer and less solid, the Nigerian Government has wasted no time in using what they have. Chinua Achebe, the author of *Things Fall Apart*, barely twenty-nine, is practically in charge of broadcasting in the Eastern region. That does not mean that he is a little bureaucrat. Not at all. He goes out into the field with tape-recording machine, and brings Nigerian life back into the studio for the Nigerian community. Cyprian Ekwensi the author of *People of the City*, holds a similar position in Lagos. Amos Tutuola, who has little formal education, and is the greatest of them all, could not be expected to do the kind of work required of Aquensi and Achebe; but the same Broadcasting Corporation has found him what looks like a sinecure. He is a 'messenger' in the radio station in Ibadan, but a most unusual messenger; for he seldom leaves the little office which he calls, 'my quarters.' In other words, the Nigerian Broadcasting Corporation in Ibadan has the unusual distinction of broadcasting regular contributions from one of its messengers. This is one difference between the West Indies and West Africa; it is the real difference between vitality that is no more than animal exuberance, and vitality which is truly dynamic. This vitality can only be achieved when the colonial castration of the West Indian sensibility has been healed.

If the politicians don't want to retire the Governors, they can, at least, begin by assaulting the snobbery of complexion in a society where the nigger signature has made its mark in nearly every blood vessel. They can help the younger generation to break with the habit of expecting social prestige by offering themselves for financial promotion; for it is this obvious idiocy which creates the fallacy of being middle class among people who have no connection whatsoever—except through Fifth Column work—with the pipe lines of power which organises money in a colony.

In his book, *The West Indies and their Future*, Daniel Guerin quotes a source which re-creates the reflection of a slave shortly after emancipation:

'When I woke up after the drunken joy of finding myself free, the hard reality that stared me in the face was that nothing had changed either for me or for my friends who'd been in chains with me. . . . Like all other Negroes, I was still here in this accursed country; the bekés still owned the land, all the land in the place, and we went right working for them as before.'

More than a century has passed since that cry; and what do we hear today? The new voice is authoritative; for it is Aimé Cesaire, perhaps the greatest of all Caribbean poets—describing the hole where he was born.

'. . . a tiny house stinking in the narrow street, a miniature house which lodges in its guts of rotten wood dozens of rats . . .; a tiny, cruel house . . .; the thinned roof, patched with tin from petrol cans. . . . And the bed of boards which brought forth my race, the bed with feet of kerosene cans . . . ; with kid-skin cover, and dried banana leaves, its rags . . .'

The politicians should consider this humiliating lack of change.

They can encourage the schools at the earliest possible stage to turn the habit of reading for examinations into the more intelligent habit of reading for exploration and discovery. The West Indian novelists have already exposed much of this squalor; but that basic work remains to be done by the national leaders of the community.

It will have to be done before any of these West Indian writers could feel relatively secure in returning to a society whose values were largely responsible for expelling them. Men who are approaching forty and fifty, and who have spent nearly all their adult life struggling to do work which they feel as part of their instinct; such people, whether they be writers or plumbers, or what you like, cannot be easily bribed by posts in a colonial bureaucracy. Otherwise they would have changed their direction long ago. Speaking for myself, I would say that I have come to the bitter conclusion that I am utterly unemployable.

It is entirely up to men like James and Williams to start this necessary work. For the whole future of the Caribbean, as a dynamic unit in the New World, depends to a large extent on the scope and urgency with which the present Trinidad Government can see and undertake its task. The other territories—in the Southern Caribbean at any rate—will follow their example; for the situation of their writers, as I have described it, is only an indication that their needs as well as their native expectations are the same.

In the Caribbean we have a glorious opportunity of making some valid and permanent contribution to man's life in this century. But we must stand up; and we must move. The novelists have helped; yet when the new Caribbean emerges it may not be for them. It will be, like the future, an item on the list of possessions which the next generation of writers and builders will claim. I am still young by ordinary standards (thirty-two, to be exact), but already I feel that I have had it (as a writer) where the British Caribbean is concerned. I have lost my place, or my place has deserted me.

This may be the dilemma of the West Indian writer abroad: that he hungers for nourishment from a soil which he (as an ordinary citizen) could not at present endure. The pleasure and paradox of my own exile is that I belong wherever I am. My role, it seems, has rather to do with time and change than with the geography of circumstances; and yet there is always an acre of ground in the New World which keeps growing echoes in my head. I can only hope that these echoes do not die before my work comes to an end.

# EVIDENCE AND EXAMPLE

•

## PARADOX

WHEN GEORGE VI died, the B.B.C. engaged one or two colonials to 'cover' certain aspects of the funeral. A press card allowed me to go inside the grounds of Windsor, an echo away from St George's Chapel where the King's family were paying their last respects. Royalty has learnt how to colonise sorrow; for no one could tell from the faces what the cousins of the Crown were thinking. Princess Margaret, I would say, came nearest to betraying an emotion which might be deciphered.

This occasion had great meaning for me, partly because I liked to get a look at people whose power demands that they should not be seen too frequently; partly because I am deeply moved by ceremony. A poor student of history, I get the feeling, on these occasions, that it is here in the context of this drama which is at once religious and political; it is in the fact and overtones of ceremony that we may get some glimpse of the past. All the history books in the world could not really show what was happening on this purple morning in and around Windsor Castle. We were witnessing, in the present, the resurrection of a way of behaving.

I forgot the demands of the B.B.C., the irrelevancies of dates and dynasties, and kept the words focused on this ceremony as an aspect of resurrection. Later someone complained in the studio that I was reading it too gravely—as though he couldn't remember what had happened at Windsor. A similar complaint would not have been made if I were reading a poem about that Windsor burial; but my script was NEWS, and NEWS demands a mechanical neutrality of tone whether the voice is giving messages about dying or delight. I was a poet in those days; and it is impossible for a poet to evoke sympathy from people who use words as a way of measuring time; and time as the measure of how much money. This attitude comes to its full obscenity in the Colonial Section which is seen—when it is seen at all—as the arse-hole of the Corporation. But it was necessary in those days for me to stay there. So a year later I was sent again with some other colonials—West Indian and North American—to 'cover' the Coronation. One West Indian, an experienced journalist, was assigned to the Facts; and I was sent, presumably, to bring back the atmosphere.

This occasion had brought together in a single city the world's most settled and average citizens. For the time being it had cancelled all individual loyalties. Republican and Royalist brushed shoulders, appearing to share a common need, a similar curiosity. So a woman who walked beside me along the Charing Cross Road couldn't bear her secret any longer. She said: 'There must be something in it after all. Could you tell me what makes people do that?' This was the eve of the Coronation. She had pointed ahead to the kerb where crowds had waited since early morning. Now it was about to rain. An old woman munched sandwiches as she looked up from under a rug at the clouds now turned heavy, black, disloyal. A child was asleep beside her, the head supported by the old woman's arm which made a pillow across a wooden stool.

I crawled along, an inch here, an inch there, wondering, too, why they were doing it; why, for that matter, had I risked getting wet in order to see those who weren't going to be defeated by the weather: people who were going to wait for another twenty-four hours. Tomorrow, I would have a seat in a stand, free to take shelter if it rained.

Trafalgar Square now opened its heart to the visiting nomads: foreign faces whose complexions made me curious about their geography, for I am spared the unfortunate privilege of categorising them according to colour. They had peopled the pavements everywhere. The fountains, fussier than ever, were making a soft spray over those who were near. The children were numerous. They patted the bronze manes of the lions and ran under the curve spurted by the water; then hurried back to make sure that their places had not been taken. Soon I had reached Parliament Square where I would be encamped on the following day; and as though I were being reminded of what was in store for that day, the rains came.

The buses pushed behind each other like monstrous crabs. They served little purpose, except to offer shelter which few people seemed to need. Soon I got inside one. I had never felt more comfortable in a bus. It crept along, and the crowds on the pavement heard the roll of the engine, but saw nothing. They had already drawn the raincoats, and the blankets and the rugs over their bodies, soaked and shivering with cold. It is, perhaps, an unfortunate comparison; but nothing reminded me more of their defiance than the transparent figures of torture in Henry Moore's war-time sketches of people asleep in the underground. In the bus, a little boy said: 'Mummy, are they going to stay there all night?' and Mummy, casual and sure, replied: 'Yes. They are waiting for Tomorrow.'

Then the showers increased. The rain was making a noise like pebbles on top of the bus. It came too thick for us to see from the bus what had happened to the people on the pavements; but we could hear them. They were singing. At first a little sadly, as though they thought it unfair that this should happen. Later the voices, each encouraging the other, achieved a little more gaiety; and finally they soared above the rain in a calculated outburst of triumph. They were determined to stay put; and they were embarked on an attitude that would annihilate the weather. I heard a foreigner making some comments on this phenomenon. In the gravest voice he could summon, he had said: 'I shall always remember it as their wettest hour.'

A night had passed. The train which was taking me to the nearest stop from the Abbey rolled into Victoria at half past five. Everyone seemed wearily settled in their seats, until a foreign voice alerted us. A father had boarded the carriage with a family of five. They were eager as a battalion. The man looked from under his navy blue beret and said: 'My friends, I've travelled seven thousand miles, been in the country only twelve hours, and I don't know where I am or where I'm going to. Tell me when I reach the place called Charing Cross.'

He had spoken to no one in particular; yet he had reported his feeling and directed his request to everyone present. Like the sudden visitation of goodwill on Christmas Eve, the word 'friends' was his name for this occasion. It was the word which could best describe the abandonment, the excitement, and the delight which would rule throughout the day. Perhaps he had spoken for all visitors; and he had spoken, too, for the majority who had grown used to this kind of pageantry; for this Coronation seemed an attempt at the greatest show on earth, a resurrection of the oldest play of the race.

The B.B.C. had sent my West Indian colleague, Thomasos, inside the Abbey. They sent me to a stand with a perfect view of the West door where the Duke of Norfolk would receive the Queen. A door to the left, the peers and their wives would enter. It was the same door which the Commonwealth and Colonial Ministers were allowed to use. It was the same door through which Mr Nehru preceded the late Dr Malan. I remember to this day how the B.B.C. voice announced, for everyone to get a look, the elegant and distinguished Prime Minister of India. When Dr Malan was announced—for they dared not omit him—he was already inside the Abbey, his back the only glimpse we could get of the man. A white American journalist who sat next to me was furious; for he thought that some loyal citizens had been robbed of their chance to boo.

But the peers were still arriving, and Queen Salote, whose presence was an atmosphere as large as the Coronation itself. It was a memorable afternoon for viewing. The air was all ermine, the peers were like divine horsemen trying out their legs on the dubious surface of this terrestrial corner where the House of Commons was watching and waiting to announce some necessary scandal. The American was now silent, reflective and solemn as a boy whose good name has occurred in the Black Book, or like a girl whose bad character has been mysteriously christened angel. Then he leaned towards me, in whisper—for some transference was now complete—in whisper and in a conspiracy of feeling, the American leaned to say:

'My boy, believe me, it's the greatest inauguration ever . . .' I knew how that guy felt.

When the peers were all tucked away and the Queen was inside, I asked the American to have a drink. He was all acceptance, and we went one flight down where the taps were noisy as windmills. It was at the bar that I remembered poor Thomasos who was honoured with a seat in the Abbey, and, therefore, had to stay until the show was over.

For a strange thing happened to Thomasos and one of his political compatriots on their arrival. I heard the story when I got back to the studio. The others were asking Thomasos: 'But how could you do that? You of all people?'

Thomasos, of all people, was an aggressive nationalist. Politics and a 'pint' were his poetry. When he was arriving at the Abbey, he saw a black man coming towards him. The man was a member of an official party from the West Indies. The people of his island had chosen him as the leader who would represent their feeling; tell by his presence alone their delight on this day. And he was dressed to match the fantasy of the morning. It is not clear why or how he selected the articles of his regalia; but it must have struck the English eye as a most 'extraordinary innovation.' To Thomasos, who had now halted, this gentleman was simply playing the ass. That hilarious get-up might have been perfect on carnival day in Port-of-Spain. But in the Abbey!

For the gentleman was wearing a morning suit—like those I saw at the Windsor funeral—those charcoal-grey trousers, whose stripes go chasing like black snakes up and down the legs, a hat tall as a mountain top with a silver-grey precipice and a mourning black band, a white glove fitted like skin over the left hand; and held—not worn—but held by the right hand was his second glove, tossed and

swung to the rhythm of his military stride, a flag of surrender showing five fingers bled white and swollen with longing for its lost hand.

Foreigners may smile, but this black apparition was no joke to
Thomasos who was now beginning to feel the arrows of civilisation
pierce his pride. The gentleman had lost his way. Nervous of the
white face, he strode towards Thomasos, his equally lost brother, his
safest rescue.

But Thomasos, of all people! Proud, courageous and strong, how
could you have done such a thing for all those English eyes to see?
For when the gentleman was about to speak, Thomasos ran! I say
Thomasos ran; and Thomasos whose pride and courage have always
been his greatest boast admitted that he ran.

The programme finished. Thomasos and I went across to the
Feathers. I wanted to hear more of what happened in the Abbey.
He wanted to hear more of what happened outside. We were now
free, free from white ears, free from black lackeys.

'But why you run, Thomasos?' I asked.

'I ain't tell them others the whole story,' Thomasos said, 'now
tell me if you wouldn't run too.'

'What happen?'

'I didn't mind the kiss-me-arse regalia an' all that,' said Thomasos,
' 'cause I know some black brains born mad. But George, if I tell
you . . .'

'What, man?'

'That on top of all that regalia,' said Thomasos, 'swingin' on all
the regalia, that son-of-a-bitch was wearing a sword. Born with chop-
per, never been to war, he was marching with a sword on all that
regalia. . . . Wouldn't you run?'

I was smiling the smile that means but never dares express for all
to know: Yes, be Jesus Christ, Yes! And why?

' 'Cause one thing I wasn't going to let happen,' said Thomasos, 'I
wasn't going to let any of those English people think that this sword-
man and me come from the same part of the world. Never, never,
never!'

It is years since I saw Thomasos; and today I wonder whether he
still has his marvellous sense of humour, his drinking comradeship,
and his racial fear?

# A WAY OF SEEING

•

Here, take this purse, thou whom the heavens' plagues
Have humbled to all strokes.   That I am wretched
Makes thee the happier. Heavens, deal so still!
Let the superfluous and lust-dieted man,
That slaves your ordinance, that will not see
Because he does not feel, feel your pow'r quickly;
So distribution should undo excess,
And each man have enough.

*King Lear*, Act IV, Scene I

I

I shall have failed to communicate my meaning if I leave the impression that I am constructing theories. I haven't got the kind of equipment which is required of men who engineer ideas; but I do believe that what a person thinks is very much determined by the way that person sees. This book is really no more than a report on one man's way of seeing, using certain facts of experience as evidence and a guide. I emphasise this point about a way of seeing because I am going to consider one or two things about colour as it affects black men living in a white society. First I shall begin by describing an episode which took place in Hampstead.

About a year ago I was sharing a flat with a West Indian called Polly. We were both expecting some important letters: he was waiting to hear about a new job and I was waiting to hear about a new loan. Our letters hadn't come on the Tuesday, so we thought they were just a day late. On the Wednesday they hadn't come, and we decided that we were being impatient. But when nothing happened on the Thursday we suspected they had gone astray. Yet how strange that both Polly's letters and mine should choose to lose themselves for the same reasons and at the same time. On the Friday morning we met on the stairs and this dialogue followed:

'George!'

'What's happening?'

'I see some envelopes.'

'You go, Polly,' I said, 'my luck isn't in.'

'No, you go,' said Polly, 'Friday ain't my day for nothing but disaster.'

So I went. There were two letters; but they were addressed to the same name which was neither Lamming nor Pollard, but Singleton whom we had never heard of. When we read the address it was our street all right; but instead of the number 70 which was our house, the number was 'X' which must have been Singleton's. We were convinced that Singleton had our letters and we had Singleton's. So we went to number 'X.' Polly rang the bell, and an old woman came out. She seemed a little afraid of Polly, and that scared Polly too. While he was trying to explain, another old woman appeared. They didn't know anyone by the name of Singleton; but they took our names and went to look. We waited, and when they came back, an old man was with them. It was a house of old people, old and now very courteous and willing to help. But our letters weren't there.

'So sorry,' the old woman said, 'I've looked at all the envelopes that came in for the last few days; and I didn't notice any BLACK stamps.'

Polly laughed so loud, the old woman could have died from a heart attack. Black stamps! We must be clear about her meaning. She didn't simply mean Negro; she meant stamps marked Africa or India, China, or the West Indies. One kind, honest and courteous old woman had fixed almost two-thirds of the world's population with one word.

You will say that the old woman is a simple example of ignorance. But I maintain that ignorant or not, it has fundamentally to do with a way of seeing. So I shall give another example where ignorance, you might think, would be less prevalent and where, nevertheless, a similar thing happened.

Now the Institute of Contemporary Arts is very contemporary and very much an institute. I hardly ever pass there these days; but shortly after I arrived in England I had been taken there by a friend; and my chief reason at the time might have been to see what certain people look like. I remember being positively scared when someone pointed out that the lady over there was Edith Sitwell whose work I had admired, but could not remember. It was exactly the kind of shock that Dame Edith might experience if, by chance and without warning, she had encountered an African witch doctor. There are many examples of this kind of surprise which overtakes the eye. Indeed, it is the kind of surprise with which a poet tries to conquer the ear.

But I want to concentrate on the eye for the time being. The

Institute of Contemporary Arts was a good place, it seemed, for seeing people. After three or four visits, I got the impression that I was not alone in this exercise of seeing people. A large number of the I.C.A. members seemed to go there to learn certain faces: the faces of important people. Certain people will say that this is a pure waste of time: just going about to watch people. Once a friend accused and rebuked me for doing just that sort of thing. But he is wrong about that; for I was a poet; and wasting time—however the waste is spent—is part of a poet's necessary business.

Interesting discoveries can be made while time is being wasted; provided you don't go to sleep. Sleeping is for me a near-waste of time. But if you can keep your eyes open, and if you do not betray their function, which is to see, then the I.C.A. can never be seen as an example of a waste of time. For I noticed that seeing important faces was only one stage from consorting with important people; and importance when it attaches itself to artists seems to work like influenza. If you are near you can catch it, so that each sneeze the great man makes will sooner or later produce a sniffle from his admirer. And this sniffle is quite genuine—I mean that the admirer does with time develop a cold, may even learn how to grow cold.

I noticed at the I.C.A. that seeing the important face soon led to being near the important person—within word reach of what he was saying—you were then able to receive his opinions in all their range of idiosyncrasy and wisdom, since they were coming from the actual voice of the great—I omit 'man' here because genius has a way of dehumanising the original creator until he, the man, gets established as it, the great. If you are within reach of that voice, and your eyes are looking straight into that scarlet and melancholy landscape that is his face, you will soon want to touch the great man. In other words, you are confronted with the moral duty—in the sacred name of contemporary art—of shaking the great man's hand.

This is the moment of two truths. Having accomplished the sacred touch, you have established one simple truth: which is that you met the great man. When envious rivals challenge your claim, you know in your deepest heart that God is on your side. For God saw when and even how it happened. The second truth is—and this could be the moment of peril—that the great man might not have noticed when he shook your hand; for he does that sort of thing as a kind of holy routine. If your rival challenged your claim, and decided to call in the great man himself as a witness, you are in serious trouble. You can't call God as your witness—for it is my impression that prayer is not popular as a method of communication among the disciples of contemporary art—so you might be left with the situation in which the great man did not see you, and has, therefore, to deny your very existence.

But that is not likely to happen: for although there are many great men who fail to pay attention, who, in other words, do not see, there can hardly be a great man who would deny the existence of an admirer whose praise is the very principle upon which his greatness is built. The great man will probably say: 'Yes, I remember!' And that is infinitely more serious. Indeed, the whole morality of the contract which binds admirer to the admired is about to break down. The great man is lying when he claims a truth which, though true, is not really the great man's truth. And since he uses this truth without acknowledging the moral fact that it is not really his, he creates in you the false conviction that you did not only meet him, but that he *recognised* you.

The next stage of promotion in your endeavour to consort with the great man is to report to those jealous rivals that you did not only meet the great man but 'as Stevie said to me.' There is nothing like the use of a first name to warn your enemy that any further rudeness of insinuation or denial will be treated as vulgarity.

Some years ago I was reading a professional complaint made by Miss Kathleen Raine about the indiscriminate use of first names by those outside the royal circle of acquaintance. I feel a little nervous now I recall this, since it threatens the truth of what I feel about great men experiencing compassion and even gratitude towards the living source of praise which enhances their fame. I can only think that Miss Kathleen Raine is not a great poet; or if she is, then the professional demands of a great man are not quite the same as those imposed by a great Dame. I hope I have not been too wrong; for, believe me, I have not gone astray. I am still very much at the Institute of Contemporary Arts; and the year is 1950.

I was there as a poet, invited to read with other poets from a platform especially prepared for the young! Interpret young here as unpublished, since a young man who is also a poet is invariably a writer whose name you will not see on that hard cover which carries an important imprint. It is a sad thing to have to say, but it is true, that a writer without a book is like a cowboy without his horse and pistols. That is how the young poets were seen on a platform that was sanctioned by a presence no less benign than that of Sir Herbert Read. There must have been quite a few great men present, for the I.C.A. was crowded that night; and crowds do not travel to watch cowboys who have neither horse nor pistols.

For the young poet, that short journey from the second or third row across the floor and up to the platform can be a kind of cruci-

fixion. And sitting beside the gentle and patient voice of Sir Herbert
Read does not help. That crowd down there may be placid, but the
young poet up on that platform is in deep waters. If he really believes
in the sanctity of the I.C.A.; if he trusts to the critical predictions
which those great men present are capable of making; if he believes
in all this, then that night can be his calvary; that solitary climb to
his full standing height may be his first and only climb to the cross;
and there simply is no resurrection for a young poet who is not
Christ. When he begins to read his hymn of melancholy longing of
love, whether it be for mother, girl or grave—he may, in fact, be
singing his own epitaph on a career that will not survive that night.
For love is not a common characteristic of the great, however contemporary they may be. Youth, meaning talent, and contemporary,
meaning fashion, are born enemies.

But some young poets are lucky. I had heard three or four poets
before I decided to leave my chair. I wanted to hear the others have
a try. I was waiting, perhaps, to get the feel of the land; and wishing
now that one of those poets would be really bad, for there is nothing
to hide mediocrity like an atmosphere of obvious and generally
acknowledged badness.

But I discovered that I didn't even need the disgrace of one of my
English cowboy colleagues; for when I got up from my chair, every
step of the journey was walked to a chorus of hands clapping my
arrival or my resurrection, God alone knows which. I knew no one
but Gloria in that audience; and I am sure that Gloria would not
have organised that gimmick although she was a West Indian and
couldn't bear the thought of her side being let down. I had absolutely
no reputation in England. The platform, in spite of Sir Herbert
Read, was a free for all. I was simply an anonymous West Indian
emigrant who could read and who, mysterious as it might seem, had
even trespassed on the territory of the literate who made fame by
writing. Nor was I a witch doctor working a boisterous magic in
their hands.

Why, then, did they clap? I ask again why and what made those
highly contemporary intellectuals clap? Why? We must be absolutely honest about this Why. You and me! I do not claim to know
the final answer; but I am convinced that it has something to do
with a way of seeing. The eyes that rejoiced down on that floor were
looking up at a black man who had the audacity to make a poet's
journey in public, and apparently unashamed. Courage! There's
nothing like courage, they may have been thinking. But there are
different kinds of courage: black courage in the face of lions they
could admire and understand; but black courage in the face of lan-

guage was pure black magic; and magic, black or white, is not easy
to accept.

I read this poem.

### THE BOY AND THE SEA

More punctual and deliberate than bird carol at dawn
While water's wedding to the wilted weeds
In crystal accents screamed across the lawn,
I would awake with a child's wild wandering will.
Before light borne shafts lacerated
The lakes of cloud in the high sky,
Or winged choirs crowned the untidy trees
With their chorusing reminiscence of mornings
I was away with this child's wild, wandering will.
Too early for lust or lullabies in love
I learnt many tales of the white lily
That grows with her green stalked companion.
In the flowering months of my soiled lane
Dressed in her dowry of dullness and disease
My fevering fancy followed the huge hedgerows
Where orchestras of colour paraded
And the populous white lilies appeared.
Through marsh and marl of the unready roads
Wild and wandering as the will of the winds
My hurrying heels hurdled the white lilies,
And carrying my prayers incomplete on my lips
I dashed through the dawn descending day
To bear my body on the broad bay.
Born on a rock islanded by wild waves
That conceal the lost continents of legend
My natural lesson in child's learning years
Was the ritual of seabathe at dawn.

Riding through eternity's green tears
That cut the coral of my rock's red face,
I wrought on the slipping scape of waves
With a keeling gesture of hands and feet
The ardour of my nine bright years,
And tossed on the outward tide of the bay
Signed my alliance with the sun
For a day that signals to my rock's red face
The season of the sea's salt eggs
And the blue scaled fish that flies.

Through driftwood and weed I waded
To where the irregular tides contend
And the water is levelled low.
First the foaming ridge arises
In a croon of crisp, caught leaves
Sparkles and sings in the bubbling light
A chorus of the wind driven waves.
Then sudden and silent as the sign
Of breaking light in a thundering dawn
The foam drops down to the surfacing edge
Of dark, green weed that sways.
As the slant of rippling glass
The water slides to meet in moss-grown beds
The rising curve of the outward tide.
The miracle of that morning
Was a sudden severance of seas
Worked by the wind and waves,
Fish ferreted about the nibbled frond
Near yet far the wooden spectacles of pride
    (Weathering yachts and the hilarious club)
Swam leisurely on the elegant tide.
And there in the valley of moss and fern
I wept with the wobble of a wind driven wave
A memory that marred my nine bright years,
Dreaming to my woken self
I was the measure of all flesh
Under and out of the cunning sea.

It was a green poem, but the applause which followed was louder
and, in the circumstances, more sensible. Yet it was no different
from the first applause. It was part of the same way of seeing.

Each young poet had to sit down after he had read and wait for
the examination questions. This is a most painful test. But I was
spared it. Someone asked, rather shamefacedly, about the West
Indies. I think this reticence might have had to do with doubt about
where I had actually come from; and one can't be guilty of this kind
of ignorance in the I.C.A. It would be like farting at the altar. But I
was spared the examination epilogue for another reason. I can read
verse much better than most English poets alive. That is a fact. And
I read exactly as I would have done in the West Indies. After all, it
was my poem. I had made it. It was my own trumpet; and I knew
the keys. If I were afraid to blow it, whom could I expect do it for
me? So I made a heaven of a noise which is characteristic of my

voice and an ingredient of West Indian behaviour. The result was an impression of authority. That's why they left me alone. Duty and conscience said that the boy had done his job. No one would want to say whether he would do it creditably in the future; but tonight he had done his job.

What, I ask you, is that job? It is this: Caliban had got hold of Prospero's weapons and decided that he would never again seek his master's permission. That is also my theme: a theme which embraces both literature and politics in our time. The real meaning of this theme: its meaning for us as well as its presence with us has never been more urgent in any previous century. It is this urgency which confronts us now and which we must respond to without reservation or denial. For what is at stake is the historic result of our thinking; what is under tragic scrutiny is our traditional way of seeing.

Contemporary art may not be far removed from contemporary crime. However different in taste and levels of education, the I.C.A. is a neighbour of Notting Hill. In spite of our difference in fortunes, the West Indian who was murdered in Notting Hill is an eternal part of the writing Caliban who has, at least, warned Prospero that his privilege of absolute ownership is over.

The time is ripe—but may go rotten—when masters must learn to read the meaning contained in the signatures of their former slaves. There may be more murders; but Caliban is here to stay.


2


Shortly after I had taken my seat at the I.C.A., someone touched my shoulder and passed me a note which had come from further back. I couldn't ask the man where the person was sitting; for another cowboy—he had no horse, but it seemed he owned pistols which were loaded—this cowboy was reading a poem which ended in a fearful row. His poem was interpreted by some important poets present as an unjust attack upon the greatest and most important of them all: an attack on Mr T. S. Eliot.

The place really started to get like Notting Hill, except that there were no knives. Mr Spender had risen first or second (I don't remember, but the artillery came according to its importance in striking power) to the rescue of the Great Man's name. To me, fresh from a noisy island, it was magnificent fun; for it's exactly how we would behave on similar occasions, with the sole difference that our arena in the West Indies would have no seniors. We were, like the Haitian army, all important officers!

Mr Spender made it clear that the poem was a misrepresentation of Mr Eliot's meaning. And Mr Spender was on safe ground here. He had two important weapons, the first of which he should not have used. He drew our attention to the fact that some part of him— I have forgotten the fraction—was Jewish; and speaking as a fractional Jew to another Jew—who was much more whole—he would definitely state that the Jewish cowboy should not have brought his pistols into the place at all.

His second weapon of attack was better, and it could have fixed the matter up once and for all. It was this: the cowboy had got Mr Eliot's *meaning* wrong. Mr Spender could have finished the matter here; for those of us who have tried to learn Mr Eliot's meanings, know that they lead to a territory in which Mr Eliot himself can sometimes stumble. For Mr Eliot's ideas are not only rendered in precise speech, his meaning has movement. And when you're looking here, it has moved there. When it is the right meaning you discover that the situation has made you wrong; for the meaning keeps moving; until meaning and movement are part of the same indistinguishable dance of a mind which has no time to engage in argument. For one of the truly remarkable things about Mr Eliot is the consistency of his relation to his work. He is a poet with a very accurate and comprehensive understanding of what is required of a poet.

The row proceeded, sophisticated and loud, major poets followed by minor poets in a massive retaliation against that solitary cowboy. No one could quite understand how Sir Herbert Read was going to deal with this situation; and it is too late now to say what he would have done, for few people realised, to our surprise, that Mr Eliot was actually in the I.C.A. A young poet at the back had, in real cowboy fashion, revealed the secret. Now the exercises in seeing and wanting to see had begun. Everyone wanted to see where this great man was sitting. And it is here that we might learn something about Mr Eliot and the problem of looking. For greatness, which can so perfectly enter the role of anonymity, is the firmest rebuke to the falsely admiring eye. What is worth mentioning here is that although all colonials cannot be great men, it is a characteristic of certain colonials to be seen and not heard, to enter and depart without attracting the right attention for the wrong reason, or the wrong attention for the right reasons.

Sir Herbert had managed his end very well, and soon the atmosphere of discreet and civilised exchange had been restored. The show was almost over. The young poets had surrendered their song; the judges had postponed punishment; and the crowd was in retreat. It is interesting how these people now decided which hands they could risk shaking, which they shouldn't. And when the slow, reluctant dispersal of the disciples was taking place, I observed—for my seeing was now at the very pinnacle of its greed—that Mr Eliot was walking towards Sir Herbert Read with the calm though somewhat nervous humility of a retired butler whom the master had kindly asked to look in.

It was now time for me to leave. A lot had happened that night, much more than I had bargained for. As I said earlier, I had received a note shortly before the poets went into action on behalf of their Master. That note had been signed by Mr Stephen Spender, a nervous and fragile scrawl which indicated that he and John Lehmann had been considering a new anthology of young poets, and would I etcetera, etcetera, etcetera. . . .

3

It couldn't have been long after the I.C.A. evening that I made a journey to St John's Wood where Mr Spender lived in those days. He wanted to hear more about the writing of poetry in the West Indies. He also wanted to include me in an exhibition of faces that were both topical and of temporary importance. Instinctively I decided that I would use this opportunity to ask him if he would take part in the B.B.C. programme 'Caribbean Voices.' He accepted, and Henry Swanzy, who was editor and producer of this programme, sent him a representative collection of poems from the Caribbean.

He was not the first English writer to contribute to this programme. Among those who had taken part were Roy Fuller, Arthur Calder Marshall, R. N. Curry, who impressed me, both as a poet and a person, as a solid though gentle gift. Harry Craig, a young Irishman just down from Dublin, was a familiar voice. These programmes were beamed to the West Indies once a week; and it is difficult to explain how important they were for those writers who had remained in the Caribbean.

In an island where local radio is an incestuous concubinage between commerce and the official administration, these writers would look forward to that Sunday evening at half-past seven. It was their reprieve. Moreover, 'Caribbean Voices' enabled writers

C

in one island to keep in touch with the latest work of writers in another island. Going through these scripts again, I detect a similarity in Fuller, who criticised the poems, and Calder Marshall, who dissected the short stories. The programme was intended to 'encourage' local talent; and it was a most salutary change when, under Henry Swanzy's direction, I'm sure, Fuller and Calder Marshall became astringent. And Calder Marshall, whose sincerity was beyond question, could be very rough.

The West Indian writers would meet in the same house and listen to these programmes. Then they would wait for the closing announcement in the hope that next week's programme would include some of their music. Since the radio was not mine or Cecil's or Clifford Sealey's, and there was no way of avoiding the commercial intrusion which followed, the writers, furious or elated according to the critics' recent judgment, would ramble to Down Town Port-of-Spain: George Street, Marine Square, harbouring for a while with the rats in Auntie's Tea Shop. And all the way they were tearing Fuller and Calder Marshall to pieces.

'Who the hell he think he is . . .?' 'Is all right for him sitting up there talking 'bout we don't take more time . . .' 'Is what we got to get is a native critic . . .' And so on.

If the English critics had arrived in Down Town Port-of-Spain in this atmosphere, they would have had a glorious time; for the West Indian writer had no reputation to lose, and he had no audience sufficiently interested to recognise that he was acquiring one. Literature was, like cricket, his native sport. The B.B.C. money was spent right there in Down Town Port-of-Spain on roti and Vat 19. Fuller and Calder Marshall, R. N. Curry and Harry Craig, would simply have been warned not to endanger their digestive system in an attempt to go native. For the West Indian, it seems, is born with a cast-iron stomach. These critics would have had a hell of a time, what with reaching Marine Square, and hearing Kitch, Growler, or Lord Melody announcing the latest Calypso. For the West Indian writer, there would have been one defect in that carnival of disputatious argument. The next day was Monday, and they were either teachers, Civil Servants, or store clerks.

But you see the magic of the B.B.C. box. From Barbados, Trinidad, Jamaica and other islands, poems and short stories were sent to England; and from a London studio in Oxford Street, the curriculum for a serious all-night argument was being prepared. These writers had to argue among themselves and against the absent English critic. It was often repetitive since there were no people to talk with. The educated middle class had 'no time for them'; and the dancing girls in the Diamond Horse Shoe simply didn't know what it was all about. In other words, it was not only the politics of sugar which was organised from London. It was language, too.

Here was a perfect example of the colonial contract as it operated in the wholesale department of culture. And if the West Indian, at the receiving end, was alive to the indignity of his role, we can safely assume that London, at the other end, must have been struck by the extraordinary privilege of being the organiser of these gifts. It must have occurred to everybody that these programmes should have been broadcast, in the first place, on the local radio stations in the West Indies. If the work ever reached London, it should have been intended as a commodity for the B.B.C. domestic services. No one bothered to pursue this line of endeavour for the simple reason that when you finally reached the traditional and elephantine authority of Commercial Radio in Trinidad or Barbados, you had reached Dead End; and no writer who was a Civil Service boy 'playing he is a poet' had the strength or prestige which earned him the right to argue with those who rule and reside in Corpse-Land. So it was London, or nothing.

Our sole fortune now was that it was Henry Swanzy who produced 'Caribbean Voices.' At one time or another, in one way or another, all the West Indian novelists have benefited from his work and his generosity of feeling. For Swanzy was very down to earth. If you looked a little thin in the face, he would assume that there might have been a minor famine on, and without in any way offending your pride, he would make some arrangement for you to earn. Since he would not promise to 'use' anything you had written, he would arrange for you to earn by employing you to read. No comprehensive account of writing in the British Caribbean during the last decade could be written without considering his whole achievement and his role in the emergence of the West Indian novel.

My emphasis on the bureaucratic waste of the B.B.C. derives from a feeling that it is not wise or safe for any employee of the Corporation to take too serious an interest in his job. And it is probably quite dangerous for an intelligent producer to know what he is doing. However extravagant this may sound, the feeling is not wholly unjustified when we are forced to ask: On which floor and in which House of the B.B.C. is Henry Swanzy working now? What is he producing? And why did he have to leave the Caribbean section? For Swanzy has gone and, as Sam Selvon always says when we meet, 'The Voices stop. Henry gone and the Voices stop.' For reasons which, apart from Swanzy's departure, no one can explain, the programme 'Caribbean Voices,' has been brought to an end. But the West Indian writers, unknown and not yet ready to migrate, continue to multiply.

4

But I discovered that this colonial situation also exists among English poets. This discovery is all part of the history of that evening at the I.C.A. An important personality who was also a poet had invited me to have drinks. . . . He was in a great hurry, since there was a small party not far away, and which he would have liked me to 'drop in' on. I could stay if I chose, but he had to leave in connection with some conference of Intellectual Freedom which was taking place in India in a very short time. He was leaving for India in a day or two. The urgency of this visit was in some way determined by Mr Arthur Koestler's presence in India at the same time; and it seemed that there had to be somebody of equal weight to challenge what Koestler was going to say about freedom or the lack of it. It never occurred to me then to ask how the passages were going to be paid for.

I never thought of poets earning the sort of money that would enable them to fly all the way out there. For India, in my colonial imagination, had always meant the East; and the East is simply the unreachable East if you are a professional poet resident in the West. But this poet was going.

It is about nine years ago. I have been to all sorts of parties since then—including some mystifying arrangements in New York. But this party was a good example of literary privilege; and privilege is one of the relations between men and men and man and society that I am very interested in.

Moreover, this book is written particularly for a West Indian audience—whether or not they ever read it—and I want to confront that audience with examples of privilege; for it is precisely the disease they are now in pursuit of.

I don't know how well these people at the party knew one another. The poet among us couldn't have known everyone, for he was being introduced from time to time. The hostess was particularly concerned that he shouldn't go; yet when he left it seemed all right. He had earned the right to leave; and one got the impression that he had earned that right by the very generosity of his arrival in the first place.

Not every poet of his generation could have done that sort of thing; and I have met some whose lack of contact with such living-rooms has created strange forms of anger. They make a deliberate mess of them if they are ever allowed in. That seems to me an absurd way for a man over forty, poet or no poet, to behave. I got the impression that there were two classes of poets: the pub poets and the living-room poets. The pub poets were as violent about the living-room poets as any American Negro could possibly be about racial segregation. If the living-room poets encountered one of his pub colleagues—and this led to a drink in the pub poet's salon which was often the public bar—then the living-room poets behaved with the sort of humility which I tried to communicate in Mr Eliot's demeanour as he made his way towards Sir Herbert Read.

Sometimes the pub poets would use this as an opportunity to vilify and attack the living-room poet for what seemed total betrayal: exactly the kind of behaviour I've seen between, say, a Jamaican peasant who had learnt the hard way up via the R.A.F., and some West Indian student class gentleman who was taking sides with the Colonial Office on the question of independence. I have wondered about these subtle and sometimes not so subtle gradations between men who are obviously involved in the same undertaking.

In the case of the West Indians, I have no doubt who is right. Any West Indian who has any reservations about the absolute necessity of independence—any colonial for that matter—is a slave, and should not be allowed the privileges of a free man at a time when the entire world is agreed on the moral difference between the two states of existence.

But what about the poets? Has a pub poet any right to outrage the living-room poet if the latter prefers to drink in the living-room; and living-rooms have, for one reason or another, offered their protection. I say 'protection,' because there are instances when one pub poet does show signs of needing protection from another pub poet, and wishes there was not a living-room, but a liveable hole where he could go into hiding. Has this got to do with ideas about poetry? Has it got to do with the gifts of the respective poets? On what is this privilege based?

The answer is obviously money, a subject which, like race, everybody understands in spite of the general reluctance, at certain levels, to talk about it. This is a matter which the colonial, poet or dentist, must consider; for I've been in two different colonial worlds recently—West Africa, to be precise—and I notice something of a similar nature creeping up in the urban centres. In order to acquire privilege they have to do a great deal of spending; and it is not

enough to buy the most worthwhile. You have to buy the particular
brand of commodity which determines your standard of taste. This
kind of commercial circus might be all right—though I don't think
is is—for people who have known money and its consequences for
centuries. But it is plain suicide among people whose children—not
necessarily theirs but the children a few hundred miles away—have
not drunk milk since the weaning came reluctantly to an end.

I have used this party and the poet's privilege as my example, not
merely because this poet was privileged, but also because the
privilege was earned by his reputation as a poet. And poetry is the
classic example of an activity which shows the correct distinction
between working and jobbing. A man's work often bears little relation to his job; and his job invariably makes it impossible for him to
do any useful work he might have been capable of.

But poetry has no worth outside its particular value; and money,
as a way of measuring work, cannot assess value unless it reduces
value to the degradation of price. All this may be perfectly clear to
Prospero; but since my society, that is a colonial society with specific
reference to the West Indies—since this is in grave danger of being
throttled by the myth which feeds upon price—I thought it should
be said, and particularly by a colonial who is not professionally
engaged in either politics or commerce; for it is commerce which has
separated the pub poets from the living-room poets, or the living-
room poets from the pub poets.

This kind of distortion reaches the height of madness when people
who haven't stolen have to feel ashamed of being rich. It is to give
the metal and Christmas paper a living and breathing reality, as
though it were really possible for Santa Claus to speak although someone played a gimmick with the lights. We all know Santa Claus
can't speak; and it's a waste of time pretending that you know
the sound of his voice. If you want to have the illusion, then go on
with it and keep it at the level of poetic illusion; but the pretence
is imbecilic.

Similarly, if money is there, and it can be manipulated in such a
way as to save the waste or increase the possibilities of work, then it's
a moral duty—for work is the basis of all moral enterprise—to see
that the circulation takes place. And if the behaviour of Santa Claus
depends entirely on your will, the collective will of those sitting or
kneeling or standing, according to their strength—around the Christmas tree, then there is no question about the possibilities of the
money. For money like the Father Christmas which it purchases can
be colonised by a human desire that is founded on creative
work.

5

What then about that living-room? I had been introduced to the lady over there and the gentleman near her. There were three young actresses, one of whom had just 'had' her first film, and who, it was said, was going to be a success. Were the arrangements being made already, I wonder? There was an American novelist whose husband was a professor of some language for which there was not, at the time, a very enthusiastic demand either by students or teachers. He had a marvellous job from the sound of it. It's the professor's involvement with a scientist which I remember most vividly.

A most beautiful blonde lady was saying in reply to a question about her husband's health, that she didn't have a clue. It wasn't many months since their difficulties had separated them; but the young wife made it sound like a total ambush.

I was colliding from time to time with the American wife. By collide, I mean that we were not always together, but whenever we met, it seemed that there wasn't really any interval. One reason might have been that she was an American. I have forgotten which State; but I do remember that the frontiers of our talk had something to do with the Mason Dixon line. She talked well, not so much about America, for she had spent some time in China when some recent fighting was going on. That is, during the struggle that ended in the present Communist Authority.

(When I use the word, communist, I am using it simply as a descriptive of a category of persons whose history is already assumed in the light of that category. That's not unlike the use of the word Negro, in seeing another category of men. I pause to state this meaning, because we weren't talking politics, and as a matter of interest, it is my experience that professional communists among my acquaintance do not often talk politics with the intelligence one would expect from hearing about the menace they represent.)

The American novelist and I were talking about the West Indies; for she had written quite a number of books, and some of these had been set in the West Indies. I assumed that she had been there, and immediately asked which island. But she had never seen the Caribbean. She re-created the atmosphere from general reading. Has this something to do with a passion for islands? Or is it the indirect colonial influence of the Tempest? The American novelist had no inhibitions about talking; nor had I after the persuasive influence of half-a-dozen martinis; for these were not ordinary drinks. These martinis were an example of alcoholic transformation.

There are certain atmospheres in which any kind of alcohol that is familiar actually challenges your tongue to prove that it is the original you know. You know it is gin in that martini; but the total act of drinking makes that ordinary Gordon do a strange camouflage. Wealthy people have a special genius for creating such an atmosphere without the slightest effort. And this atmosphere can sometimes postpone the paralysis which drink can so easily bring about if you are disloyal or a stranger to it.

It was at this stage that I noticed the professor and the scientist. For their convictions were beginning to take a strange turn. I would have ignored this if they were Americans for whom argument and noise are a perfectly sensible way of saying what you think. But in this atmosphere, gentle as twilight until this moment, those voices (accents deliberate and not altogether dissimilar) were doing the most astonishing thing that one professional man can do to another. Each was telling the other that he didn't know what it was all about.

No one can blame me if I say categorically that some critics of my work have no idea what they are talking about. I saw it happen between two men of considerable sophistication and breeding, and on a subject which is most illusive. But I will leave the subject until I have stated their positions. One was saying that this example had nothing to do with theory; for it was a fact of his experience. He was absolutely sure that he was right, for he had got out of his bed—it was some first hour of the dawn—and hurried outside to make sure. He was convinced he had heard the noise.

The scientist argued—and he was using that mobile sneer which can be understood by the changing size of the smile—he argued that it was simply impossible. He wasn't guessing; for the facts, meaning the accumulated knowledge that is fact, made it impossible for such a noise to make itself heard at that particular time.

The professor, with poetic realism, said that a noise was a noise; and if you recognised a certain noise, there was no point in clouding the issue by bringing up the scientist's kind of facts. This is a most dangerous accusation; for it is trespassing on the very premises, bringing into doubt the actual validity about certain kinds of investigation. I am no scientist, but colonial or not, I know that the scientist will not let that one pass without coming to the defence of his work, which is a man's life.

So the scientist countered with a challenge which the professor, who was not a poet, could not possibly have dealt with. The scientist said that he understood the professor's error, for it was not uncommon in certain cases of hallucination. (I may have missed one or two things for it was nine years ago, but I think the reconstruction is correct.) Now there was a pause, a change of temperature, and soon we were about to go. I was offered a lift by the professor and his wife, and I accepted since it was hurrying towards dawn.

To my utter astonishment I discovered that this furious war of wits, involving knowledge, status and possibly friendship, had been caused by a bird.

The professor admitted the uniqueness of his experience; but he insisted that he had actually heard the bird singing that morning. The scientist refused to abandon his world of causality and fact. Ears or no ears, no one could have heard that bird then; for it was a good three months too soon for that particular note which he had made his special study.

At the time I was impressed by two things. In the first place, I like to see people break a pattern of behaviour in order to defend what they believe. Life is at work in that kind of attitude. But what made it more splendid, more magnificent in its gravity, was the fact that it had to do with a creature so beautiful (and if the professor is right), a creature so dutiful as to start its notes at dawn.

Today it occurs to me that neither of these men might ever have bought an ounce of seed in all their bird reviewing days. And I think there is something wrong in taking the bird's feed for granted, if you believe that song must be kept alive.

6

I think it is necessary and appropriate to establish as I best can the connection between the I.C.A. and Notting Hill. I am not so silly as to suggest that the activities in the two places—or the respective defects in these activities—are identical, but I feel their connection since I see them as expressions of a similar deficiency in the national life of the country. It will be important to discuss the violent occurrences of racial discrimination which we have been made aware of during the last few years. It's not a disorder which people at the I.C.A. would care to consider for too long; but it is the kind of misfortune—like a death in the family or an unexpected betrayal—which gives us an opportunity to clarify some of our attitudes. We must forget, for the time being, all talk about equality, and consider the evidence of our attitudes, particularly those attitudes which are never expressed except in occasional slips in discussion about racial differences.

Intellectuals take refuge in the absurd habit that it is enough for two people to share similar ideas in order to claim a certain identity of outlook. If I appear to deviate from that common assumption of outlook, and the conversation centres upon questions of Race—about which we are bound to have different private experience—I am sooner or later confronted with a charge which says: 'You have a chip on your shoulder.' It is made with such authority, with such apparent regret, that my friend anticipates silence or a denial from me. He expects that I will argue: no, that's not true, and by such a denial try to re-establish the ground of our common understanding.

But it is both unnatural and unreasonable of me to do such a thing; and he appears hurt when I express the view that his charge, his expectation of agreement, embodies an entire attitude which he has always tried to obscure or conceal by his expression of goodwill. Moreover, it is an attitude which implies indifference or a liveable contempt. He does not say that I am anti-white (which he would know to be a lie) and which would, in any case, have made our friendship impossible. He uses a form of rebuke which gently suggests my fall from a certain standard of concurrence in matters which civilised men feel no need to speak about. The current phrase is 'talking one's language'; for if you and I talk the same language of ideas, there is no need to wade through explanations; and when the subject is Race, naturally the whole matter is excluded as being no part of our agenda for serious talk. We may speak about what's to be done to stop racism in a way that plumbers may consult with each other about the defects of a pipe line; but the pipe line has nothing to do with the plumbers. Similarly, the flow of racial antagonism does not really pass from me to my friend. We are, by the ideal nature of our relationship, already outside the orbit of such barbarous irregularities.

Hence the word, chip, if I appear to deviate; for he cannot believe that my fall is complete. It does not occur to him that he is making me an offer of equality, or reminding me of his original disposition to grant me that much. He is horrified if I say that his equality, on the evidence of his charge, is an abstract equality. It does not grow from a felt recognition of my capacity for experience, my particular way of seeing. Unfortunately for him, it is not possible to dismiss me by branding me ignorant of his world, for that world is also a part of mine. Moreover, I am capable of situating him in it by examining the history of his relations to it. He will now try to drop the whole matter by asking 'Can I press you to have another drink?' But our glasses are full. In his state of confusion, he has forgotten that we cannot arrive at the next drink until we have finished these. This offer of generosity has nothing to do with my thirst. It is abstract like the equality which he imagines to be my destination, my ambition, the sanction of our friendship. Either we should agree to throw the drinks away and order the same again, or we should call for a change of drink, if we think it necessary to have glasses of a different size. Hence the imagined chip! Had he said: 'You're black my dear boy, and that must put a real forest on your back,' we would have had some honest reason for talking about race. He would have been more accurate in the choice of his images; for my back takes up more room than my shoulder, and racism is more akin to the jungle. After all, what is a chip but a tiny splinter with which I may pick my teeth. When I am finished cleaning the crevices I spit it out. You can't do that with your skin, or your shoulder. A man is always resident in the castle of his skin. If the castle is deserted, then we know the Devil has been at work.

But this use of the word 'chip' to define one's involvement in a predicament that is news in the daily paper can often be an indication of an attitude other than indifference or contempt. It can be imposed as a tactic of evasion. In this case, it is no more or less than the language of betrayal. And why betrayal?

One reason is that my English friend knows, in a sense deeper than intellectual, that my urgency is no simple attempt to start an argument. If he is of working-class origin—and most young intellectuals seem to have migrated from that source—he knows with a certain intimacy what I am talking about. For what I am emphasising is the inherited feeling of *difference* which is his privilege and my source of discomfort. He travels by Tube and bus, circulates in remote social sectors where it is scarcely known that there are blacks around. He hears and may sometimes argue against expressions of disapproval in certain pubs, in the foyer of cinemas. His passion for cricket forces him to recall the Constantine scandal. He knows that this atmosphere exists. It is revealed through whispers, the glance of unwelcome, the calculated suspension of all courtesy. My friend with the 'chip' image knows all this; and it is precisely because he knows, that he reduces the vast acreage of the jungle to the relatively tiny distortion called, chip.

He is doing this for two reasons. He wants to exempt himself from any responsibility or active involvement in race discrimination. After all, our friendship is the absolute proof of his 'difference' from his aunt. His second motive has to do with involving me with this 'difference.' He wants to protect me from the experience of being excluded by granting me the honour of being exceptional, that is, 'different' from most other blacks. He and I, along with a few others, can, with time, establish that there are still saints in the land of increasing terror.

In order to rebuke his aunt, he may marry my niece. I have not only been colonised by his humanity, I have been situated most firmly in the family circle. And everyone knows that families should not quarrel among themselves. It would be silly of me to raise the colour predicament with any member of the family, for we all know that what's wrong is the simple business of a 'chip'; and we also know that *we*, on the inside, are really '*different*' from *those*, meaning black and white—who are on the *outside*. For it must not be forgotten that white people also have shoulders that are getting more and more 'chipped' every day. We are all in the same sea. The tides are treacherous; but *our* family boat is now seen as a special boat.

In these circumstances, I want to know which divinity under or beyond the sea gave us this most extraordinary blessing of uniqueness. If it is true, I would like to know why the divinity chose me and my new family; and since it is highly unlikely that the divinity will intervene at this stage with explanations, we should try to examine the nature of this blessing; for it may be an example of the gift in its most destructive form. It may be the worst form of colonisation: colonisation through a process of affection.

This is the way I want to speak about this colour predicament. I use the word predicament because I think we are all likely to fool ourselves if we approach each other with the attitude that racial discrimination is a specific 'problem' for which we have the following logical 'solutions.' It is not problem and solution which we must deal with exclusively. We must accept that racial antagonism in Great Britain, is, after Notting Hill, an atmosphere and a background against which my life and yours are being lived. Our duty is to find ways of changing the root and perspectives of that background, of dismantling the accumulated myth, both cultural and political, which an inherited and uncritical way of seeing has now reinforced. And our biggest weapon, our greatest and safest chance lies in education: education among the young; for it is my feeling that two-thirds of the parents are beyond redemption.

One of the paradoxes of Notting Hill was that the vast majority of the people in this country felt a deep sense of outrage. They genuinely felt that it was wrong and beastly that such a thing should happen. It's one reason those English kids were so severely sentenced (a decision which I thought at the time, and still do now, was not altogether sound). It was not altogether sound because it was done as a way of informing the world how this country felt about Notting Hill. But a large number of the people who felt so bitterly about the incidents in Notting Hill feel no less bitterly about the presence of these black men in this overcrowded country.

Nothing has really happened within these people to change their traditional way of seeing; and the whole predicament is likely to have international significance.

I believe a large section of the American public were as relieved in conscience that Notting Hill had happened, as a large section of people in this country were relieved, for reasons of their own pride, when the Russians put up the sputnik before the Americans.

Those colonial Americans, with their traditional arrogance in the face of Nature, had been put in their place. And who put them? Not just a vast peasantry ordered to work for this particular achievement. Not just the anonymous skill of those Russian hands, but a great brain whose seeds of understanding may have been nourished by the gentle soil of Cambridge.

In other words, if you take a calm and long range view of the matter, you might say that the first sputnik was, to a large extent, the baby of Cambridge. It is the gift from Prospero to Caliban all over again. But Caliban has a most strange way of behaving some-times, and he gets some curious ideas into his head even when he has not got the unreliable crutches of scholarship. For shortly after the sputnik went up, Lord Kitchener, the Trinidadian calypsonian, sang about it. An English communist was furious with me when I told him what the calypso was about. He was furious because the refrain of the song was:

Columbus didn't need no dog.

Kitch is no intellectual; he can see in his own way, and he com-municates with song. I am sure he has read little or no history, but note the instinctive return to the theme of Christopher Columbus. Kitch is himself a kind of Columbus in reverse; for his music has made a most welcome invasion on the English spine. That spine is no different from my spine; but it needed, perhaps, to be fertilised by a change of rhythm. And that is all to the good.

I am not suggesting, though, that racial antagonism should be approached by weekend get-togethers with Kitch in the chair, and some important M.P. 'dropping in' for an hour or so to give the thing some *tone*, with general circulation through the dubious eye of commercial telly. Not at all; for that leads right back to the old myth.

Here is one example of the myth. Recently Sam Selvon came to see me about a project he was commissioned to do for one of the Sunday papers. He had been asked to interview a poor Jamaican who was utterly disorganised in feeling by some of the things which had hap-pended to him in England. Sam related one incident which had to do with English factory girls creeping up behind the Jamaican, trying to lift his jacket in the hope of discovering his tail. The Jamaican peasant was deeply shaken by this reduction of his person to the status of an ape. They had colonised him by their particular kind of interest; and he was too scared to realise that those girls knew he had no tail.

In Jamaica it would have been clear to him that they knew. But England had undermined his confidence. He could not realise, therefore, that the girls were not looking for his tail. They were looking for something else which was there, which they had received from a traditional mythology, and which they felt was worth investigating. They were curious to see his prick in order to get eye evidence of its size. They had heard about *It*, and asked themselves the genital question: 'Would the native black steel rise to its fantastic stature?'

The working-class English girls were curious; and although I would not allow this method of curiosity, what the girls were really after seems a perfectly just reason for being curious, a perfectly decent expression of desire between a woman and a man. After all, you can't know until you have found out, although it is not likely that a simple look at It will help you discover the potency of It.

Perhaps there are Negroes who don't mind this look and spend most of their time on a wild, pussy-collecting campaign. But what has this got to do with colour since it is generally known that some men, among them English, are simply c——struck.

Which takes me back to the other example of Contemporary Art. The I.C.A. is simply culture-struck. And the factory where those gross and innocent working-class girls felt their curiosity to be a privilege bears an important relation to the Institute which regards itself as the custodian of contemporary taste. If colour did not obscure the Jamaican's essential humanity, then his lack of opportunity would have made him equal with the factory girls in the eyes of the I.C.A. ladies. For the I.C.A. is not concerned with culture as a national enterprise in expression. It is democratic in the sense that any slippery charlatan with a ready-made vocabulary of isms is allowed to have his say; and the less intelligible he is, the more important he might become. Any name that has stumbled or been elevated by commerce into a popular success is an eligible investment in prestige. The subsequent attention from the peripheral herd, the sudden conversion of the popular press to a new concern for the arts, the autograph witch-hunt: it is all part of the conspiracy of colonisation. Both artists and art lovers are suddenly transformed by the magic of a new Name.

Culture-struck!

Name-struck!

Colour-struck!

After the sirens of Notting Hill had given their warning, I experienced a change in my curiosity about English people who were walking towards me. I didn't live in England during the war, but I imagine it is a feeling you might have had in the early stages of the bombing. The planes might not have been in the sky; but the warning had somehow geared your attention to expect something from above. You might look up, quicken your step; or in a moment of exaggerated anticipation, miss your step, increase your speed, or wonder where the nearest air raid shelter might be. All this could happen without any actual warning that the Germans were on their way. Similarly with me after the sirens of Notting Hill.

It is at this point that one experiences the tremendous disadvantage of being black. I am not speaking about equality or justice, for the time being; I am speaking of strategy. For there are occasions when the gentlest creature must abandon its nature in order to protect its spirit from either destruction or disgrace. Dignity itself can weep in order to declare that there is a change in tactics, an order for preparation; for weeping can be a method of self-defence. Similarly with the West Indian in this atmosphere of preliminary violence. He asks himself the question: If this happens, what do you do next? But if it takes that form, what alternatives have you got? And so on.

A good example is the encounter I had with a West Indian writer a few days after the first attacks upon the West Indians. We were not resident in Notting Hill; but we were not so foolish to think that locality was a matter of importance. (It has been brought to my attention that there are West Indians who have actually tried to argue that it is not by accident that the worst 'type of West Indians' live in the part of London where the riots started. I'd like to know who the hell has got hold of the barometer that measures type. But more of this later.)

I met Peter, who had lived in England throughout the war, a much older man than myself, with a greater and more varied experience of practical matters. Peter was calm, as usual; but there was a new severity in his manner. He has a manner of speech which makes it impossible for you not to smile; and I was laughing when he started to outline a plan of self-defence. It sounded like real war, and returned me to the High School where I was a cadet. For I was at school during World War II; and when the news came through that France had fallen, the exercises of the school's army were intensified. My shoulder, though not chipped, aches to this day from the stag-

gering of the rifle butt against my body as the bullet swerved a yard
from the target. I was a bad shot; but I was playing toy soldier at
the orders of a school which, though far away and ignorant of the
causes or implications of the war, was determined to play its duty on
behalf of the Mother Country.

But Peter's outline for a method of defence was not in a toy
atmosphere; and I got desperately serious when he mentioned the
possibility of fire. What would the Boys do in case of fire? It is interesting to note here that most West Indians who knew each other
would refer to the West Indian community as the Boys. The Boys
were all those (type my backside!) who, in such crises, would not be
separated. Peter made me think of a number of things. The fire
brought me up sharp, because I had collected notes for a new book,
and there were bits and pieces of writing which I couldn't afford to
lose. It was at this point that I listened to these tactics with the
greatest care. He outlined the plans for dealing with fire. In other
words, equipment for dealing with fire should be ready long before
the enemy had even thought about moving into your territory. Peter
was once a priest of the Anglican Church, and obviously a man who
had served on all sorts of committees, including those for dealing with
the liquidation of the Devil. For it was the Devil we were up against.
The Devil was at work in Notting Hill; and there is no point
trying to say it was the Teddy Boys.

Having heard Peter's plans, I decided that I should pass on these
details. A matter of great interest here is that, among Peter's plans,
there was not a single bit of advice on methods of attack. He suggested that some of us should ask for temporary refuge in France. He
thought that, in the circumstances, the Boys should try not to get
actually involved; they should avoid walking after night. They
should resist carrying weapons in public, since they might confuse
their case if asked to explain the presence of the instrument.

For Peter's plans had taken care of the legal aspects. His defence
was determined by the uncertainty of prompt police protection, but
he believed there would be a chance of holding out until the Law
arrived. The West Indian, until then, had an implicit faith in the
Law, and some ancient certainty that the police would be on his side.
Where the Law was concerned, the West Indian was colour blind.
Hence his duality in the face of an enemy.

I mention Peter's suggestions in order to show the psychology
which Notting Hill had produced in men who, after long sojourn in England, could not believe what they were reading or
seeing from day to day. I recall a feeling of utter stupefaction; for I
had argued in America—a year before—that it was difficult to draw

parallels in spite of the prejudice, for Georgia or Alabama just could not happen anywhere in England. It was in Georgia where I told some Negro professionals that the likelihood of a Tull episode (Tull was a twelve-year-old boy murdered on a charge of rape by staring)—happening anywhere in England—would be like having a National Health Service organised and functioning throughout the United States in a matter of weeks.

So this was the kind of duality the West Indian was involved in. This duality had to do with his way of seeing. And one example is a discussion I was having with Neville Dawes, the Jamaican novelist, who lived in Ghana. He had come to London for his summer holiday. We were trying to explain Neville's fear the night before when he thought that two men at a Tube station were going to strike him. The point is that in this situation the West Indian will not pre-judge the other.

I am walking up the street, and three men are walking towards me. I do not think that they are the enemy from Notting Hill; nor do I think that they are not. I simply do not know, for there is no way of telling. It is my particular way of seeing which creates this doubt, in spite of all I have read about what was happening. And it is in this moment of doubt that my life is endangered, for while I wonder and watch and wait, the men and I are actually getting nearer. I begin with the grave disadvantage that if they are the enemy, then they have seen their target long ago. While I am working out the possibilities, they have already chosen unanimously the result. There it is. I am completely in their power by the fact that experience has not trained me to strike without the certainty of the enemy's presence. I am completely immobilised by all my social and racial education as a West Indian.

This could not possibly happen to an American Negro. His experience prepares him for any situation of racial emergency. He can smell it, and every nerve is summoned to deal with the arriving odour. As soon as the Notting Hill siren went, the American Negro would have replied that the war was on. No question about that. For no American—and Baldwin has stated this in different ways—would be capable—by the references of his experience which is all he has—to feel doubt about that man coming towards him. It would be like an English soldier in battle wondering whether the German over there was in the war or not. If he were catapulted out of passive resistance, that was too bad, but a war was a war and you were you. And either I had to get you or it would be your duty to get me.

The best way of explaining this difference would be to notice the language which West Indians use to introduce the battle of Notting Hill with the language of an American Negro who had been asked the same question. 'What do you think about Notting Hill?' The American Negro would begin: 'So at last it gave way.' The West Indian would begin: 'Man, if you had told me a year ago . . .' Both men are correct according to the particular orientation in these matters.

And it is my impression that one purpose behind Notting Hill was that the West Indians should strike back. Notting Hill would have been a nasty episode in this country's peace-time history if those boys had struck back. For they are not afraid. That must be borne in mind. They sense, in some curious way, not only that the odds are against them numerically, but that waiting is wiser. But waiting is ineffective without the certainty of legal protection. And the point I have to make now is this: the West Indians who lived through the terror of Notting Hill have lost their confidence in the police. I am not guessing about this. I have spoken to several of them. They believe that the police were not really in sympathy with them. It is not my business to say whether that is so or not; but it ought to be known; for it leads to a question which the Home Secretary must answer. He owes it to those West Indians, for their restraint, to answer. For it is his answer which may help restore their confidence in the Law.

Why didn't the Home Secretary intervene, positively intervene? There can be one of two answers to this. Either he did not think the situation sufficiently urgent and calculated that the matter would solve itself, or he realised its urgency, but had reasons for postponing his decision about intervention.

If his thinking took the first turn, then I am saying—and the West Indian community in Notting Hill are the best evidence— that the Home Secretary committed a serious error of judgment. Perhaps he was misinformed.

If he realised the urgency of the situation, what was the motive, what was the thinking behind his procrastination? The debate on Race which was held much later should have been held during the Notting Hill crisis.

If politicians explain the moral decadence of their society by saying that ours is an age of juvenile delinquency, we cannot wonder at the gradual decline of artistic expression authorised by an eye which complains that it sees despair everywhere.

I have not got the sort of importance which can plant 'chips' in the shoulders of the I.C.A.; but it is my right, while things remain as they are—to speak; and it is my responsibility as a writer who is also a colonial to report honestly my feelings about matters which deeply concern us both. I could not accept any uniqueness of privilege in an atmosphere which is capable of gratuitous murder.

## 7

Knives are too messy for the I.C.A., but what happens if we pass from the colour-baiters to the culture-vultures?

It is an atmosphere that breeds enemies, for some naïve foreigners often make the unforgivable blunder of asking whether the work of the NEW-NAME is worthy of serious attention.

It is at this point that the charge 'chip' may surrender its true meaning. The original lapse from offer of equality acquires a new meaning, enters a new category of disgrace. Caliban is now seen not only for who he is, but for what he has always been. He becomes a condition which can provide us with a multitude of examples. When he has been baptised ungrateful and the sources of his ancient deformity have been resurrected, there is nothing left for him but a passionate gesture of forgiveness.

It is usually left to the innocent voice to introduce this theme. It is not yet Prospero's turn to speak, for he is considering more sinister matters. Moreover, he can allow his daughter to perform this obvious chore since she and Caliban, different as they may be, have shared a common source of instruction, a common Master.

But Caliban's descendant has had some variety of experience. He has inherited a legacy of dispossession, but he and his generation really belong to the age of negotiation. He has travelled further forward than his past. He has arrived at Prospero's home. He is received as though he were a lost Crown Prince, innocent enough to ask for his throne. He is offered a vision of thrones to remind him how painful it can be to take one's place, alone, and in the public gaze. He takes his place, and everyone helps him with approval, encouragement, prediction, until he begins to ask for some alterations in this particular throne.

He thinks it is not large enough. He would like more freedom to turn, swing, stretch or be rigid in his way. They remind him that the thrones are all the same size; they have always been the same size, that's how he found them. He agrees that this is true for his sight is as good as theirs. But Caliban's strength is his racial insensitivity. It doesn't allow him to traffic in discretion. The age and uniformity of the thrones have nothing to do with his request for a new throne.

This is his first concrete demand: a new throne. The atmosphere soon changes; and the people who once clapped soon adopt an attitude that Caliban is getting tiresome. He is not the same Caliban they used to know. Indeed, he has become a bore. They adopt the attitude that Caliban understands, but he pretends not to hear, like a drunk calculating trouble. But Caliban is no longer nervous. He has had a long experience in dealing with adopted attitudes. In fact, he has found it necessary to learn some himself; and he is not in the least worried about 'charges': particularly the charge of conceit. He simply repeats his wish: to change the shape of the throne.

Now there is a great deal of deliberation, patient, elaborate and courteous. It is an interval which shows the fruits of a civilised awareness; an awareness which can see two sides of any one-sided question. So the first concession is granted. Of course the shape of the throne can be changed. But it is a theoretical concession; for they now proceed to involve Caliban in an intricate discourse on relations: the relations of the separate parts of the throne to the totality which is that particular throne, the relation of one throne to another. And during this pursuit, one simple fact of security, of permanence, is suggested. It would not be in the interest of any throne to build a new throne until they had settled the relation of all the thrones to the original Idea of throne. Caliban has learned not to curse these speculations as nonsense. He simply says that it's going to take a hell of a long time to get the new throne, not to mention the insoluble difficulty of who will then be allowed to sit on it; for a man's size is not constant; it is not fixed. They wait for Caliban to speak; but, instead, he thinks; he is in dialogue with himself. He tells himself that Prospero doesn't really want the change to come about. He is even inclined to think that Prospero doesn't mind him occupying one of the thrones indefinitely, provided that it is the old throne. But any change of throne will require a corresponding change in Prospero himself. This will be his second change. The first was Caliban's admission to the Kingdom of Possibilities. He has had enough.

Prospero lives under the pressure of traditions; moreover, the immediacies of life are becoming too many and too dangerous to risk a change of vision whenever we are assaulted by a new fact of awareness. A continuous process of change will allow no rest for evaluating the progress of change. Prospero fears that change itself will become a contagion. Caliban is sympathetic; for he knows the pain it has cost him to realise the change within himself. He is a child of the backward glance with recollection of a time when he was not even accorded the right to be angry. He has known what it means to have one's past appropriated, then languageless as his aboriginal neighbours. What, someone has asked, could the first exported slave-mother say to her child? But Caliban accepts this predicament as part of his historic acre of ground. He has been precipitated into his change. He has made it, and it has made him. Now it is Prospero's turn to submit to the remorseless logic of his own past.

It is the future, not Caliban's but theirs, which now threatens to reduce Prospero to madness or impotence. It was a divine recognition of privilege which made Prospero's past, the divinity which gave him the right to colonise the unarmed and excluded Caliban is the witness which waits for this decision. He cannot deny that past; nor can he abandon it without creating a total suicide of all those values which once sanctified his acts as a coloniser. He cannot commit his name and history to the unforgivable vice of ingratitude against the once divine grace which had offered him eternal protection against the dumb conscience of the Infidel; the grace which still promises to wash him clean of any crime resurrected in the name of colonisation. Guilt is a waste of emotion. Glory is pure camouflage. Withdrawal is impossible. He must act; and he must act with Caliban; or he must die, not so much from spears, as from the slow and painful diminution of an energy he used to call human dignity. To change or not to change? That is the question which has already set up an atmosphere of change in Prospero. It is the question he has encountered by surprise, the atmosphere he must breathe for ever. It surrounds him everywhere. In every conscious act, it beckons him; it orders him forward; it urges him to enter the unknown territory of a life which can no longer be excluded. Colonised by his own ambition, Prospero's role is now completely reversed. Prospero is once again face to face with what is urgent and near-impossible. And he is terrified.

# CONFLICT AND ILLUSION

I

DURING MY stay in West Africa, I met a West Indian who had spent most of his life among the Africans of two countries. In his youth he had been a thorn in the side of English District Commissioners. The freedom which we have come to take for granted is, for him, the history of a dream which has come true. But age, disappointment, as well as a Victorian austerity of conscience have turned him sour. The tropics haunt him, and the African proximity to the Caribbean rhythm of spirit, fills him with nostalgia for his original native residence.

His Christian virtues as well as his Christian vision are absolute. He has never been at home among the African gods; for he thinks that this multiplicity of gods, with their debased habits of intervening in human affairs, is a betrayal of the One and Only God. He can forgive the Greeks for a similar worship since they had the misfortune to be born before Christ. But his judgment is austere when he considers this defect in the African. If he dates the existence of the African after the birth of Christ, it is because he conceives of existence, in the sense of reflective self-consciousness, as identical with possessing the Word.

This use of Word means the whole language of cognitive thought. (I shall say more about this in the following section.) The African did not achieve the Word because he acquired a phenomenal aptitude for wickedness. God separated him from the Word so that he might sojourn in a state of illiteracy; and in this state, he would be punished by the greed, the deception, the cruelties of literate men. Apart from the ultimate loss of Heaven, this separation from the Word is the severest punishment God could inflict on His children. And God did this to the African because the African was once His favourite child. He had once given the African the keys to Heaven; and with this privilege the African made straight for Hell.

'There is no hope for them,' said Uncle, 'no hope in Heaven or Hell.'

'You mean they are going to inherit the earth?' I asked.

86

Uncle wasn't sure that this would happen while life remained liveable on the land; but he was adamant in his prophecy of the African's future which would be eternal persecution with long intervals of gratuitous torture.

This didn't sound very Christian to me, and I wanted to know why it was no longer within the power of Christ to save the African who, after all, was once the favourite child of God. It seemed unworthy of any spirit that jealousy should assume such vindictiveness.

'Not even Christ can help?'

'Christ could help,' said Uncle, ' 'cause there's nothing Christ can't do. But to save the African, Christ would have to be crucified three times. And I don't know whether God would want that for His only Son.'

Even if this were so, I took the view that there is one thing God and the African would have in common. If they were both on trial, one against the other for some charge of treason, they would make a similar request of their Judge. However bitter their opposition, both God and the Negro would be agreed that, in no circumstances, should the Devil be allowed to give evidence.

For they have both got an inside knowledge of the Devil's techniques. There is a sense in which the Negro's technique of survival in a foreign environment bears a relation to the Devil's technique of universal temptation. It is not merely because the Negro is black, and we have racial fantasies about the night. It is because he can, like Ariel, deal with you according to the result which is required. He is there and he is not there. His colour makes him the easiest object to see in broad daylight; and it is precisely this obviousness which makes him the most difficult presence to recognise. As a member of a minority group—living, that is, in England—he has paid most careful attention to the weaknesses of his adversaries. It is important that he acquires a perfect knowledge of their defects; for it is from their defects that they derive their way of seeing him. He will then proceed to offer the self which they are looking for; and each self changes with the white need and the white situation which wants to exploit or embrace him.

Black artists whose recent gifts are confined to the guitar are experts at this kind of chameleon transformation. Insecurity has made them attentive. Entering a room of important people—television producers, for example—the Negro will assess in a flash the possible meanings of this situation. If it appears they want an intelligent Negro who also plays the guitar, he will invent a relation to the guitar which he knows they will interpret as intelligent. He may speak of the guitar as his second and not so passionate love. He has stuck to the guitar because he needs it, and he can use it; and if given the right circumstances, he can use it well.

He risks this disloyalty because he has judged the man who is about to employ him in the role of guitarist; and he has noticed from the emphasis of that man's talk that the television is not his first, and will never be his passionate love. This producer wants to be an artist, perhaps novelist or poet. He justifies his work in television by believing in his sensibility. It is a sensibility which knows whom and what to choose as material for intelligent entertainment. For the trouble about entertainment, he has said earlier, is that it lacks intelligence. This is another way of saying what is wrong with his colleagues. The Negro agrees that it is precisely his trouble with 'most Negroes.' All they are after is money which is precisely why this Negro is there, as we shall see in the contrasting example.

Or the Negro may enter a situation which tells him by its vibration that a Negro drummer is required: some black god whose music will order the jungle to enter and impose its turbulence upon the simple and ossified domesticities of every suburban living-room. If it's telly they want; it's telly they will get. The same Negro transfers from the melancholy of last night's guitar music to the ancient thunder of the drum. He hears the order and he learns its requirements. 'I want you to beat it, man.' If the black gods are reluctant, the producer can turn him into a god by making an appeal to his deepest nerve. In a voice, wholly invented to express anger, the producer may rave: 'Nigger, have you forgotten where you learnt that drum.' There may be a terrible ambivalence in the Negro drummer, but the money god now conspires with the drum god to work a hateful turbulence in this Negro's hands. It is terrific. The camera men said so; the make-up girl said so; and they are right, for the next morning awakes the suburb relaying one fearful question: 'Did you see that African last night?'

That African was actually a West Indian from the Victorian outpost of Barbados where the Drum is entirely the property of the Salvation Army whose rhythms have a different intention, whose themes are stated every Saturday in the order:

> Onward Christian soldiers,
> Marching as to war
> With the Cross of Jesus,
> Going on before.

But it was terrific. It worked. The Negro may tell the producer that they must speak later. The producer, genuinely apologetic, names the nearest pub. At the bar where no ultimate judgments can be made, they will argue about the methods used to make that drum explode. The Negro questions the producer's choice of language; the producer tries to explain the contingencies of the imagination, the range of realistic licence which freedom has bestowed on all theatre. And at closing-time, they may be heard reaching some bitter compromise over their last black pint of sacrificial blood.

2

A month ago I was leaving the B.B.C. Bush House after a long discussion about this same matter, the Negro in the role of Devil meaning absent guide, when I lost my way somewhere between Holborn and the Strand. It was about eight o'clock, and I was in a hurry to get back to Magdala pub, because I knew there was going to be some important trouble in the small bar that evening. Anyway, I needed information. So I turned to a man who had just entered the same street and asked him which was the shortest way to the nearest Tube station. He was most attentive. A man, I would think, between the age of forty and sixty. Very spruce, brisk, friendly, sort of Gentleman of the World, bowler hat and the lot, but not a dressed-up monkey. He wore those clothes in a way which told you that he belonged to them. In Baldwin's sense of time, that man had been wearing that bowler hat for a few centuries.

'Where are you going?' he asked.

'Belsize Park,' I said.

'I'll show you the way,' he said, 'I'm going to the Tube myself.'

This seemed to me perfectly natural. In fact it is precisely what I would do for him in the back streets of Port-of-Spain which I know like the palm of my hand. His behaviour was a fulfilment of the unsigned but irreducible contract between one man and another.

'Are you often in this area?' he asked.

'No,' I said, which was perfectly true and which the Boys at Bush House can confirm.

'Are you just walking around?' he asked.

'Of course not,' I answered. 'I never walk around in places where I don't live.' (I meant here that walking around is perfectly natural for me to do in Hampstead. It is that necessary loitering, that state of creative idleness which every poet has direct experience of.)

'To the left,' he said, preparing to guide me down a street whose black heart I didn't like the look of. As Nature and the Law would have it, I then noticed two policemen standing on the kerb. We were about to pass them when I decided I would check about that Tube.

"Which way to the nearest Tube?' I asked.

'Keep straight ahead, sir,' one of them said.

Turn left! Keep straight ahead! These were contradictory guides. In spite of Notting Hill I still believed the police. So I took the advice of the police and kept straight ahead. When I turned to say good night to that amicable stranger who had suggested a left turn, he was not there. He was, in fact, several yards down the left street.

I forgot all about him until I saw him standing at the Tube. In other words, his left turn was correct; and so was the bobby's keep straight. Therefore, my friend, the stranger, must have been most indignant. Indeed, that's why he was waiting. He bought a ticket ahead of me, and waited until I had bought mine. He was deciding that he would let me know what he thought of me, the exact punishment I and all like me would receive for such suspicion.

'You thought I was lying,' he said.

'Not necessarily,' I said. 'You strike me as being very English in a good sense of English, but your familiarity in questions strikes me as being most un-English. I just wasn't sure.'

I don't even know whether he was listening; for he had something to get off his chest.

'I just want to tell you,' he said, 'that *I will never speak to a coloured man again.*'

I would have laughed—West Indians are in the habit of laughing at every goddam thing—if I had not realised how much this attitude contained. I wonder what that man expected me to feel or think in reply. I wonder! For he seemed to think I was talking Chinese when I said that it was entirely his business whom he chose to speak with; and that there should be no Law here or above the sun to make him speak to coloured people or any people, for that matter. That choice was his business, his responsibility—not mine.

I am sure that the man belongs to an average middle-to-lower-upper middle class home. Not all members of that category belong to that way of thinking; but I am also sure that the attitude which his annoyance took is part of a privileged way of feeling in nearly every English home of similar circumstances and origins. I do not hold it against him or any other English person for inheriting such a habit of mind and emotion; for I can't see what other habit they could have inherited. What I do hold against that man is his assumption that he didn't have to pay attention to that savage and colourful noble to whom he was giving information. He did not refuse to pay attention. He simply did not feel, by habit could not feel, that this occasion merited attention. What's done is done; but you and I—both black and white—will be guilty of a criminal deceit if we allow that man's children to reach their father's age in such a state of tragic and mindless illusion. David Pitt, the Labour candidate for Hampstead, demonstrated this by the way he conducted his campaign.

For Hampstead is, in some ways, not unlike Port-of-Spain in the cosmopolitan mixtures of the two places: Port-of-Spain with its Indians, Chinese, Syrians: Hampstead with its central European immigrants, its Indian and African students, Canadians, Australians, South Africans, who have all settled into what has become for many of them a tolerable refuge away from their original home. It is also the home of both foreign and native intellectuals. From street to street, the sound of typewriters, in the early hours of the morning, is as frequent as rain. Also, Hampstead is a great place for talking. There is no subject under the sun that does not come up for dissection in pubs and cafés. Hampstead and Port-of-Spain do share in such a community of interests as they have shared, at different times, in the experience of having David Pitt involved, at an important level, in their political affairs.

A man's sensitivity is also his capacity for being wounded. But David Pitt never once lost his temper. He would shout his replies when the devil's disciples came to heckle. And that is as it should be; for there is no voice which can make more noise in argument than the West Indian voice—students should remember that their land-ladies are not used to that kind of barracking after midnight—but David Pitt never once lost his head. And his greatest moment of that campaign was the night before the election. I was hoping that this would happen at some time. When some young Conservative was pestering him about pensions (what state of degradation can allow a young man to think of his pension? The next stage will be to accuse the Government of not providing for his grave?) when this young man was talking about pensions, David Pitt was making another and more important emphasis.

'We must not be fooled by Tory Summit gimmick. More important is our relation to a colonial world on which we have depended and whose good faith we shall need in the future. It is not we who matter so much as the children. We must not go to our graves knowing that our children hate us for having given them a legacy of circumstances which make their life unbearable.'

As a doctor he must have seen and made friends with lots of English children; and as a colonial of African descent he embodied a predicament which it is often difficult to communicate. But he was a West Indian with lived experience of a community in which different races worked towards the same end. In thinking of England and Africa, he would have been hoping that parents would not postpone the day when their children could walk any street south of the Sahara in the certain knowledge that no African would throw stones at them. For they had earned the right to be there serving by their skills, contributing to an enterprise that is of their own time. He was trying to communicate a vision of this young English boy or girl learning to adjust to a new environment through a spirit of freedom which would be a rebuke to any African's assault. This attitude from a colonial has nothing to do with generosity or forgiveness. It is the minimum requirement for earning the right to be alive.

3

The University of Woodford Square is, perhaps, the only academy of its kind in the New World. It occupies the banks of the Dry River, it neighbours the Trinidad public library in Port-of-Spain; and it is hardly a red brick's throw from the Legislative Assembly. The Prime Minister of Trinidad, Dr Eric Williams, a former professor of Social Science in Howard University, gives his most important lectures in this arena. The courses which are not classified are free. Indeed, the whole enterprise has to be a free for all, since the classes are conducted in the open air, and microphones are evident everywhere.

This experiment has been fiercely attacked by the local intelligentsia; and the attack would not have been possible if it were not for the conspiracy of the most influential daily newspaper. But it has made no difference to the vast numbers of men and women who crowd to hear a few facts about the circumstances of their lives, both now and in the past. In his reply to certain critics, Dr Williams said:

'Somebody once said that all that was needed for a university was a book and the branch of a tree; someone else went further and said that a university should be a university in overalls. With a bandstand, a microphone, a large audience in slacks, a topical subject for discussion, the open air, and a beautiful tropical night, we have all the essentials for a university. Now that I have resigned my position at Howard University in the U.S.A., the only university in which I shall lecture in future is the University of Woodford Square and its several branches throughout the length and breadth of Trinidad and Tobago.'

This was his preamble to the lecture which was then introduced in this way:

'Our subject tonight, constitution reform in Trinidad and Tobago, is eminently suited to university discussion. It is in this spirit that I propose to approach it—to examine the history of constitution reform in the light of reason and experience and to attempt the drafting of a constitution consonant with the needs of Trinidad and Tobago, and harmonising with the aspirations of its inhabitants.'

It was during this lecture that Williams attempted to analyse by quotation and historical description of context the way in which this whole problem of reform had been seen by three distinguished men of English culture: Anthony Trollope, Thomas Carlyle, and James Anthony Froude who was Professor of Modern History at Oxford which, by the way, was also Williams's first university. Carlyle had never visited the West Indies which, according to Williams, 'allowed him to speak with the greatest authority.' But Trollope was there in 1859; and Froude went in 1884. It is Froude who is most relevant to my meaning, and the passage I am going to quote emphasises his greatest concern in considering the problem of constitution reform.

'A West-Indian self-governed Dominion is possible only with a full negro vote. If the whites are to combine, so will the blacks. It will be a rule by the blacks and for the blacks. Let a generation or two pass by and carry away with them the old traditions, and an English Governor-General will be found presiding over a black council delivering the speeches made for him by a black Prime Minister; and how long could this endure? No English gentleman would consent to occupy so absurd a situation.'

Throughout this book, I have been trying to suggest the legacy of myth which is behind this form of contemporary prejudice; and Froude's comments lead naturally into Lord Montgomery's approach to the problem of reform in South Africa. We have heard a great deal from him, and the danger of his statements must not be obscured by the obvious silliness of their content. It is important to remember that Montgomery has devoted the greater part of his life learning how not to lose wars. South Africa is a minority dictatorship; and it is not improbable that the South African Government might have used the opportunity of Lord Montgomery's visit to discuss matters affecting military strategy on the African continent. Dr Chike Obi, of Ibadan University, has already drawn attention to this danger.

'The South African threat to Nigeria is real and very real indeed: there is no doubt as to what will be the effect of a really strong, independent Nigeria on the status of the white usurpers of South, Central and East Africa.'

Dr Obi is a Nigerian; and Lord Montgomery may simply be contributing to a suicidal illusion if he imagines that there are not Africans, both north and south of the Zambesi, who have not already thought out two or three alternatives to their present situation. In the light of these remarks, we can say farewell to Lord Montgomery as he emerges in the following extract.

Asked at a press conference held on November 20th, 1959, at the home of Major-General Sir Francis de Guingand in Johannesburg whether he would see Mr Albert Luthui, President of the African National Congress, Lord Montgomery said: 'Is he a good buy? I have never heard of him.'

But it is salutary to know that we can end these reflections on a wiser note, one which helps to sharpen the nature of the previous illusions. In his farewell speech to the people of Ghana, the Duke of Edinburgh said:

'The British Administration here would have been a failure by every standard if the demand for freedom and independence had not been heard sooner or later. I believe both our peoples can take justifiable pride that our association has resulted in the thriving go-ahead nation which is Ghana today.'

There is an obvious conflict between the Army, Culture, and the Crown. England must choose.

# A MONSTER, A CHILD, A SLAVE

•

Eia for those who never invented anything
Eia for those who never conquered anything
But who in awe give themselves to the essence of things
Ignorant of the shell, but seized by the rhythm of things
Not intent on conquest, but playing the game of the world
True and truly the first born of this world
Receptive to every breath of the world
Brotherly enclosure for all the winds of the world
Bed and not gutter for all the waters of the world
Sparks of the holy fire of the world, trembling in the world's tremble

AIMÉ CESAIRE

*The Tempest* is a drama which grows and matures from the seeds of exile and paradox. Through a process of poetic schematisation, it contains and crystallises all the conflicts which have gone before. It is the poet's last will and testament; but the details of the legacy read like an epitaph: an apology for any false dividends which Art—meaning all method and experience of transformation—may have brought home.

> Now my charms are all o'erthrown,
> And what strength I have's mine own,
> Which is most faint: now, 'tis true,
> I must be here confin'd by you,
> Or sent to Naples. Let me not,
> Since I have my dukedom got,
> And pardon'd the deceiver, dwell
> In this bare island by your spell;
> But release me from my bands
> With the help of your good hands:
> Gentle breath of yours my sails
> Must fill, or else my project fails,
> Which was to please. Now I want
> Spirits to enforce, Art to enchant;
> And my ending is despair,
> Unless I be reliev'd by prayer,

Which pierces so, that it assaults
Mercy itself, and frees all faults.
As you from crimes would pardon'd be,
Let your indulgence set me free.

It is the Epilogue which reminds us that the Voyage is not over.
Indeed, we are right back where we started:

### ACT I. Scene 1

(On a ship at sea a tempestuous noise of thunder and lightning
heard)

Will the magic of prayer help Prospero and his crew safely towards
Milan where the marriage of Miranda and Ferdinand may remind
them that Innocence and Age are two sides of the same coin; that
there are no degrees of forgiveness; that compassion will not exclude
any? Will Prospero, no longer interested in temporal success, enter
his grave without admitting that his every third thought remains
alive? For where, we wonder, is our excluded Caliban? And what
fearful truth will Caliban discover now the world he prized has
abandoned him to the solitude of his original home: the Island which
no act of foreign appropriation ever could deprive him of.

It is not only aesthetic necessity, but the *facts* of lived experience
which demanded that the territory of the drama had to be an island.
For there is no landscape more suitable for considering the Question
of the sea, no geography more appropriate to the study of exile. And
it is that ruthless, though necessary wreck, which warns us that we
are all deeply involved in the politics of intrigue. The tides have
turned treacherous. Thunder is talking a language which everyone
understands; and in this moment of peril we are reminded by the
loyal that there are very important people on board: a King and his
heir, the King's brother, a Duke who has important connections not
far away. There is panic among the great; and the old counsellor,
Gonzalo—loyal even to his mistakes, Gonzalo the perfect embodiment of servitude, thinks not of himself but of his master's safety:

GONZALO: Nay, good, be patient.

BOATS: When the sea is. Hence! What cares these roarers for the
name of King? To cabin: silence! trouble us not.

GONZALO: Good, yet remember whom thou hast aboard.

It is an expression of the perfect colonial concern: what will happen if the edifice of one man's presence crumbles? But these sailors
have always sojourned with danger. Their harbour is no more than a
postponement of peril. The sea is their kingdom, and they don't
give a damn about the King who is essentially a land-crab. That's

how they think; and confidence demands that they should say so: BOATS: None that I more love than myself. You are a counsellor; if you can command these elements to silence, and work the peace of the presence, we will not hand a rope more; use your authority: if you cannot, give thanks you have lived so long, and make yourself ready in your cabin for the mischance of the hour, if it so hap. Cheerly, good hearts! Out of our way, I say.

It is a fine piece of straight talking and is in direct contrast to the forgivable stammering which comes from dear, old Gonzalo. We shall draw attention to another contrast when we encounter Ariel and Caliban in a similar situation of servant and master. But this wreck strikes terror in every heart; for it was Nature combined with Art which brought it about. Men seem to think that it is their last chance to call a spade a spade; and there is a good deal of bad language as the ship surrenders its sails to the total embrace of the sea. But the sea in conspiracy with the Art which also created these characters has returned them to safety.

According to plan they will reach shore; for it's on land and among the living that the awkwardness of the past must be resolved. Yet there must have been an interval of absolute hell: the purgatorial journey from origins to some landmark which reminds that you are always in transit. Ariel, in a spirit of pure and diabolical delight, gives a first-hand account of their suffering:

ARIEL: Not a soul
But felt a fever of the mad, and play'd
Some tricks of desperation. All but mariners
Plung'd in the foaming brine, and quit the vessel,
Then all afire with me: the King's son, Ferdinand,
With hair up-staring,—then like reeds, not hair,—
Was the first man that leap'd; cried, 'Hell is empty,
And all the devils are here.'

To which Prospero replies: 'Why, that's my spirit!'

A most appropriate parallel in contemporary history is the unforgettable transport of slaves from Africa to the Caribbean . . .

'On ship the slaves were packed in the hold on galleries one above the other. Each was given only four or five feet in length and two or three feet in height, so that they could neither lie at full length nor sit upright. . . . In this position they lived for the voyage, coming up once a day for exercise and to allow the sailors "to clean the pails." But when the cargo was rebellious or the weather bad, then they stayed below for weeks at a time. The close proximity of so many naked human beings, their bruised and festering flesh, the foetid

D

air, the prevailing dysentery, the accumulation of filth, turned these holds into a hell. During the storms the hatches were battened down, and in the close and loathsome darkness they were hurled from one side to another by the heaving vessel, held in position by the chains on their bleeding flesh. No place on earth, observed one writer of the time, concentrated so much misery as the hold of a slave ship.'

That purgatory of the Middle Passage lasted six thousand miles; and like Prospero commending his 'brave spirit,' there was the captain of the slave ship with so clear a conscience that one of them, in the intervals of waiting to enrich British capitalism with the profits of another valuable cargo, enriched British religion by composing the hymn:

'How sweet the name of Jesus sounds!'

But these 'savage and deformed slaves' arrived; and like the character who or which fits this description in *The Tempest*, they worked, and were rebellious and often went wild with the spirit of freedom, and were imprisoned, and yet, like Caliban, they survived as though there were some divinity which made them unique in their capacity to last.

We are back, then, to the Island, once the birthright of Caliban, and now the Kingdom of a Duke who lives in exile.

If we consider the politics of the Island, the size of its population as well as its relation to the world beyond its shores, we are left with a remarkable example of a State which is absolutely run by one man. Absolute is the only word for a power which does not even require an army. Prospero has no need of bureaucrats. Caliban is his slave, which means, among other things, his physical survival:

> But, as 'tis,
> We cannot miss him: he does make our fire,
> Fetch in our wood, and serves in offices
> That profit us. What, ho! slave! Caliban!
> Thou earth, thou! speak.

We are trying to suggest the way in which Prospero saw himself in relation to the immediate neighbourhood around him. It is in his relation to Caliban, as a physical fact of life that we are allowed to guess some of Prospero's needs. He needs this slave. Moreover, he must be cautious in his dealings with him, for Caliban contains the seed of revolt.

After the slaves were encamped in Haiti, torture became a common method of persuading them to work. In some cases, they were roasted; others were buried alive up to the neck, their heads smeared with sugar that the flies might devour them; they were fastened to nests of wasps, made to eat their excrement, drink their urine, and lick the saliva of other slaves. A great pastime too, was to fill them with gunpowder and strike a match somewhere near the hole of the arse. There is a similar sadism in Prospero whenever he is moved to threaten Caliban for his rebellion:

PROSPERO: For this, be sure, tonight thou shalt have cramps,
Side-stitches that shall pen thy breath up; urchins
Shall, for that vast of night that they may work,
All exercise on thee; thou shalt be pinch'd
As thick as honeycomb, each pinch more stinging
Than bees that made 'em.

But Prospero dare not dynamite Caliban; for there is one slave only, one pair of hands that labour. To murder Caliban would be an act of pure suicide. But Caliban is more than his source of food as we shall see. Caliban haunts him in a way that is almost too deep and too intimate to communicate.

But we must return to the politics of the island, to Ariel's function in this drama of intrigue. For Ariel, like Caliban, serves Prospero; but Ariel is not a slave. Ariel has been emancipated to the status of a privileged servant. In other words: a lackey. Ariel is Prospero's source of information; the archetypal spy, the embodiment—when and if made flesh—of the perfect and unspeakable secret police. It is Ariel who tunes in on every conversation which the degradation of his duty demands that he report back to Prospero. Of course, he knows what's going on from the very beginning. Ariel is on the inside. He knows and serves his master's intention, and his methods are free from any scruples:

ARIEL: All hail, great master! grave sir, hail! I come
To answer thy best pleasure; be 't to fly,
To swim, to dive into the fire, to ride
On the curl'd clouds, to thy strong bidding task
Ariel and all his quality.

But it is a dangerous partnership, and Prospero never hesitates to remind him of his servitude. Like some malevolent old bitch with a bad conscience, Prospero's habit is to make you aware of his power to give. He is an expert at throwing the past in your face. And Ariel is no exception:

PROSPERO:                    Dost thou forget
From what torment I did free thee?

ARIEL: No

PROSPERO: Thou dost, and think'st it much to tread the ooze
Of the salt deep,
To run upon the sharp wind of the north,
To do me business in the veins o' th' earth
When it is bak'd with frost.

ARIEL:                          I do not, sir.
PROSPERO: Thou liest, malignant thing! Hast thou forgot
The foul witch Sycorax, who with age and envy
Was grown into a hoop? hast thou forgot her?
ARIEL: No, sir.
PROSPERO: Thou hast. Where was she born? speak; tell me.
ARIEL: Sir, in Argier.
PROSPERO:                  O, was she so? I must
Once in a month recount what thou hast been,
Which thou forget'st. This damn'd witch Sycorax,
For mischiefs manifold, and sorceries terrible
To enter human hearing, from Argier,
Thou know'st, was banish'd: for one thing she did
They would not take her life. Is not this true?
ARIEL: Ay, sir.
PROSPERO: This blue-ey'd hag was hither brought with child,
And here was left by th' sailors. Thou, my slave,
As thou report'st thyself, was then her servant;
And, for thou wast a spirit too delicate
To act her earthy and abhorr'd commands,
Refusing her grand hests, she did confine thee,
By help of her more potent ministers,
And in her most unmitigable rage,
Into a cloven pine; within which rift
Imprison'd thou didst painfully remain
A dozen years; within which space she died,
And left thee there; where thou didst vent thy groans
As fast as mill-wheels strike. Then was this island—
Save for the son that she did litter here,
A freckled whelp hag-born—not honour'd with
A human shape.
ARIEL:                          Yes, Caliban her son.
PROSPERO: Dull thing. I say so; he, that Caliban,
Whom now I keep in service. Thou best know'st
What torment I did find thee in; thy groans
Did make wolves howl, and penetrate the breasts
Of ever-angry bears: it was a torment
To lay upon the damn'd, which Sycorax
Could not again undo: it was mine Art,
When I arriv'd and heard thee, that made gape
The pine, and let thee out.
ARIEL:                          I thank thee, master.
PROSPERO: If thou more murmur'st, I will rend an oak,

And peg thee in his knotty entrails, till
Thou hast howl'd away twelve winters.
ARIEL: Pardon, master:
I will be correspondent to command,
And do my spriting gently.

It is at this point that we can offer the contrast between Ariel and Caliban in a similar encounter with Prospero. Caliban is a victim of mental torture. It weakens him; and sometimes it seems that his confidence is lost. But the spirit of freedom never deserts him. When he makes his first appearance in the play, it is at the order of Prospero.

PROSPERO: Thou poisonous slave, got by the devil himself
Upon thy wicked dam, come forth!

*Enter* CALIBAN

CALIBAN: As wicked dew as e'er my mother brush'd
With raven's feather from unwholesome fen
Drop on you both! a south-west blow on ye
And blister you all o'er!
PROSPERO: For this, be sure, tonight thou shalt have cramps,
Side-stitches that shall pen thy breath up; urchins
Shall, for that vast of night that they may work,
All exercise on thee; thou shalt be pinch'd
As thick as honeycomb, each pinch more stinging
Than bees that made 'em.
CALIBAN: I must eat my dinner.
This island's mine, by Sycorax my mother,
Which thou tak'st from me. When thou cam'st first,
Thou strok'st me, and made much of me; wouldst give me
Water with berries in't; and teach me how
To name the bigger light, and how the less,
That burn by day and night: and then I lov'd thee,
And show'd thee all the qualities o' th' isle,
The fresh springs, brine-pits, barren place and fertile
Curs'd be I that did so! All the charms
Of Sycorax, toads, beetles, bats, light on you!
For I am all the subjects that you have,
Which first was mine own King: and there you sty me
In this hard rock, whiles you do keep from me
The rest o' th' island.

Caliban has not lost his sense of original rootedness; and for this reason Prospero must deal with him harshly. The rock imprisonment is, in our time, a form of the emergency regulation which can forbid a son of the soil to travel outside a certain orbit; marked out and even made legal by a foreign visitor. But Caliban keeps answering back, and it is his refusal to be silent which now bullies Prospero into the crucial charge:

> PROSPERO:                    Thou most lying slave,
> Whom stripes may move, not kindness! I have us'd thee,
> Filth as thou art, with human care; and lodg'd thee
> In mine own cell, till thou didst seek to violate
> The honour of my child.
> CALIBAN: O ho, O ho! would't had been done!
> Thou didst prevent me; I had peopled else
> This isle with Calibans.

What an extraordinary way for a slave to speak to his master and in the daughter's presence. But there is a limit to accepting lies and it was the Lie contained in the charge which the man in Caliban could not allow. 'I wish it were so.' But he does not wish it for the mere experiment of mounting a piece of white pussy. He goes further and imagines that the consequence of such intercourse would be a fabulous increase of the population.

> I had peopled else
> This isle with Calibans.

Is there a political intention at work? Does he mean that he would have numbers on his side; that he could organise resistance against this obscene, and selfish monster. But why, we wonder, does Caliban think that the population would be Calibans? Why would they not be Mirandas? Does he mean that they should carry the father's name? But these children would be bastards and should be honoured no less with their mother's name. Or were there other possibilities?

Did Caliban really try to lay her? This is a case where the body, in its consequences, is our only guide. Only the body could establish the truth; for if Miranda were made pregnant, we would know that someone had penetrated her. We might also know whether or no it was Caliban's child; for it is most unlikely that Prospero and his daughter could produce a brown skin baby. Could Prospero really have endured the presence and meaning of a brown skin grandchild. It would not be Miranda's own doing. It would not be the result of their enterprise. It would be Miranda's and Caliban's child. It would be *theirs*: the result and expression of some fusion both physical and other than physical: a fusion which, within himself, Prospero needs and dreads!

Prospero is a Duke who has been deprived of his kingdom.

Through the logical treachery of his brother, Antonio, and the conspiracy of the neighbouring King of Naples, Alonso, Prospero was thrown out of his kingdom. Miranda, his heir, was then no more than three years old. Father and child were hurried on a bark, taken out to sea and then dumped on

> A rotten carcass of a butt, not rigg'd
> Nor tackle, sail, nor mast; the very rats
> Instinctively have quit it: there they hoist us
> To cry to th' sea that roar'd to us; to sigh
> To th' winds, whose pity, sighing back again,
> Did us but loving wrong.

But all this happened twelve years before the wreck which brings some visitors on to the island, and Miranda, now grown into a virtuous beauty, is hearing about these events for the first time. She is at the ripe and provocative age of fifteen, a virgin and, like her father, curious about the facts of life. She had witnessed or had some vision of the wreck which has just taken place; and it is an appeal on behalf of those, presumably dying at sea, which leads to her father's recapitulation of the times before they were expelled from Milan. She tries to explain what of the wreck she has seen; and her vision of their suffering is also the measure of the pain she feels on their behalf.

> MIRANDA: O, I have suffered
> With those I saw suffer! A brave vessel
> (Who had, no doubt, some noble creature in her,)
> Dashed all to pieces. O, the cry did knock
> Against my very heart!
> PROSPERO: Be collected:
> No more amazement: tell your piteous heart
> There's no harm done.

It is this contrast of attitude towards a common disaster which introduces the noble and compassionate nature of Miranda on the one hand, and the supernatural power of her father on the other. Equally noble in their origins, Father and Child are different only in the degrees of their knowledge. What comes between them is the distance which separates Age that apprehends, from Innocence which can only see. Prospero who is also her first and only teacher now gives Miranda a lesson in their domestic history. She learns that the wrecked crew will land safely on this island; and she learns, stage by fastidious stage, the circumstance and purpose of the happy misfortune. And so her curiosity, an essential logic of the drama, forces Prospero to give a hurried lesson in domestic history. He begins, as his custom with all people, by drawing her attention to her limitations:

PROSPERO: I have done nothing but in care of thee,
Of thee, my dear one; thee, my daughter, who
Art ignorant of what thou art; nought knowing
Of whence I am, nor that I am more better
Than Prospero, master of a full poor cell,
And thy no greater father.

Now the search for time lost has begun. He traces the orbit of memory in which she will travel back to find some image of her infancy. And the first landmark, the first anchor which comes to mind is a memory of her maids. She can remember three or four. Prospero assures her there were many more. He coaxes her to dig up some more evidence of that lost infancy; but she can't get much further.

PROSPERO: What seest thou else
In the dark backward and abysm of time?
If thou rememberest aught ere thou cam'st here,
How thou cam'st here thou mayst.
MIRANDA: But that I do not.

What impresses us here is the fact that she has, it seems, absolutely no recollection of her mother. Nor does she raise the question until Prospero's ambiguous way of explaining relations forces her to ask:

MIRANDA: Sir, are you not my father?

To which he gives a reply characteristic of his method of rendering information:

PROSPERO: Thy mother was a piece of virtue, and
She said thou wast my daughter; and thy father
Was Duke of Milan; and his only heir
And princess, no worse issued.

It is the first and, if I am not mistaken, the very last reference we have to Miranda's mother who was, presumably, Prospero's wife. Is she alive? Or did she die in the treacherous *coup d'état* which led to Prospero's exile? But Prospero does not mention her again; for he is busy giving his daughter a summary account of events which led to his brother's conspiracy with the King of Naples, who, with his son, Ferdinand, is among the survivors destined for this Island. So is the old counsellor Gonzalo who was given the job of designing Prospero's downfall. The whole gang are alive and well, but ignorant of what's in store for them.

Resurrected from the water, innocent and guilty, offer a striking parallel with the Haitian ceremony of Souls. Prospero is the bitter reality which they cannot avoid; and Miranda is no more than an initiate who is being briefed at lightning speed about the necessary facts. These are carefully chosen, for the techniques of propaganda are not unknown to Prospero; and he emerges swiftly, but surely, as the outraged martyr: the embodiment of an original nobility, a criterion of virtue which bears witness to the disgrace of his degenerate adversaries.

This is the only light in which Miranda can see him; for she has no experience of the world beyond this island, no instruments for making a comparative judgment. Caliban is the only other man she has seen; but his whole relation to the condition meant by Man is gravely in doubt. Her father's account of history—which is no more than a schematic arrangement of necessary and self-protective emphasis—fills her with an admiration which she can only express through regret. She regrets that she should have been so much trouble to him.

MIRANDA: Your tale, sir, would cure deafness.

Her case is perhaps not unrelated to what, in our time, is called brain-washing. Virtue, nobility, chastity and beauty, degeneracy, bestiality, lust, and physical deformity are the antithesis which she has thoroughly absorbed and which will, in the course of time, be exemplified by those she meets. Caliban, her first experience of a stranger, is already the black temple of every tendency that characterises the beast, and he serves as a reminder to any noble spirit which may be tempted to overreach the laws of its nature. It is against this moral background of opposites that Miranda learns how it came about that her father could have lost his dukedom.

PROSPERO: I pray thee, mark me.
I, thus neglecting worldly ends, all dedicated
To closeness and the bettering of my mind
With that which, but by being so retir'd,
O'er-priz'd all popular rate, in my false brother
Awak'd an evil nature; and my trust,
Like a good parent, did beget of him
A falsehood in its contrary, as great
As my trust was; which had indeed no limit,
A confidence sans bound. He being thus lorded,
Not only with what my revenue yielded,
But what my power might else exact, like one
Who having into truth, by telling of it,
Made such a sinner of his memory,
To credit his own lie, he did believe

He was indeed the duke; out o' th' substitution,
And executing th' outward face of royalty,
With all prerogative;—hence his ambition growing,—
Dost thou hear?

MIRANDA: Your tale, sir, would cure deafness.

PROSPERO: To have no screen between this part he play'd
And him he play'd it for, he needs will be
Absolute Milan. Me, poor man, my library
Was dukedom large enough: of temporal royalties
He thinks me now incapable; confederates,
So dry he was for sway, wi' th' King of Naples
To give him annual tribute, do him homage,
Subject his coronet to his crown, and bend
The dukedom, yet unbow'd,—alas, poor Milan!—
To most ignoble stooping.

MIRANDA: O the heavens!

PROSPERO: Mark his condition, and th' event; then tell me
If this night be a brother.

MIRANDA: I should sin
To think but nobly of my grandmother:
Good wombs have borne bad sons.

And when she asks the pertinent question:

MIRANDA: Wherefore did they not
That hour destroy us?

He congratulates her on the acuity of her attention, and proceeds to explain that his survival was due entirely to the love his people—meaning the common herd of men and women—bore him.

His absence could probably be explained in much the same way that the political exile of African chiefs could be given 'some rational interpretation.' The present Asantehene, Otumfuo Sir Osei Agyeman Prempeh II, K.B.E., suffered a similar fate when he was banished by a British Administration to the Seychelles. . . . It was some years before he was returned. So also did King Jaja of Nigeria, who, for some odd reason, was removed to Barbados, the island of the author's birth. The latter episode enriched the almost absent folk music with a tune about Jaja.

Prospero is not only a ruler, but a philosopher as well; and we can assume that this combination: the Philosopher-King—the here-

ditary right to rule people and the spiritual need to organise reality—
is directly related to that creative will to conquer the absolute: a
will which finds its most perfect vessel in the infinitely expanding
powers of transformation that characterise the timeless frontiers of
the Poetic Vision. This is the total atmosphere of expectation in
which Miranda lives. Her father will arrange her future; and all will
be well provided the references of truth are not disturbed by some
fearful contingency. Sooner or later the wrecked crew will come
safely to shore; ignorance will be dispelled by Prospero's light. Like
the miraculous discovery of one's empty purse, the guilty will find
their conscience. The magic of birth will sail Miranda, young,
beautiful and a virgin, into the arms of a King's only son. Her eye
will show her at one glance who is her heart's desire. The rest is forgiveness and preparation for a marriage whose future must remain
promising and absent as paradise.

> Was Milan thrust from Milan, that his issue
> Should become Kings of Naples? O, rejoice
> Beyond a common joy!
> . . . . .

Caliban cannot be revealed in any relation to himself; for he has
no self which is not a reaction to circumstances imposed upon his
life. He is not seen as a possibility of spirit which might fertilise and
extend the resources of any human vision. Caliban is the very climate
in which men encounter the nature of ambiguities, and in which,
according to his desire, each man attempts a resolution by trying to
slay the past. Caliban's history—for he has a most turbulent history
—belongs entirely to the future. It is the wind which reminds us that
trouble has gone into hiding. In all his encounters with his neighbours—whether they be Kings or drunken clowns—Caliban is never
accorded the power *to see*. He is always the measure of the condition
which his physical appearance has already defined. Caliban is the
excluded, that which is eternally below possibility, and always beyond reach. He is seen as an occasion, a state of existence which can
be appropriated and exploited for the purposes of another's own
development. Caliban is a reminder of lost virtue or the evil vigour
of the Beast that is always there: a magnetic temptation, and an
eternal warning against the contagion of his daemon ancestry.

The difficulty is to take from Caliban without suffering the pollution innate in his nature. To yield to Caliban's natural generosity is
to risk the deluge: for his assets—such as they are—are dangerous,
since they are encrusted, buried deep in the dark. It is not by accident
that his skin is black; for black, too, is the colour of his loss; the

absence of any soul. If he shows an aptitude for music, it is because the perfection of harmonies can strike some chord in his nervous system.

> CALIBAN: Be not afeard; the isle is full of noises,
> Sounds and sweet airs, that give delight, and hurt not.
> Sometimes a thousand twangling instruments
> Will hum about mine ears; and sometimes voices,
> That, if I then had wak'd after long sleep,
> Will make me sleep again: and then, in dreaming,
> The clouds methought would open, and show riches
> Ready to drop upon me: that, when I wak'd,
> I cried to dream again.

Caliban is in his way a kind of Universal. Like the earth he is always there, generous in gifts, inevitable, yet superfluous and dumb. And like the earth which draws attention to age and therefore to the past, he cannot be devoured. Caliban is, therefore, the occasion to which every situation, within the context of the Tempest, must be related. No Caliban no Prospero! No Prospero no Miranda! No Miranda no Marriage! And no Marriage no Tempest! He confronts Prospero as a possibility; a challenge; and a defeat.

> This thing of darkness
> I acknowledge mine.

He confronts the drunken butler Stephano, and the jester Trinculo, as a commercial speculation, a promising investment:

> STEPHANO: This is some monster of the isle with four legs, who hath got, as I take it, an ague. Where the devil should he learn our language? I will give him some relief, if it be but for that. If I can recover him, and keep him tame, and get to Naples with him, he's a present for any emperor that ever trod on neat's-leather.

> CALIBAN: Do not torment me, prithee; I'll bring my wood home faster.

> STEPHANO: He's in his fit now, and does not talk after the wisest. He shall taste of my bottle: if he have never drunk wine afore, it will go near to remove his fit. If I can recover him, and keep him tame, I will not take too much for him; he shall pay for him that hath him and that soundly.

But it is the difference in these intentions which suggest the difference between Prospero and Trinculo; it is a difference which has to do with birth and the inescapable law of heredity. Caliban's incapacity to see that Trinculo and Stephano are crooks, his readiness to accord them the worship he had once given Prospero, are proof of his condition. And it is this condition which Prospero, in the role of philisopher, would like to experiment with. The problem of learning is now firmly stated. Education, meaning the possession of the Word —which was in the beginning or not at all—is the tool which Prospero has tried on the irredeemable nature of his savage and deformed slave. We are brought to the heart of the matter by the cantankerous assertion, spoken by Miranda, but obviously the thought and vocabulary of her father.

MIRANDA: Abhorred slave,
Which any print of goodness wilt not take,
Being capable of all ill! I pitied thee,
Took pains to make thee speak, taught thee each hour
One thing or other: when thou didst not, savage,
Know thine own meaning, but wouldst gabble like
A thing most brutish, I endow'd thy purposes
With words that made them known. But thy vile race,
Though thou didst learn, had that in't which good natures
Could not abide to be with; therefore wast thou
Deservedly confin'd into this rock,
Who hadst deserv'd more than a prison.

There is no escape from the prison of Prospero's gift. This example of deformity was a challenge to Prospero's need to achieve the impossible. Only the application of the Word to the darkness of Caliban's world could harness the beast which resides within this cannibal. This is the first important achievement of the colonising process. This gift of Language is the deepest and most delicate bond of involvement. It has a certain finality. Caliban will never be the same again. Nor, for that matter, will Prospero.

Prospero has given Caliban Language; and with it an unstated history of consequences, an unknown history of future intentions. This gift of Language meant not English, in particular, but speech and concept as a way, a method, a necessary avenue towards areas of the self which could not be reached in any other way. It is this way, entirely Prospero's enterprise, which makes Caliban aware of possibilities. Therefore, all of Caliban's future—for future is the very name for possibilities—must derive from Prospero's experiment which is also his risk.

Provided there is no extraordinary departure which explodes all of Prospero's premises, then Caliban and his future now belong to Prospero. Caliban is Prospero's risk in the sense that Adam's awareness of a difference was a risk which God took with Man. Prospero believes—his belief in his own powers demands it—that Caliban can learn so much and no more. Caliban can go so far and no farther. Prospero lives in the absolute certainty that Language which is his gift to Caliban is the very prison in which Caliban's achievements will be realised and restricted. Caliban can never reach perfection, not even the perfection implicit in Miranda's privileged ignorance.

For Language itself, by Caliban's whole relation to it, will not allow his expansion beyond a certain point. This kind of realisation, this kind of expansion, is possible only to those who reside in that state of being which is the very source and ultimate of the language that bears them always forward. The difference between Caliban and the sinner is this. A sinner remains a child of God, and redemption is not so much an order as a natural duty. Grace is the sinner's birthright. But Caliban is not a child of anything except Nature. To be a child of Nature, in this sense, is to be situated in Nature, to be identified with Nature, to be eternally without the seed of a dialectic which makes possible some *emergence* from Nature.

Such is Caliban, superfluous as the weight of the earth until Prospero arrives with the aid of the Word which might help him to clarify the chaos which shows its true colours all over his skin. But he can never be regarded as an heir of that Language, since his use of Language is no more than his way of serving Prospero; and Prospero's instruction in this Language is only his way of measuring the distance which separates him from Caliban. If it were possible for Caliban to realise Language as his perfect inheritance, and if, in spite of this new power, Prospero could still appropriate and imprison him at will; then Prospero would have achieved the triplicity which he is pursuing: 'The Power and Fortune of a King, the knowledge and illumination of a priest, and the learning and the universality of a philosopher.' The seeds of this triplicity are within Prospero; but there is one disqualification which hounds him slowly to despair. Prospero is getting old, and the powers he would claim are associated in his mind with youth. Caliban at twenty-four is certainly young. But he has no *sight*. He is without that necessary light which is the very origin of Language, the light which guides Prospero, and which, at the same time, Prospero is trying to surpass.

Caliban may become Man; but he is entirely outside the orbit of Human. It is not Prospero who keeps him there; nor is it his own fault that he is there. It is some original Law which exists even beyond Prospero's seeing. It is this Law which has ordained the state of existence we call Caliban. If Caliban turns cannibal, it is not because human flesh may appear a necessary substitute for food which is absent. It is rather because he is incapable of differentiating between one kind of reality and another. His hunger is too large—not his greed but his hunger—too large to be harnessed by any process of selection. He cannot distinguish between Man, the object, and Human, the form and ideal which auras that object. He could not recognise the difference of quality between Prospero and Trinculo or between Stephano and Ferdinand. Language may help him to describe the physical attributes which nobility calls beautiful; but language will not help him to distinguish between separate personalities. Word and concept may be part of his vocabulary; but they are no part of his way of seeing.

Caliban is not allowed to distinguish, for the eyes that register personality must belong to, must derive from a consciousness which could be regarded as person. And Caliban is a condition.

Hence the charge of rape. Caliban would think no more of raping Miranda than he might of eating her if she were alone, and he was hungry or feeling too idle to go swimming.

This is precisely Miranda's view of Caliban also; for her father and only teacher throughout her life is Prospero. It would not be difficult for Miranda to accuse Caliban also of having actually raped her; for she probably dreams about him, and does not trust his heredity when she is asleep. If she dreamt that Caliban had raped her, she would not be able to tell whether it had happened or not; for Caliban, as the descendant of a Devil, may have inherited that traditional power which allowed Devils to put their female victims asleep while they had their pleasure. It is through Miranda, the product of Prospero's teaching, that we may glimpse the origin and perpetuation of myth coming slowly but surely into its right as fact, history, absolute truth.

Throughout the play we are impressed by the affinities, the likeness of circumstance between Miranda and Caliban. Like many an African slave child, Miranda has no recollection of her mother. The actual Caliban of *The Tempest* has the advantage—regrettable as he makes it sound—of having known the meaning and power of his mother Sycorax.

But Miranda has a deeper affinity than this likeness of circumstance. She was no more than an infant when she and her father met Caliban on the island. Prospero says she was scarcely three. Caliban would have been about twelve. As time passed, and Prospero grew more and more occupied with his Book, Caliban and the child, Miranda, must have grown closer by the necessary contact of servant and mistress. Before the emergency regulation which imprisoned him in a rock, Caliban must have taken this child for walks about the island. He probably had to carry her on his back, the way we have seen African servants showing their affection to European children. Between the age of three and five Miranda must have spent a lot of time playing with Caliban, the way European children, during their parents' absence, monopolise the African servant's rest hour.

Miranda and Prospero may be equal in their assumed superiority of origins over Caliban. But Caliban and the Duke's daughter have a bond that is not easily broken. They are alike in their ignorance; and there are parallels in their response to strangers from the world beyond these shores. The moment Miranda sets eyes on Ferdinand— handsome, noble and a prince—she suffers a genuine attack of love-sickness.

MIRANDA:                   What is 't? a spirit?
Lord, how it looks about! Believe me, sir,
It carries a brave form. But 'tis a spirit.

PROSPERO: No, wench; it eats and sleeps and hath such senses
As we have, such. This gallant which thou seest
Was in the wrack; and, but he's something stain'd
With grief, (that's beauty's canker) thou mightst call him
A goodly person: he hath lost his fellows,
And strays to find 'em.

MIRANDA:                   I might call him
A thing divine; for nothing natural
I ever saw so noble.

And Ferdinand who is her equal in vigour and her other half in chastity lets her know exactly his intentions.

FERDINAND: O, if a virgin,
And your affection not gone forth, I'll make you
The Queen of Naples.

Ferdinand does not yet know that his father is alive; hence his promise to Miranda that she will be queen. It is at this point that Prospero intervenes to supply us again with the kind of stuff he is made of: an imperialist by circumstance, a sadist by disease; and, above all, an old man in whom envy and revenge are equally matched. Immediately after Ferdinand's offer of marriage, Prospero says:

PROSPERO:                   Soft, sir! one word more.
(*Aside*) They are both in either's pow'rs: but this swift business
I must uneasy make, lest too light winning

Make the prize light. (*To Ferdinand*) One word more; I charge thee
That thou attend me: thou dost here usurp
The name thou ow'st not; and hast put thyself
Upon this island as a spy, to win it
From me, the lord on't.

FERDINAND:                         No, as I am a man.

MIRANDA: There's nothing ill can dwell in such a temple:
If the ill spirit have so fair a house,
Good things will strive to dwell with 't.

PROSPERO:                          Follow me.
Speak not you for him: he's a traitor. Come;
I'll manacle thy neck and feet together:
Sea-water shalt thou drink; thy food shall be
The fresh-brook mussels, wither'd roots, and husks
Wherein the acorn cradled. Follow.

It is possible that Prospero envies and admires the passion which
is an essential part of the couple's youth. It is likely that he had never
experienced any such feeling towards his wife. His imperialism is like
an illness, not only in his personal relationships, but in his relation
to the external and foreign world. This island belongs to Caliban
whom he found there; yet some privilege allows Prospero to
assert—and with an authority that is divine—that he is lord of the
island.

Sadism is characteristic of this type. He approves of the union of
Ferdinand and his daughter. Indeed, it is a part of his overall
arrangement; but youth and innocence must be punished before
they can partake of the pleasures and paradox of love. He accuses
Ferdinand of being a spy when he knows that the shipwrecked boy
is occupied with sorrow for the imagined death of his father. He
tells Miranda that she must not rush these things; and
again that loathsome habit of cutting people down to size is
revealed:

PROSPERO: Thou think'st there is no more such shapes as he,
Having seen but him and Caliban: foolish wench!
To th' most of men this is a Caliban,
And they to him are angels.

His accusation of espionage is also intended to test Ferdinand's
nobility. Enraged, the boy draws his sword, and is immediately
charmed into immobility by Prospero's magic. Even Miranda, who
has not long heard what an excellent specimen of nobility and
wisdom her father is, even she is shaken by the appearance of

the monster in Prospero. Torn between her love for the young prince and her tribal allegiance to Prospero, she tries to cheer Ferdinand up:

> Be of comfort;
> My father's of a better nature, sir,
> Than he appears by speech: this is unwonted
> Which now came from him.

An opinion which we know to be in direct contradiction with the facts; for the obscenity of Prospero's rage knows no bounds in his dealings with Ariel and Caliban: the two agents of labour and public relations without whom he would be helpless. It is this innocence and credulity in Miranda which—were it not for a difference in their degrees of being—would have made her and Caliban almost identical.

For Caliban also has this tendency to take people at their face value. Whereas Prospero's fear springs from a need to maintain his power—for to lose his power is to lose face—and it is only through power that the world knows him; Caliban is the epitome of a pure and uncalculated naïveté Having been deprived of his freedom, it seems that Caliban has nothing to lose but his goodwill; and one meaning we can extract from this is that the suspension of a man's freedom can have the effect of returning him to the fundamental sources of integrity. Temporary imprisonment is the greatest service an imperialist can do to a nationalist leader. It is in the solitude of the cell that he gets a chance, free from the indulgence of his followers, to think things out. When he is freed—as we shall see with Caliban—he returns to the streets with a formidable power born of suffering and reflection. But it is this original tendency to welcome which gets Caliban into trouble. We recall what he tells Prospero:

> CALIBAN: This island's mine, by Sycorax my mother
> Which thou tak'st from me. When thou cam'st first,
> Thou strok'st me, and made much of me; wouldst give me
> Water with berries in't and teach me how
> To name the bigger light, and how the less,
> That burn by day and night: and then I lov'd thee,
> And show'd thee all the qualities o' th' isle,
> The fresh springs, brine-pits, barren place and fertile:
> Curs'd be I that did so!

And later, in his state of utter displacement brought about by Prospero's betrayal of love, Caliban makes the same mistake again.

Trinculo is a jester, a man who lives at the mercy of a successful joke. Stephano is a butler and an irresponsible and adventurous drunk. In their original home, they bear much the same relation to royalty that Caliban here bears to Prospero. They are scum. It is to these innocent bandits that Caliban turns for help. He is plotting revolution with them; but they have absolutely no idea what it means for Caliban that he should get Prospero out of the way. To them, it is no more than cutting another throat. To Caliban it is an enterprise of colossal importance. Yet it is to these men that Caliban will surrender his secrets:

> CALIBAN: I prithee, let me bring thee where crabs grow;
> And I with my long nails will dig thee pig-nuts;
> Show thee a jay's nest, and instruct thee how
> To snare the nimble marmoset; I'll bring thee
> To clustering filberts, and sometimes I'll get thee
> Young scamels from the rock. Wilt thou go with me?

In some real, though extraordinary way, Caliban and Miranda are seen side by side: opposite and contiguous at the same time. They share an ignorance that is also the source of some vision. It is, as it were, a kind of creative blindness.

In different circumstances, they could be together in a way that Miranda and her father could not. For Prospero is alone. He hates and fears and needs Caliban. The role of father demands that he should pay Miranda some attention, equip her with a few basic prejudices; but he is not really interested in her as a person. The education he bestows is in the nature of a formality. Miranda herself has told him that he was always postponing to tell her certain things.

It has taken him twelve years to tell the child one or two things which any decent parent of his intelligence would have passed on long ago. When she asked him: Are you not my father? he talks about the chastity of her mother; and we realise—with some knowledge of this type—that he is taking refuge in the lesson of chastity in order to evade or obscure any talk about the woman who is supposed to be his wife. Who, we are left to wonder, was really Miranda's mother? And what would she have had to say about this marvellous monster of a husband who refuses us information?

An interesting contrast is seen in his dealing with Caliban on the same subject. For some reason or other, the memory of Sycorax, Caliban's mother, arouses him to rage that is almost insane. For all that he is a Duke and noble, Prospero can't conquer that obscene habit of throwing the past, turning your origins into a weapon of blackmail. In Caliban's case it takes the form of his mother being a so-and-so.

We ask ourselves why a Duke should debase himself to speak in such a way. The tone suggests an intimacy of involvement and concern which encourages speculation. But we could not speak with authority on the possibilities of this defect until we had heard from Sycorax and Miranda's mother. They are both dead; and so our knowledge must be postponed until some arrangement comparable to the Haitian Ceremony of Souls returns them to tell us what we should and ought to know.

We begin to distrust this Duke. Why should we believe, in the light of all that has happened now, that the people of Milan really loved him. For it's a difficult love: the love of a dispossessed crowd for a rich and absent idol. Prospero contributed in no uncertain terms to his brother's treachery. If he wanted to retain the honour and privilege of Duke, then he should have been prepared to undertake the responsibilities. If the Book dominated his deepest interest; then he should have told the people that in the interest of learning which would be to their benefit, he would have to abdicate. It was the only decent thing to do.

Antonio can be forgiven for usurping the rights and privileges that were not his. Prospero sees this as another occasion of ingratitude. When he hears of Caliban's conspiracy to overthrow him, he is again plunged into rage. For this is seen as ingratitude of a most bestial nature. Caliban whom he had given Language conspiring with men not much better than himself to sabotage the divine hierarchy of which he is the most privileged on earth!

PROSPERO: He is as disproportion'd in his manners
As in his shape. Go, sirrah, to my cell;
Take with you your companions; as you look
To have my pardon, trim it handsomely.

One wonders whether it is ingratitude that bothers Prospero. Could it not be a shattering kind of self-knowledge, the knowledge that he really deserves such ingratitude? Prospero's gifts are no part of his concern for those who receive. Could it be that Prospero didn't really care any more about the people of Milan than he cared about his wife? Is it that age and the pressure of a simple honesty had forced him to see his total indifference to his neighbour as a perfect example of human degradation? For the real sin is not hatred, which implies an involvement, but the calculated and habitual annihilation of the person whose presence you can ignore but never exclude.

What can he feel when he recalls the statement which tells us what Caliban truly felt?

CALIBAN:                              When thou cam'st first,
Thou strok'dst me, and made much of me; wouldst give me
Water with berries in't; and teach me how
To name the bigger light, and how the less,
That burn by day and night: and then I loved thee.

Will the Lie upon which Prospero's confident authority was built be discovered? For tomorrow they will take to sea, rehearsing again the distance and purgatory which have always separated them from their forgotten slave.

We can assume that they are gone. Dawn has rigged their sails; the clouds have dispersed; and the sun is loud as wedding bells. But no one bade them farewell.

Tonight, in his deformity and his solitude, Caliban, like Ishmael, is left alone.

# CALIBAN ORDERS HISTORY

●

You know that it is not out of hatred for other
races that I am the toiler of this unique race . ..
AIMÉ CESAIRE

### TO TOUSSAINT L'OUVERTURE
Toussaint, the most unhappy Man of Men!
Whether the rural Milk-maid by her Cow
Sing in thy hearing, or thou liest now
Alone in some deep dungeon's earless den,
O miserable chieftain! where and when
Wilt thou find patience? Yet die not; do thou
Wear rather in thy bonds a cheerful brow:
Thou fallen Thyself, never to rise again,
Live, and take comfort. Thou hast left behind
Powers that will work for thee; air, earth, and skies;
There's not a breathing of the common wind
That will forget thee; thou hast great allies;
Thy friends are exultations, agonies,
And love, and Man's unconquerable mind.
WORDSWORTH

THE ENTIRE Caribbean is our horizon; for Caliban himself like the
island he inherited is at once a landscape and a human situation.
We can switch from island to island without changing the meaning
of Language in *The Tempest*. The Empress Josephine, a planter's
daughter from Martinique, may be Miranda all over again; and
although the altar was erected in France, and not Milan; although
the divine right of royalty had been assaulted by the crowd, the
legacy of Prospero's absolute claim was still alive. Napoleon was no
duke, but a Titan at the very summit of an expanding ambition.

Familiar with triumph over men and over race, it was this birthright of Language which blocked his hearing when a new Caliban
ordered his attention. It was not in Europe, but in Haiti that the
Emperor met his match. He hated Blacks; but hatred is a feeble
weapon beside genius. Colour and race were irrelevant to the achievement of one slave whose work would remain a monumental contribution to every Tempest which wrought freedom on the nineteenth
century. We shall never explode Prospero's old myth until we

118

christen Language afresh; until we show Language as the product of human endeavour; until we make available to all the result of certain enterprises undertaken by men who are still regarded as the unfortunate descendants of languageless and deformed slaves.

One glorious chapter in this enterprise takes the form of a West Indian classic; and it is the product of a great West Indian working at the height of his powers. *Black Jacobins* should be Bible-reading for every boy who would be acquainted with the period in question. For in it C. L. R. James shows us Caliban as Prospero had never known him: a slave who was a great soldier in battle, an incomparable administrator in public affairs; full of paradox but never without compassion, a humane leader of men. It is not by accident that a document so rich in facts, so beautiful in narrative organisation, should have remained out of print for over twenty years. Space will not allow more than a sample of the mind which made it.

'In 1789 the French West Indian colony of San Domingo supplied two-thirds of the overseas trade of France and was the greatest individual market for the European slave-trade. It was an integral part of the economic life of the age, the greatest colony in the world, the pride of France, and the envy of every other imperialist nation. The whole structure rested on the labour of half-a-million slaves.

'In August 1791, after two years of the French Revolution and its repercussions in San Domingo, the slaves revolted. The struggle lasted for twelve years. The slaves defeated in turn the local whites and the soldiers of the French monarchy, a Spanish invasion, a British expedition of some 60,000 men, and a French expedition of similar size under Bonaparte's brother-in-law. The defeat of Bonaparte's expedition in 1803 resulted in the establishment of the Negro state of Haiti which has lasted to this day.

'The revolt is the only successful slave revolt in history, and the odds it had to overcome is evidence of the magnitude of the interests that were involved. The transformation of slaves, trembling in hundreds before a single white man, into a people able to organise themselves and defeat the most powerful European nations of their day, is one of the great epics of revolutionary struggle and achievement. Why and how this happened is the theme of this book.

'By a phenomenon often observed, the individual leadership responsible for this unique achievement was almost entirely the work of a single man—Toussaint Louverture. Beauchamp in the *Biographie Universelle* calls Toussaint Louverture one of the most remarkable men of a period rich in remarkable men. He dominated from his entry until circumstances removed him from the scene. The history of the San Domingo revolution will therefore largely be a record of his achievements and his political personality. The writer believes, and is confident the narrative will prove that between 1789 and 1825, with the single exception of Bonaparte himself no single figure appeared on the historical stage more greatly gifted than this Negro, a slave till he was forty-five.' [*Black Jacobins*.]

We speak nowadays of men who are enslaved by machines, enslaved by the rigours of a political régime; but it is impossible to project ourselves into the condition which meant 'slave' for those Africans exiled in Haiti. These men were property as a plough is the property of any English farmer. They were fed, kennelled, and pushed around as ploughs may be polished, transported, and stacked for safe keeping. And in the eyes of their owners, they had no language but the labour of their hands. If these hands, like the prongs of the plough, showed signs of weakening, the property was disposed of; buried or burnt while it was still alive. If this property risked any deliberate signs of inactivity, the most ingenious experiments in torture were devised. This property (male or female it did not matter) was hounded by dogs, dynamited for the sheer fun of seeing human flesh blow up. The whip was regular as wind, no less brutal on the bones than any hurricane which ripped open the land. From dawn until midday with a brief interval for fodder, from two in the afternoon until an hour before midnight. This was the curriculum of work, the punishment which those slaves endured. . . . One Swiss traveller has left this first-hand account of that human energy at work:

'They were about a hundred men and women of different ages, all occupied in digging ditches in a cane-field, the majority of them naked or covered with rags. The sun shone down with full force on their heads. Sweat rolled from all parts of their bodies. Their limbs, weighed down by the heat, fatigued with the weight of their picks and by the resistance of the clayey soil baked hard enough to break their implements, strained themselves to overcome every obstacle. A mournful silence reigned. Exhaustion was stamped on every face, but the hour of rest had not yet come. The pitiless eye of the Manager patrolled the gang and several foremen armed with long whips moved periodically between them, giving stinging blows to all who, worn out by fatigue, were compelled to take a rest—men or women, young or old.'

It is 'that mournful silence' as well as the sublime lack of distinction between the sexes which strikes our attention. No less impressive is that utter incapacity of the civilised Frenchman to distinguish between age and youth; for it allows us to see the great division which he had constructed between what was human and what was not.

We may guess the age of a man; but a plough, like the land it opens, cannot evoke a similar interest. For it was not human, but the category of nature to which masters had relegated these savage and deformed slaves. Yet there was one paradox which remained to perplex this new Prospero.

'The difficulty was that though one could trap them like animals, transport them in pens, work them alongside an ass or a horse and beat both with the same stick, stable them and starve them, they remained, despite their black skins and curly hair, quite invincibly human beings; with the intelligence and resentments of human beings. To cow them into the necessary docility and acceptance necessitated a régime of calculated brutality and terrorism, and it is this that explains the unusual spectacle of property-owners apparently careless of preserving their property; they had first to ensure their own safety.' [*Black Jacobins.*]

The effect on the slave was even more bewildering. It must have been clear to the owner that the mournful silence of this property contained a danger which would last as long as their hands were alive. One day some change akin to mystery would reveal itself through those man-shaped ploughs. The mystery would assume the behaviour of a plough which refused contact with a free hand. Imagine a plough in the field. Ordinary as ever, prongs and spine unchanged, it is simply there, stuck to its post beside the cane shoot. Then some hand, identical with the routine of its work, reaches to lift this familiar instrument. But the plough escapes contact. It refuses to surrender its present position. There is a change in the relation between this plough and one free hand. The crops wait and wonder what will happen next. More hands arrive to confirm the extraordinary conduct of this plough; but no one can explain the terror of those hands as they withdraw from the plough. Some new sight as well as some new sense of language is required to bear witness to the miracle of the plough which now talks. For as those hands in unison move forward, the plough achieves a somersault which reverses its traditional posture. Its head goes into the ground, and the prongs, throat-near, stand erect in the air, ten points of steel announcing danger.

It is a transformation of such dimensions which the owners must have anticipated; but the property could never be encouraged to think of itself as a source of possibility. Every method was therefore employed to separate the slave from a logic of a spirit which might soon declare his future on the side of freedom. Committed to a régime of bestiality, no civilised Frenchman could afford to turn back.

'The slaves received the whip with more certainty and regularity than they received their food. It was the normal incentive to work and the guardian of discipline. But there was no ingenuity that fear or a depraved imagination could devise which was not employed to break their spirit and satisfy the lusts and resentment of their owners and guardians—irons on the hands and feet, blocks of wood that the slaves had to drag behind them wherever they went, the tin-plate mask designed to prevent the slaves eating the sugar-cane, the iron collar. Whipping was interrupted in order to pass a piece of hot wood on the buttocks of the victim; salt, pepper, citron, cinders, aloes, and hot ashes were poured on the bleeding wounds. Mutilations were common, limbs, ears, and sometimes the private parts, to deprive them of the pleasures which they could indulge in without expense. Their masters poured burning wax on their arms and hands and shoulders, emptied the boiling cane sugar over their heads, burned them alive, roasted them on slow fires, filled them with gunpowder and blew them up with a match; buried them up to the neck and smeared their heads with sugar that the flies might devour them; fastened them near to nests of ants or wasps; made them eat their excrement, drink their urine, and lick the saliva of other slaves. One colonist was known in moments of anger to throw himself on his slaves and stick his teeth into their flesh.' [*Black Jacobins.*]

It produced an extraordinary reaction in the slaves. It seemed that they had come to identify all movement with whipping; and sometimes they would not move until they were whipped almost to the point of death. In a sense they were giving a lesson in pain to the agents of their torture. This attitude of deliberate fatalism undermined the effects of the owners' bestiality. Whatever the owner pretended, the slave's choice of conduct had set up a reciprocity between them in this total contract of master and slave. The master could not withdraw; for he was the embodiment of his orders, and the orders had to proceed if his régime were to survive according to his will.

Sometimes the slaves entered the role of camouflage; but it was not a camouflage of imposing their personality. It was the camouflage of self-negation. They would affect to be the perfect embodiment of stupidity. Drawing his sources from the most acknowledged French authorities on the period, James reports anecdotes that strike us as pure fantasy:

'Why do you ill-treat your mule in that way?' asked a colonist of a carter. 'But when I do not work, I am beaten, when he does not work, I beat him—he is my Negro.' One old Negro, having lost one of his ears and condemned to lose another, begged the Governor to spare it, for if that too was cut off he would have nowhere to put his stump of cigarette. A slave sent by his master into his neighbour's garden to steal, is caught and brought back to the man who had only a few minutes before despatched him on the errand. The master orders him a punishment of 100 lashes to which the slave submits without a murmur. When caught in error they persisted in denial with the same fatalistic stupidity. A slave is accused of stealing a pigeon. He denies it. The pigeon is discovered hidden in his shirt. 'Well, well, look at that pigeon. It take my shirt for a nest.' Through the shirt of another, a master can feel the potatoes which he denies he has stolen. They are not potatoes, he says, they are stones. He is undressed and the potatoes fall to the ground. 'Eh! master, the devil is wicked. Put stones, and look, you find potatoes.'

Their method, it seemed, was part of an attempt to punish their masters by making all life appear irrelevant; that is life in a régime of slavery. The next step from stupidity and irrelevance was the logical act of suicide. Death became an act of revenge against their owners. It became also the political appropriation of the masters' whole means of survival. The land would have no existence without the labour of these slaves; and since suicide involved one death only, one loss of property, they would have terrible seasons of homicide.

Some masters didn't think the female slaves unfit for bed, and commanded them to have intercourse whenever they chose. Sometimes a slave's dexterity under the sheets might earn her the status of a regular mistress. Since she had a stake in her master's passions, she had some power over his possessions. When the master discarded her, she would poison his whole family, wife and every child, as well as all his slaves.

Now and again the slaves would poison the younger children of their master 'to ensure the plantation succeeding to one son. By this means they prevented the plantation being broken up, and the gang dispersed.' But the slaves also poisoned each other. The fewer their numbers, the more modest would be the master's enterprise in agriculture. Therefore, they would reduce their own numbers in order to cut down on the work for those who survived. Slave children as well as slave wives met their death in this way. During her trial, one slave who had worked as a nurse, confessed that for many years she had poisoned every child which she had attended at birth. 'The most dreaded of all this cold-blooded murder was, however, the jaw-sickness—a disease which attacked children only, in the first few days of their existence. Their jaws were closed to such an extent that it was impossible to open them and to get anything down, with the result that they died of hunger. It was not a natural disease and never attacked children delivered by white women. The Negro midwives alone could cause it, they alone could preserve children from it, and it is believed that they performed some simple operation on the newly born child which resulted in the jaw-sickness. Whatever the method this disease caused the death of nearly one-third of the children born on the plantations.'

The African woman's bond to the child is proverbial; but murder against their own blood was the only weapon of defence at their disposal. Infanticide was their way of protecting the children from the horrors of slavery as they had known it. These acts were not purely negative. They were also done as a way of boosting their own morale for an undertaking which was always present in their minds. They had given awful trouble during that dreadful crossing from the African West Coast to the Caribbean. They were a constant threat to the lives of the sailors; and this spirit of revolt never deserted them.

Among themselves they would plot ways and means of realising this intention. Hence the duality of their behaviour. The day was for that 'mournful silence' which the Swiss traveller observed. After work they became different. Night was their opportunity for consultation; and their conferences were conducted in song. Long before Napoleon sent his brother-in-law to crush them, these slaves had chosen their life's work which they sang every night:

> Eh! Eh! Bomba! Heu! Heu!
> Canga, bafio te!
> Canga, moune de le
> Canga do ki la
> Canga, li!

'We swear to destroy the whites and all that they possess; let us die rather than fail to keep this vow.'

Every attempt was made to stop this song, but the night was theirs: the night and the future of Haiti.

One night in July, 1791, there was a terrible storm. The forests shook with wind. Rain washed everything clean. Lightning burnt the leaves. But the thunder was elsewhere. It did not descend from a great burst of cloud. It rose, instead, from the preparations of the slaves. There were about 12,000 slaves in the mountainous north. Half were men; and they were already organised. Their plan was to fire all the plantations in this part of the island. When the fires showed against the sky, that would be the signal for the slaves in the plain to complete both the massacre of the whites and the destruction of their estates.

There were other risings before, but this undertaking would be the result of their previous experience in organisation. Following their leader, Boukman, they lit their way with torches and marched through night and rain into the forest. They sacrificed a pig, and after the ceremonial incantations which had survived with them, Boukman spoke this prayer:

'The god who created the sun which gives us light, who rouses the waves and rules the storm, though hidden in the clouds he watches us. He sees all that the white man does. The god of the white man inspires him with crime, but our god calls upon us to do good works. Our god who is good to us orders us to revenge our wrongs. He will direct our arms and aid us. Throw away the symbol of the god of the whites who has so often caused us to weep, and listen to the voice of liberty, which speaks in the hearts of us all.'

Language had changed its name. A new word had been spoken. Action and intention became part of the same plan. Without the least hesitation they went to work; and in less time than the birds were allowed to fly, the whole place was a furnace. Poison had given way to fire. The war was a straight fight between masters and slaves. Casualties would happen in the course of burning, but nothing could restrain their vengeance. If all Haiti dropped down dead, that would have been no less a triumph. Their prison would have crumbled. They burnt and tortured as they had seen their owners burn and torture those slaves whose death would be sanctified by these fires. Haiti could sink with fire under the sea; but the miracle had happened. The ploughs had spoken. The human spirit had been redeemed, inscribed in fire by one act of freedom.

It meant the impoverishment of the land and the laceration of the slave himself by a history of crimes which had almost dragged him down to madness. And it is at this point that the genius arrives to impose some order on this chaos. The man who would be a thorn in Napoleon's side was almost old. But age was irrelevant. The future had found its architect in Toussaint Louverture.

Toussaint was one of the few privileged slaves. Unlike Dessalines and Christopher who were to become his indispensable lieutenants, he had not known the ferocity of the whip. He worked as a steward of the livestock on his master's plantation. He was, so to speak, on the inside; and he applied his gifts to this privilege. He could read, and he made use of the books which came his way. He had studied Caesar's Commentaries; he was familiar with the revolutionary writing of the Abbé Raynal on the East and West Indies. It is not unlikely that he had already seen himself as the man who had been described in the following passage:

'If self-interest alone prevails with nations and their masters, there is another power. Nature speaks in louder tones than philosophy or self-interest. Already are there established two colonies of fugitive negroes, whom treaties and power protect from assault. Those lightnings announce the thunder. A courageous chief only is wanted. Where is he, that great man whom Nature owes to her vexed, oppressed and tormented children? Where is he? He will appear, doubt it not; he will come forth and raise the sacred standard of liberty. This venerable signal will gather around him the companions of his misfortune. More impetuous than the torrents, they will everywhere leave the indelible traces of their just resentment. Everywhere people will bless the name of the hero who shall have re-established the rights of the human race; everywhere will they raise trophies in his honour.'

Yet a whole month of unrest and revolution had passed before Toussaint decided to join forces with the slaves. He had stayed on to protect his master, his family and their plantation. His decision to fight was no part of an attraction for violence; and this extraordinary concern to save the life and property of his former master was to reveal itself in other ways during his career. But when he had made up his mind, there was no turning back. He found the slave leaders: Biassou, Jean François and Jeannot, and offered his services. He was a subordinate among them; but they were immediately sensitive to his gifts, and used him to the greatest advantage. They were men of entirely different character from Toussaint. Biassou was a reckless adventurer, and he drank too much. Jeannot had tendencies towards cruelty. His imagination had been weakened by the crimes of slavery; but he was a ruthless and necessary leader. Jean François was handsome, and proud. He had run away from his master's estate and never returned.

But Toussaint's life had been orderly. He had married and settled down with his family, he lived in a state of comfortable servitude.

Toussaint was, therefore, among men whose lack of opportunity had made them fierce. He found many of the slaves naked, or barely covered in rags and filth. They had started a colossal insurrection; but how were they going to continue? They hardly had any weapons apart from a few pistols and guns which they had found or stolen off their enemy. They had fought with anything that came to hand: sticks, bottles, pieces of iron, stones, any object which could injure. The horses in their possession, were either old or hungry. This was the state of the slave army which would certainly have to pay in blood for the consequences of that night in the forest.

But they were equipped with a will which they had already translated in song; and they had an inordinate and instinctive feel for drama. In order to impress the rank and file, these half-naked leaders honoured themselves with degrees of military status which many a French soldier had failed to achieve after many years of active service. Biassou took upon himself the rank of brigadier. Jeannot said he too would be a brigadier. And Jean François, true to his proud spirit, gave himself the formidable title of 'Admiral, Generalissimo and Chevalier of the Order of St Louis.' He was born in San Domingo, and he had probably never set foot on a ship; but it didn't matter. Subsequently he and Biassou got involved in some dispute; and as though to establish a point of precedence, Biassou changed his title from Brigadier to 'Viceroy of the Conquered Territories.' Toussaint became a subordinate to the new Viceroy's regiment.

The Colonial Assembly retaliated with characteristic brutality. They refused to refer the insurrection to France, and took things into their own hands. They built scaffolds and 'broke twenty or thirty blacks on the wheel every day.' It was a way of terrifying the slaves who might have felt the urge to revolt. But the method of intimidation had the opposite effect, and the slave army increased its number to 100,000 in a matter of weeks.

On the initiative of the slaves, the Mulattos now decided to press for full equality with the whites. These Mulattos were not slaves; but their half-and-half status had exposed them to the most wounding indignities. The whites hated them; while they themselves, born of black mothers, retained an attitude of superiority to the Blacks. Their intervention at this point was of great value to the slave; for although Mulattos and Blacks were no friends, they had a common enemy.

The whites increased the pressure on the Mulattos, and the result was insurrection. Some of the Mulattos were highly educated and very trained men. Memory was like a fuel to their wounded passions, and they returned the atrocities which they had suffered at the hands of the whites. Their ambitions were not the same as the slaves; nor did they care very much for the freedom of the slaves; but strategy demanded an alliance. The situation assumed quite frightening proportions; for the Blacks, joined by Mulattos, were attacking in the north; and the Mulattos, joined by Blacks, were making headway in the south.

The English who had a huge stake in the Caribbean started on their familiar role of backing whichever horse might win. They had always been jealous of French power in the Caribbean; so the double revolt was exactly their cup of tea. Their imagination searched every corner where a seed of mischief and confusion could be sown. The local Assembly had still not called on the Home Government for help; and the first news of the San Domingo uprising reached Paris through a London newspaper. As a result three commissioners were sent from France to restore order.

The Colonial Assembly gave them a splendid welcome; and for the time being the slave revolt had to be postponed. After four months of solid fighting, there was nothing the Black leaders could do. They could burn the crops, but if they wanted to win a war, it was important that they should have food. They were at a standstill.

And now something, at once extraordinary and familiar, took place. These great leaders, Biassou and François, who had won the confidence of thousands of people, decided that something had to be done. They wanted to bargain with the Commissioners. That instrument of negotiation called the Commission is one of the most insidious forms of hypocrisy in colonial history. It always creates confusion, and plunges men into disloyalty. For both Biassou and François now promised the Commissioners that they would stop fighting if a few hundred of them were granted liberty. A few hundred out of some 100,000! They went so far as to promise the Commissioners that on this condition, they would even join the King's troops and hunt down those slaves who refused to surrender. Toussaint played his part in all this, for he was the man assigned to do most of the negotiating.

This correspondence to the Commissioners emphasised every virtue which the French gentlemen would have been pleased to hear. These Black leaders apologised for the devastation they had caused. They were loyal to the Mother Country. And finally, as though it were a matter which could not be avoided, they made some mention of the slaves. 'It would be even to your interest that if you declared, by a decree bearing the sanction of the Governor, that it is your intention to concern yourselves with the lot of the slaves, knowing that they are the object of your solicitude.'

The implication is that if the top-brass among the Blacks had got freedom and full political rights, they would be in a position to control the slaves on behalf of the Mother Country. But if they were betraying the spirit of people who so freely offered their lives, they were also sowing the seeds of a very useful dissension. The Commissioners were persuaded to consider their proposals; but the local whites—as is always the case—would tolerate no such thing. Certain that they would soon be able to kennel these black dogs and crack the whip once more, they offered and swore to forgive only those slaves who went straight back to work. Their reply to the Black negotiators finished with the order: 'Get out!'

Biassou, the recent self-appointed Viceroy of the Conquered Territories, was hurt to the quick. He swore that he would have all white
prisoners slaughtered; and it was Toussaint who had to persuade
him from this certain act of violence. The Commissioners had had a
setback; but they tried again. A meeting was arranged with Jean
François, and in spite of one unfortunate incident, it ended amicably.
He promised to return the white prisoners in exchange for his wife
who had been captured.

But the colonial Assembly was furious with the Commissioners for
receiving this Black, and they did everything to discredit the importance of the Commissioners in the eyes of the slaves. Toussaint was
now doing these negotiations on his own. He had asked that 400
slaves be freed. Impossible! So he reduced the number to sixty.
It made no difference to the local Whites. They accused the Commissioners of treachery, and stood firm in their decision to exclude
the Blacks from any kind of negotiation.

How did Toussaint conceive of his life if he were free with a swarm
of slaves living in the same conditions around him? His career, from
this moment, contradicts any notion that the attainment of her personal freedom would have been the end of the slave revolt. But it is
impossible to say what he was thinking during those treacherous
negotiations. Anyway, the road was now clear. The Whites had
created exactly the situation which was required. Their absolute and
contemptuous refusal was the first clear signal that Toussaint had
found his vocation. How could he forget the Abbé Raynal's words:
'A courageous chief only is wanted. Where is he that great man whom
Nature owes to her vexed, oppressed and tormented children?'

As he returned to break the news of their failure, Toussaint had
already embarked on the road to freedom. The only justification for
his existence would be the liberation of every slave. It would not
come about by chance. It would never be given by such people in the
Assembly. It would have to be won by their own efforts. When he
met Biassou, François and the others, he explained what had happened, and told them quite bluntly that no one in future was to look
to the Commissioners for anything. For the first time Toussaint
shared in military status. He assumed the rank of Brigadier-General,
and applied himself to the work he was best fitted for. He was a born
leader, and a born administrator. Immediately he began to train his
army.

The colonial Assembly was at war with the Commissioners, at
war with the Mulattos, at war with the slaves. They had even put
the Governor under arrest. They were plotting to murder one of the
Commissioners. There was total disorder. Paris was alarmed; for the

E

English sharks were prowling near by, ready to pounce from Jamaica if their chances looked good. The Paris mobs were not asleep. The King was still head of the Army and Navy; but the revolutionary embers were alive in France. The San Domingo Blacks didn't know what was happening in Paris, but Paris knew what was happening in San Domingo. The great palaver of debate started in the Constituent on the colonial problem, which was no longer an overseas matter. It had been brought right on the ordinary Frenchman's doorstep. Troops would have to be sent to deal with the slaves and the Mulattos. Would the Whites continue to be awkward? What side would the strengthened Left Wing of the Constituent take on these questions? After all, the Paris mobs weren't so far away, and the Rights of Man meant precisely what it said. Speaking on the question of freed slaves, Mirabeau had already made the issue clear:

'You claim representation proportionate to the number of the inhabitants. The free blacks are proprietors and tax-payers, and yet they have not been allowed to vote. And as for the slaves, either they are men or they are not; if the colonists consider them to be men, let them free them and make them electors and eligible for seats; if the contrary is the case, have we, in apportioning deputies according to the population of France, taken into consideration the number of our horses and our mules?'

The word 'slave' had become as explosive a sound as the noise 'nigger' in certain gentle circles. One French delegate put the case for the colonists, and his account, not unlike some speeches in the House of Commons, today is a classic example of what happens to some of us in 1960. We don't know the facts; and we easily assume that things may not be so bad after all. Here is Millet, talking about the condition of men who had been roasted, dynamited and often buried alive:

'We live in peace, gentlemen, in the midst of our slaves . . . Let an intelligent and educated man compare the deplorable state of these men in Africa with the pleasant and easy life which they enjoy in the colonies . . . Sheltered by all the necessities of life, surrounded with an ease unknown in the greater part of the countries of Europe, secure in the enjoyment of their property, for they had property and it was sacred, cared for in their illnesses with an expense and an attention that you would seek in vain in the hospitals so boasted of in England, protected, respected in the infirmities of age; in peace with their children, and with their family . . . freed when they had rendered important services: such was the picture, true and not embellished, of the government of our Negroes, and this domestic government perfected itself particularly during the last ten years with a care of which you will find no model in Europe. The most sincere attachment bound the master to the slave; we slept in safety in the middle of these men who had become our children and many among us had neither locks nor bolts on our doors.'

Consider the physical predicament of the slave; and ask: 'What in the name of Jesus and all the Saints should we do with a man who operates at such a diabolical level of lies?'

If Millet and his colleagues in crime were prepared to treat this revolt as a minor difficulty, it wouldn't take long for anyone to predict the future. These political tongues argued in France to their hearts' content about matters which didn't touch them personally. They might lose money if things went badly in San Domingo; but none of them were likely to have their testicles cut off for being black.

In San Domingo the Assembly was waiting to hear what would come out of these debates; but there was one man who had absolutely no time for arguing on points of order. Toussaint was hard at work. Thousands of slaves had fought; many of them had no idea what to do with a gun. Illiterate and always deprived of any experience of formal learning, they were no more than human energy which had to be disciplined and taught. With the foresight of genius, Toussaint established for himself the limitations within which it would be possible to get anything done. Unlike some ambitious imbeciles, he didn't go herding all of them together for instruction; since he knew that numerical superiority meant little or nothing if it were not supported by efficiency. He had watched the men closely; and finally he selected the hundred he thought most able by intelligence, physical power and daring. He worked on this fertile core, increasing their numbers gradually. Some months later he had around him some five hundred men who had now understood the important distinction between throwing bottles at white people and capturing, dead or alive, an important regiment. Toussaint was more or less ready; and the moment was ripe.

The debate over in France, a new lot of Commissioners were sent to San Domingo; and to assure the colonial Assembly that order would be maintained, fifteen ships also sailed from France with four thousand National Guards, and two thousand troops.

These might have been enough to postpone any trouble from the slaves; but their composition was itself a serious disadvantage. The Commissioners were Left Wing, among them Sonthanax who was a Jacobin. The commanding officers served the King. The National Guards were products of the revolution, whereas the troops were the soldiers of the King. They quarrelled from the time they set foot on the ships. Since any concession involved prestige, they were always splitting hairs about how quite simple things should be done. And it didn't help since their subordinates were always near enough to over-hear these disputes. As James remarks: 'The Commissioners carried the revolution on board with them. They went to meet it. But what was of infinitely more importance for the slaves, they had left it behind them.'

For the Paris mob was about to conquer the streets. The Commissioners left France in July; and before they reached San Domingo, August 10th had happened. They didn't know that the Paris crowds had already begun to take things into their own hands. A revolution was in full swing. The Royal Family had been imprisoned; the Legislature dissolved; and a new parliament summoned. The Paris workers did not only bring things to a halt, they wouldn't let their enemies out of their sight. These French revolutionaries had had enough; and as though there was some law regulating the sectors of suffering, they were identified in spirit with the slaves in San Domingo. A new phrase gained currency: 'Aristocrats of the skin,' and it referred directly to the affairs of San Domingo. Whether or not they knew, the Black leaders had allies in France (not intellectuals and political opportunists) but among the ordinary peasants and servants. Some of these were so horrified by the condition of the slaves, that they stopped drinking coffee, believing that it was 'drenched with the blood and sweat of men turned into brutes.' The accumulation of factors leading to the new situation in San Domingo reminds us of a truth which James defines with great restraint and clarity: 'The first sign of a thoroughly ill-adjusted or bankrupt form of society is that the ruling classes just cannot agree how to save the situation. It is this division which opens the breach, and the ruling classes will continue to fight with each other, just so long as they do not fear the mass seizure of power.'

Yet this division between the Commissioners and the officers of the King created confusion in the minds of the Blacks. The sole purpose of this Commission was to regularise the rights of the Mulattos. The conflict between Commissioners and local Whites happened all over again; but Sonthonax, a Jacobin, was a much tougher character than his predecessors. He was set on granting the Mulattos equal rights; and any dissenting voice was christened with the new disgrace: 'aristocrat of the skin.'

The soldiers of the King and the revolutionaries who took sides with Sonthonax attacked each other as though they were back in France. Geography made no difference; they were enemies. The Mulattos joined up with Sonthonax, and the Royalist leaders were soon sent packing back to France. The slaves were now almost out of the picture. It was the Mulatto issue which seemed to dominate the politics of the moment. Toussaint was in serious trouble. Mulattos who would have helped to swell his ranks now saw their chance in Sonthonax. Moreover, famine was killing off many of the slaves. The Black leaders had not yet started to think in terms of Independence. Their enemy was the local Whites, and their main ambition was freedom from the horrors of slavery; so they remained loyal to the letter of the French Constitution. Then the news came that the King had been executed.

The revolutionary forces in France were gaining ground. Its repercussions were always present in San Domingo, and no opportunity would ever be lost by a man like Sonthonax for pressing an advantage. First the death of the King, now France was at war with Spain; and shortly afterwards with Britain. The slaves could not be sure who was fighting for whom. Where did they stand in this conflict between France and France on the one hand, and France against Britain and Spain combined on the other? Their loyalties instinctively forced them to join forces against the republic which had killed a king, and they did not hesitate to accept an offer from the Spaniards at the other end of the island.

It was an opportunity to get arms, food, clothing. Moreover, the Spaniards would be in sympathy with their shooting down their former owners who were French. Biassou and François were made officers in the Spanish army. Toussaint insisted on keeping his group independent. They had, so to speak, deserted their native claims. But Toussaint had not been deserted by his capacity for swift calculation. The Spanish made him a colonel. His men now numbered six hundred, and he started to conceive the most daring plans.

He suggested he would help the Spaniards in capturing the French part of the colony on the condition that all the slaves would be freed. The Spanish Governor thought it too risky, and refused. In a few months Toussaint wrote to Laveaux, the French Governor of San Domingo, and promised that he would help in capturing the Spanish half of the colony for the French on the condition that Laveaux would free the slaves. Laveaux refused; and since there was no other part of the island under foreign domination, there was no one else to turn to.

He bided his time with the Spaniards. The French knew his worth, and since things were going rather badly for them, one of Sonthonax' Mulatto officers wrote begging Toussaint to return. He would be granted the 'protection' of the Republic if he came with his forces under his command. To their stupefaction, Toussaint replied that the Blacks wanted a king. He was having no truck with the republic in their war against royalty.

From now on, the soldier in Toussaint becomes a politician. Any horse is worth riding, provided it can get you home. But Toussaint's home was part of a most noble purpose. He was not fighting for profits or conquest of foreign lands. The freedom of the slaves was his whole ambition; and if neither side would help; then, as James ironically suggests, he was determined to use all.

He was learning as fast as he could. The French invitations to join them continued, but he wouldn't budge. Some of the royalist soldiers deserted and chose to serve in Toussaint's independent army rather than enlist with the Spaniards. He made these men teach his own soldiers. He persuaded all the Blacks near by to learn as well as teach him the lay-out of the land. There wasn't a single map anywhere, so he made one himself on the basis of what he had heard from those who lived in the neighbourhood. He simply had no time to waste; for he had come to learn that these alliances either with Spanish or British could not be relied upon. They were not interested in freeing the slaves; and that was his consuming passion. He would help Spain if it served his noble end. Similarly he would appear to be in league with the British; but he was convinced that these two sharks, Spain and England, would not hesitate to swallow him whole if it suited their interests. More decent by virtue of his cause, he was often their match in duplicity and cunning.

It is during this period that he met the slave whose name would become synonymous with massacre. Dessalines was one of the local men who taught him this part of the country. Dessalines was illiterate, and remained so nearly all his life. But his will had been shaped by the punishment of the whip. Unequivocal and stern, the white face was his conception of a target most suited for complete obliteration.

Toussaint's forces had now increased to four thousand. The French were after him again; but he didn't think it time to offer his services. Jean François and Biassou were beginning to yield to the flattery of the French colonists who had escaped into Spanish territory. But Toussaint's cause served also as a threat. Any trouble from the Spanish Governor, and he was ready to rouse all the slaves in that colony. They praised Biassou and Jean François; they called Toussaint a traitor, and threatened to have his head. But no one dared touch him. The Spanish were gaining heavily in the north; and everyone knew that these advances were largely due to Toussaint's disciplined army. His investment in that solid core of one hundred was beginning to pay off. Foresight was his great strength. He commanded the coast on the west while the Spaniards gained post after post in the north. The French were now in serious trouble, and the

British chose this moment of general confusion to make an attack on San Domingo.

For a long time the French planters had been asking the British for help; but they refused until they thought they saw a chance to capture the whole colony. The British arrived from Jamaica in September, and all the property owners went to greet them. France was at war with England, but it made no difference to these wretched and Christian subjects of France, the Mother Country, that it was the enemy whom they were embracing. Integrity is a foreign word in any language where greed is determined to have its way. It was the property they wanted to save; and they knew that the British would, among other things, defend their right to go on having slaves.

A British victory in San Domingo would be a victory over the republican forces which had grown out of the revolution. Clarkson and Wilberforce were somewhat surprised to see Pitt's gradual loss of interest in the fate of slaves. The British were moving through the Caribbean at lightning speed. Sailing up from their blessed little hide-out called Barbados, they had captured, all the way, Martinique, St Lucia and Guadeloupe. If San Domingo could be conquered, it would leave them masters in those seas. The French colonial empire would be finished in the Caribbean. The profits from this 'pride of France, the envy of every other imperialist nation' would be redirected to Britain. And James maintains that Britain would then have been able to 'return to Europe and throw army and navy against the revolution.'

In other words, this campaign which now involved the British, the French, the Spanish and the slaves under the command of the unpredictable Toussaint was a conflict of the greatest importance in world history. The Jacobin, Sonthonax, saw this clearly. San Domingo had to be saved from Britain in the interest of the French revolution. He was a desperate man as his appeal to his followers shows: 'If it is necessary to hide in a double and triple range of hills, I will show you the way. We shall have no other asylum than cannons, no other food than water and bananas, but we shall live and die free . . .' And later he wrote: 'If we are defeated we shall leave for the English only bones and ashes.'

The British demanded the surrender of Port-au-Prince. Sonthonax refused. The British resorted to bribes. It was not difficult to find traitors in a country that was at once so harassed by war and so confused about their allegiances. The French émigrés were at one with the British in their attack.

By June the capital had been captured.

It is against this background of incomparable odds that Toussaint emerges as a universal figure. The British occupation of San Domingo would be the last blow to his ambition. If the British won, he knew the Spanish wouldn't think twice of crushing him lest he made trouble among the slaves. And the revolutionary Government in France had not yet spoken on the question of abolition. Where should he turn next?

The colonial question was up again for debate in France. Sonthonax, with his progressive thrust, had sent deputies from San Domingo to take part. They were bound to create a strong impression on the Convention; since one was white, another Mulatto, and the third a free Black. Their credentials were accepted. When Bellay, the Black, and Mills, the Mulatto, entered the hall, colour was given an aristocratic welcome. The applause was loud as war. The Deputies went through all the necessary ritual. And when the President gave the fraternal kiss, all hands went wild again with clapping. It was the Negro, once a slave, who spoke on the question of abolition: and without any further palaver the motion was put by Levasseur:

'When drawing up the Constitution of the French people we paid no attention to the unhappy Negroes. Posterity will bear us a great reproach for that. Let us repair the wrong—let us proclaim the liberty of the Negroes. Mr President—do not suffer the convention to dishonour itself by a discussion.' And that was that.

The French Assembly rejoiced; for it was at this session that slavery was declared abolished . . . '. . . all men without distinction of colour, domiciled in the colonies, are French citizens, and enjoy all the rights assured under the Constitution.'

It was an act of the greatest importance for the future of San Domingo. Delight took strange forms in the French Assembly; and one deputy remarked on the joyful collapse which the revolutionary spirit had inflicted on a lady in the audience:

'A citizeness of colour who regularly attends the sittings of the Convention has just felt so keen a joy at seeing us give liberty to all her brethren that she has fainted (applause). I demand that this fact be mentioned in the minutes, and that this citizeness be admitted to the sitting and receive at least this much recognition of her civic virtues.' . . . 'The motion was carried and the woman walked to the front bench of the amphitheatre and sat to the left of the President, drying her tears amidst another burst of cheering!' [*Black Jacobins.*]

We need not seek motives for this act which led to such rejoicing; but if it was meant to bring happiness to the slaves, it was certainly going to get the British and their allies into trouble. For it helped to clarify the position of the slaves. 'The English are done for,' Danton shouted, 'Pitt and his plots are riddled.'

On June 4 news broke that seven ships, under a Mulatto named Victor Hugues, had escaped the British fleet. They had made for Guadeloupe. They were one thousand five hundred men strong; but what was more important was the message which Hugues had brought from the Convention in Paris. This Mulatto set to work on the slaves in the British captured island, furnished them with the uniforms of the republic, and drove the British off Guadeloupe.

Until this moment Toussaint was lost for a stratagem. But the news from France was precisely what he needed. A new fox among experienced foxes, Toussaint remained loyal to his purpose which was always the freedom of the slaves. Freedom had been sanctioned by the French Government; and republican or royalist, it could not matter now. He promptly wrote to the French Governor, Laveaux, and offered to join the French forces against Spain and Britain. Toussaint would be a formidable asset, and they knew it. Laveaux offered him the rank of Brigadier-General and before San Domingo knew what was happening, Toussaint was right back where he started.

The political question having been resolved, he was free to give all his attention to the fighting. Experienced and renowned as a soldier, he now recaptured for the French all the camps that he had previously captured from them for the Spanish. The British had strengthened their position and were just waiting to mark out how much of San Domingo they would plunder. They were about to realise their heart's ambition when Toussaint made his assault on their forces, taking most of their positions and finally chasing them across the river towards St Marc on the coast.

With these successes, Toussaint enters a new phase. Each situation, it seemed, had revealed a new side of his character. His exploits as a soldier were legendary. His political acumen had saved him from many a crisis. France, and therefore San Domingo, was still at war with Britain and Spain; but the position of the slaves was more assured. Now he emerged as the administrator and the citizen. He could take no chances with the enemy; but he had his eye on the development of the country as well. His troops were made up of Blacks, Mulattos, Whites. They represented a possible future which San Domingo could be, united and without the inhibitions of race. He was their commander, and he commanded on behalf of France and in the interest of San Domingo. 'All my ambition,' he writes later, 'is to give myself an advantageous basis for war and at the same time to protect and advance agriculture.'

He was a man with an impeccable sense of priorities. Revenge was almost absent from his emotions as we shall see in his dealings with those who had deserted his ranks, or even tried to betray him. It was lacking also in his dealings with the French Whites, the planters, and all who had inflicted such barbarities on the slaves. He wanted to start afresh. And it is during this period that one sees all the forces at work in his personality.

The great ambition of the slaves was to be free. They had fought and died to achieve it. The spirit which demanded it had transformed men who lived like brutes into soldiers of considerable intelligence and daring. It had revealed the genius which resided in a man whose gifts had been relegated to the care of his master's livestock. It had created a new situation, and the situation was now in the process of creating new people. But this gift of freedom was in the nature of a paradox. If it brought joy to the hearts of the slave army, it also introduced them to a fear they had never known before. Yesterday their passions were consumed by the need to be free. Freed at last, they now lived in the awful fear that slavery might be restored. The service which they had once given to realise freedom would now have to be doubled and tripled against any enemy who tried to plunge them back into their original state. And there were such enemies around. Moreover, the war was on, and France wasn't doing so well in San Domingo. Suppose Britain and Spain won here, what would be the future of Toussaint and his men? They had every reason not to relax in their efforts to help France win this war in San Domingo.

Sonthonax had returned to France. Laveaux, the Governor, was in charge of the colony's affairs; but the whole fate of the island was in Toussaint's hands. His army was made up of all sorts of people. Many had fought against each other at one time or another: Mulattos whose jealousy of the Blacks was understandable; French Whites who might have contributed to the humiliation of the Mulattos. How could you hold such a group of men together? Moreover, the army had been weakened by lack of food, lack of ammunition. Toussaint's letters to Laveaux make painful reading:

'I have absolutely no powder . . . I beseech you for Heaven's sake to send me some good gun stones. I have not got one. . . .'

'My soldiers are naked, they have no food, they receive no pay.' . . . 'You cannot imagine how I suffer at not being able to help them.'

Imagine the situation with the British at his heels, ready not only to shoot but to buy those men whom hunger might have made weary. But Toussaint's personality (like Churchill's voice in those dark hours) had the most astonishing effect on these men. When he got ammunition, it turned out that most of the guns weren't any good.

They were either too short or too rusty. But the men made what they could of them. Toussaint's orders were like a sermon in endurance and valour. Hear him describe this bond which existed between himself and that decisive circle of comrades:

'I put before them the position of the enemy and the absolute necessity of driving him off. The brave republicans: Moïse, J. B. Paparet, Dessalines and Noel answered in the name of all the chiefs that they would brave any sort of danger, that they would go anywhere and that they would follow me to the end.'

Moïse! Dessalines! These men had become as necessary as his hands. How did he achieve this loyalty? How could he get men to do what they probably would never have dared under a different command? Was it because they were all slaves together? Partly, but the reason is also part of Toussaint's character. For all his humane and compassionate understanding of men, there was an autocrat alive somewhere within him. He knew how badly equipped they were; yet when he had cause to rebuke their loss in battle, he would make their failure sound as though it were his personal martyrdom:

'But I see, Citizens, with much pain, that the orders which I have given you three times running to move on to the territory of our enemies and drive them from it, have not been put into execution. If you had condescended to execute the orders which I had sent to you, all the camps on the other side of the Artibonite would have been destroyed. . . . You have trampled my orders into the dust.'

Good God! What more, we ask, could he expect from them? And the simple answer is: More. But the enemy were not his sole preoccupation. There were always rumours of insurrections among the slaves who would complain that the Whites, in their part, had continued to treat them as though the freedom had not been declared. Naturally! Constitutions are a change of laws; but no constitution can guarantee a transformation of character. In some cases, the White had refused to tell some of the illiterate slaves what had happened. Whenever these difficulties arose, Toussaint dealt with them himself. He went to the spot where the trouble had been reported, and spoke to all who were involved. He had begun to develop that fear—it is familiar in new post-colonial territories—that something would go wrong if he didn't do it himself.

Now he is writing to send advice to Rigaud and the valiant Mulattos who are fighting elsewhere; now he is explaining strategy to the French commander; now he is trying to persuade some nervous group that they should not allow the British to bribe them; now he is imploring his soldiers not to remember the past, not to hold it against the Whites. 'No reprisals, no reprisals!' He said it time and again. Whenever they had won a campaign, and it was likely the men would use their victory as a weapon of revenge against their former owners. 'No reprisals, no reprisals.' Constitutions can change laws, and laws can produce new situations. But no constitution, with its repertoire of laws, can create the spirit of the man who, in spite of his bloody past, is still able to tell his slave brothers: 'No reprisals, no reprisals.' Nor have we any reason to doubt his sentiments when he writes the Governor:

'My heart is torn at the fate which has befallen some unhappy whites in this business.'

He and the Governor grew closer and warmer in their respect every day. He became an example of reliability. Of all the Blacks, he was the one whom the San Domingo Whites would trust. It was this range of sympathy which cut across all divisions. And when he writes to Laveaux, it is not exclusively concerned with war. He is anxious to know about the Governor's health. 'Here is something important. I send you some truffle. Be so kind as to accept them from him who wishes you the best of health, and who embraces you with all his heart. All my officers assure of their respect and fidelity.'

Laveaux needed this respect, Toussaint knew his own power; and yet his sense of order demands a certain respect. He makes it clear that he is subordinate to the Governor. And he identifies the wishes of the black soldiers with his own. In moments of great crisis, when Laveaux would appear to weaken, Toussaint would write as though there were no need to panic. He was a source of confidence to all of them.

Yesterday, a steward ordering livestock about! Today—only five years later—still small in stature, ugly of features and black by skin, but a presence which transcended colour, an aristocrat of the spirit!

He had survived traitors, insurrections, and the growing devastation of his country. Finally his army, both Black and Mulatto, had expelled the British. Both Sonthonax and Laveaux had already returned to France. The new agent, Hédouville, was determined from the start to ruin Toussaint. He had got himself thoroughly briefed on the kind of man he would have to work with; and he did everything to undermine Toussaint's influence both with the British and among his own people.

It was intolerable. Either by innuendo or open insolence, this French scum now arrived to destroy the foundations which were so strenuously built by these ex-slaves and Mulattos. Toussaint was feeling the strain of the war, the colossal responsibility of reconstruction; and he wasn't young when he started. We get some insight into his state of mind when we read his long letter to Hédouville, asking permission to retire:

'. . . If I have asked permission to retire, it is because, having honourably served my country, having snatched it from the hands of powerful enemies who fought for possession of it, having extinguished the fires of inter-racial war to which it was for long a prey, having too long forgotten a cherished family to which I have become a stranger, having neglected my own interests, sacrificed my time and my years to the triumph of liberty, I wish now to save my old age from an insult which would shame my children. I would feel it the more inasmuch as I shall know that I have not deserved it and I shall certainly not survive it. I do not conceal from you that, as you seem to be delaying indefinitely to accede to my request, I shall make it to the Directory itself. Men in general are so inclined to envy the glory of others, are so jealous of good which they have not themselves accomplished, that a man often makes himself enemies by the simple fact that he has rendered great service. The French Revolution has furnished many examples of this terrible truth. Many great men have expiated in exile or on the scaffold the services that they have rendered to their country, and it would be imprudent for me to remain any longer exposed to the shafts of calumny and malevolence.

'An honourable and peaceable retreat in the bosom of my family is my sole ambition. There, as at the head of my armies, I shall always be ready to show a good example and give the best advice. But I have learnt too much of the heart of man not to be certain that it is only in the bosom of my family that I shall find happiness.'

But he knew that solid foundations had been laid; and he trusted to the courage and experience of men like Dessalines, Moïse, Christophe. He had fought beside these men; he knew where they started; how hard they had worked; what they had achieved. Their passions were also his. The work he had shaped would be defended by them.

But there was to be no rest for Toussaint. Soon a serious dispute occurred between Moïse and a black officer who was receiving orders from Hédouville. This man was to assume command over Moïse who was second to none in skill. Moïse was adamant. Hédouville or no Hédouville, he wasn't going to yield. The troops were ordered to fire, and Moïse had to flee for his life. One of his brothers was killed in this stupid and unnecessary arrangement of Hédouville. And to add to the folly of his situation, Hédouville now ordered that Moïse was to be dismissed from service. Failing to offer himself up,

Moïse was to be hunted and caught, dead or alive. It was this incident which summoned Toussaint back to the field. He had no time
to waste in argument with Hédouville. He summoned his dreaded
Tiger, Dessalines, and gave him orders to march on Le Cap. Hédouville was to be arrested. Toussaint went to Fort Liberté where the
whole episode had occurred; and he addressed the crowd. Here was
a new Toussaint:

'I reinstate Moïse in his former functions. . . . Who reverts to the
sword will perish by the sword. . . . Hédouville says that I am against
liberty, that I want to surrender to the English, that I wish to make
myself independent; who ought to love liberty more, Toussaint
Louverture, slave of Bréda, or General Hédouville, former Marquis
and Chevalier de Saint-Louis? If I wished to surrender to the
English, would I have chased them away? . . . Remember that there
is only one Toussaint Louverture in San Domingo and that at his
name everybody must tremble.'

Bonaparte had now come to power in France. He appointed a new
commission. He postponed making any direct contact with Toussaint; but he gave the order that Toussaint should be confirmed in
the post of Commander-in-Chief. This couldn't have been more than
a trick on Napoleon's part. For Bonaparte hated blacks. Later we
find in his instructions to LeClerc who led the expedition against
Toussaint's San Domingo that these ex-slave generals had wounded
his pride. He told LeClerc that not a single epaulette was to be left
on any black shoulder.

But it was necessary for the time being to parry with Toussaint.
Rigaud, the distinguished Mulatto general, had broken with Toussaint. This was largely the work of Hédouville, and it remained one
of the most tragic experiences of the war; for it opened wide those
tensions and reservations which had always existed between the
Mulattos and the Blacks.

Rigaud got to France and achieved an interview with Bonaparte.
This courageous Mulatto spoke at great length about the affairs of
San Domingo, and his break with Toussaint. Napoleon was getting,
at first-hand, the atmosphere and feel of the place for which he had
made 'special laws,' and where, no doubt, it was his intention to
restore slavery. He made no attempt to interrupt Rigaud. But when
the latter was finished, Napoleon replied in thirteen words of
memorable consolation: 'General, I blame you for only one thing,
not to have been victorious.'

The Mulattos were confronted with a new humiliation. They had
fought with the Blacks against their common oppressors. Their great
soldier, Rigaud, had given invaluable service to Toussaint and the

cause of freedom. And this was the end. Toussaint almost in complete control of San Domingo!

There was obviously going to be a lot of trouble ahead for Toussaint. What, he wondered, did Napoleon really mean by these 'special laws'? He could no longer rely on the troops who had served under Rigaud, and loved Rigaud no less than Dessalines and Moïse loved Toussaint. He set about, therefore, purging Rigaud's army in order to make sure that the south would be secure. Toussaint had never lost his humanity; but there were occasions when he had ordered with great sternness. He did not want to widen any further that breach between Mulattos and Blacks. For this reason, he had asked one of Rigaud's commanders to do the job of purging unreliable elements. Either it had to be done by a Mulatto in the hope that his authority would soften the wound of Mulattos; or it had to be done by a Black who could be relied upon to succeed. The Mulatto refused, so the job fell quite naturally, and very unhappily, to Dessalines.

The result is a sad story which Toussaint's enemies often used against him. In his notes C. L. R. James says that the figure of ten thousand Mulattos murdered 'is just nonsense.' But Dessalines did begin by shooting three hundred prisoners in Leogane, 'and another fifty others in Port-Republicain.' Most of them were officers; and Toussaint whose character and reputation were in direct opposition to this kind of massacre, intervened and stopped Dessalines from going any further. His famous words to Dessalines were: 'Jacques, I said to prune the tree, not to uproot it.'

The south was safer after Dessalines. The next place to secure was Spanish San Domingo. Both Toussaint and Bonaparte realised what this would mean. For Toussaint it would safeguard him against any attack from those quarters. To Napoleon, it meant simply that annexation of the Spanish colony would put the whole island, both French and Spanish, into Toussaint's hands. It is for this reason that Napoleon had ordered that Toussaint should, in no circumstances, annex the Spanish colony. It was the new Commissioner's job to see that Napoleon's word was carried out. The clash was clear.

Toussaint, formal in every undertaking, now approached Roume, the Commissioner, and asked his authority to annex the Spanish colony. But who was Roume to disobey Napoleon Bonaparte's orders? He tried to evade the issue by turning Toussaint's attention to British trade representatives who were still in San Domingo. Toussaint was asked to chase these British off the island. He wouldn't allow Roume to get round his original request. He said he was leaving the British traders alone. But he wanted the Commissioner to sign his authority to this annexation of the Spanish colony. Roume asked that he be allowed to return to France. Toussaint could have let him go about his business and gone ahead with the annexation of the colony. But he was a stickler for legality. He refused to let Roume return to France.

Moïse and all Toussaint's supporters were aware of this conflict. They were eager to march on the Spanish colony; for Toussaint had claimed earlier that the Spaniards were stealing Negroes on the border and selling them into slavery. Ex-slaves were back at the slave war again; and Roume or no Roume, they weren't going to take that threat lightly. So thousands of them marched on Le Cap and threatened to make complete havoc if Roume didn't sign. Roume repeated that he could not. Toussaint explained what his refusal would probably mean. 'If you do not sign the decree . . . it means the end of all the Whites in the colony, and I shall enter Spanish territory with fire and sword.' Roume signed, but not without warning the Governor, who was told not to hand over the island. Toussaint arrested him although the decree had been signed; and with Roume's authority, Moïse and his troops marched on Spanish San Domingo. In no time at all, the matter was over. The whole island of San Domingo was French, and under the control of Toussaint. But what was Napoleon going to do? Toussaint didn't know, but he wrote Bonaparte as soon as the annexation was completed:

'Having decided to take possession by force of arms I found myself obliged before setting out to invite Citizen Roume to desist from the performance of his duties and retire to Dondon until further orders . . . He awaits your commands. When you want him, I will send him to you.'

And he continued:

'Whatever may be the calumnies that my enemies have seen fit to write to you against me, I shall abstain from justifying myself; but although delicacy enforces silence upon me my duty prescribes that I prevent Roume from doing harm.'

Toussaint had now made himself Governor of all San Domingo; but the island was still a French colony. At what point would Bonaparte decide to strike? Toussaint's army had expelled the British. By the annexation of the Spanish colony, he had defied Napoleon's orders. What would happen next? Toussaint must have known; but he was faced with an appalling choice.

For twelve years his people had been fighting either among themselves or against Britain and Spain. 'Of the thirty thousand Whites in the colony in 1789, only ten thousand remained . . . of the forty thousand free Mulattos and free Blacks, there were still about thirty thousand, while of the five hundred thousand Negro slaves perhaps one-third had perished.' The country was in a state of disorder. And now Napoleon, the terror of Europe, would be at their heels? What was Toussaint thinking? Everything. But he said nothing to his nearest and oldest comrades. Would Napoleon really arm against them? And what would be the outcome?

Toussaint kept silent, but that black Tiger, Dessalines, blunt and ruthless as his slave-past, was giving an answer to his troops:

'The war you have just won is a little war, but you have two more, bigger ones. One is against the Spaniards, who do not want to give up their land and who have insulted your brave Commander-in-Chief; the other is against France, who will try to make you slaves again as soon as she has finished with her enemies. We'll win those wars.'

And history proved him right. Toussaint's genius had led this world of slaves through a long and perilous night; but the day would be won by Dessalines.

What really happened to Toussaint? First of all he set about re-organising the whole administration of the country. He set up courts; applied all his energies to the improvement of agriculture; abolished all those duties and taxes that were an obstacle to the proper functioning of the state. Turning to the Spanish colony which had been taken, he set about building roads, one of them two hundred miles long. A grand hotel had been built at Le Cap; and for the first time Blacks, Whites, Mulattos, Americans met in an atmosphere of social equality.

Colour was losing its traditional meaning of inferior and debased; for the ex-slaves had gained a new confidence. It was one of their own kind who ruled San Domingo. As he himself had had cause to say later, 'If Bonaparte is the first man in France, Toussaint is the first man in the Archipelago of the Antilles.' There was hardly a man alive on that colony who would question that judgment. Certainly not Dessalines or Moïse, his necessary and incomparable lieutenants. Toussaint knew that; and it would seem that this knowledge was the seed of that separation which was now taking place between himself and his people. He was reluctant to share his intentions with them. They knew that his mind was always at work; that every thought was on their behalf and for their safety, but he did not tell them what he was thinking.

The result of his work was obvious for all to see. The country was finding its feet. Cultivation was beginning to show signs of a new prosperity. Laws existed where, formerly, there were none. Men in every walk of life felt safer. Toussaint was making plans for a peaceful future. He had sent Black and Mulatto children to be educated in France, so that they might be able on their return to complete this mighty task of reconstruction which he had begun. Among these new men of San Domingo would be his own two sons who were now being entertained in the expensive and contradictory presence of the Empress Josephine.

The monstrous slander of race was beginning to receive its first fatal opposition; for Toussaint did not hesitate to appoint Whites to very important posts in the administration. His first concern was for efficiency and the resurrection of San Domingo from its long history of degradation. This was no time for reprisal. He worked at a fantastic rate, and took responsibility for everything he did. He seemed to be present everywhere and at the same time. He would ride more than one hundred and twenty-five miles, almost every day. He dictated letters by the hundred. He appeared and disappeared without warning. Sleep was a brief interval of two hours every night. Two bananas and a glass of water were enough to keep the machine going for days. He had often come so near to being killed that death had ceased to be a part of his thinking.

But his most unfortunate defect was this new secrecy. As James remarks, it was dangerous, no doubt to explain what he was thinking, but it was even more dangerous not to explain. And so his behaviour often confused the people. Some of the soldiers thought he had marched on the Spanish colony because Negroes were being stolen and sold into slavery. But there was Toussaint, their own Toussaint, fraternising with Whites who were their sworn enemies not long ago. It would even seem that he favoured some of these Whites. Moreover, the harshness of some of his laws, in the interest of his agricultural programme, was being interpreted by his enemies as the old slavery with shorter hours.

Was he trying to put up a good front? Did he think that these manœuvres would give the impression in France that White life was safe? Was it his way of postponing what he knew was bound to happen: the arrival of Bonaparte's forces. He did not say; and his old associates were given no clue. Then came his own Constitution carrying the stamp of his own principles. Slavery would never happen again; and every man, irrespective of colour, could earn his place at any level of the society. It was his first positive step towards independence of the colony; for he did not abandon the colony's allegiance to France, but the Constitution did not allow any post for French officials. When this grave omission was pointed out to him,

Toussaint replied: 'The French Government will send Commissioners to speak with me.'

His courage knew no limits. At the same time he had been working out ideas for an enormous campaign to liberate Africans. He would take a thousand of his finest soldiers to Africa, and after invading slave territory, invite millions of slaves to be 'free and French.' He was getting on to sixty when this colossal enterprise fired his imagination. And he meant to implement it, for he had already sent a vast sum of money to America for the preparation of that liberation campaign in Africa.

He published his constitution without consulting anyone. Moïse and Christophe disapproved of it. Moïse, who had always called him Uncle, was more furious than ever. Of course Toussaint had ambitions, and ambitions are always personal. But it was not power, in the sense of conquest or prestige, which increased his isolation from the men whose loyalty he felt he could always assume. His greatness was a natural target for criticism; and his genius was impatient of any apparent obstacles. And it was particularly this stern silence that was getting him into trouble. Toussaint was haunted by the certain prospect of Bonaparte, and he concentrated his attention on France to the serious neglect of those who simply wanted him to say what was going to happen. 'Whatever my old uncle may do,' said his beloved Moïse, 'I cannot bring myself to be the executioner of my colour. It is always in the interest of the metropolis that he scolds me; but these interests are those of the Whites, and I shall only love them when they have given me back the eye that they made me lose in battle.'

Toussaint was losing contact at the very moment when it should have been closest. Trouble started again in Le Cap. The lives of the Whites were in danger from attack by those who had shared Moïse's feelings. The crowd had begun to shout: 'Long live Moïse!' That could mean one thing only. Toussaint's place might soon be taken by Moïse. But the steadfast Dessalines was still there. The insurrection was swiftly crushed. Moïse was arrested, and on Toussaint's orders turned over to the Commission. Toussaint could not have been unaware of the consequences. Moïse was tried, and finally sentenced to death. The troops were present when he was about to be shot, and they heard, with the deepest grief, his last and most memorable words: 'Fire, my friends, fire.' It is one of those strange and, perhaps, meaningful coincidences that he was executed on the very day which Napoleon had fixed for the departure of his expedition.

Bonaparte was ready; and there was Toussaint in a moment of unbearable paradox, the death of Moïse like a corpse on his back.

He had come face to face with the ultimate fact of his situation. He had to choose between one of two appalling situations: the restoration of slavery which was impossible, or war against France with the unbearable consequences of complete devastation. The fruits of all that labour would have to be burnt again. He never escaped this paradox. 'I took up arms for the freedom of my colour, which France alone proclaimed, but which she has no right to nullify. Our liberty is no longer in her hands: it is in our own. We will defend it or perish.'

On December 14th twenty thousand troops left France for San Domingo. 'It was the largest expedition that had ever sailed from France.' One general gave his judgment of the quality of the troops. 'The army of LeClerc was composed of an infinite number of soldiers with great talent, good strategists, great technicians, officers of engineers and artillery, well educated and very resourceful.' Some of these officers had taken part in Napoleon's most important campaigns. Their victory over San Domingo must have been regarded as a foregone conclusion; for LeClerc, Napoleon's brother-in-law, took along his wife, Pauline. And she had, for company, a host of musicians and artists. They were all going to celebrate, in song and dance, the return of the Blacks to slavery.

They arrived towards the end of December. Toussaint was standing alone on a peak which gave a view of Samana Bay. He saw the fleet arriving with the first detachment of twelve hundred troops. He had done all his fighting on land; he had no experience of a fleet; and now their number seemed legion. Walking back to join some of his men, he cried: 'We shall perish. All France is come to overwhelm us.'

It is at this point that C. L. R. James becomes completely immersed in the fortunes of his hero. There is a note of painful ambivalence as he strikes the contrast between Toussaint and Dessalines: his admiration for the clarity and exactitude with which Dessalines would now meet his new situation, and the tone of acerbity sharpens in his judgment of Toussaint: 'He ignored the black labourers,' says James, 'bewildered them at the very moment that he needed them most, and to bewilder the masses is to strike the deadliest of all blows at the revolution.'

But James cannot overcome the bond which Toussaint's glory has sealed between the historian and the soldier, and a page later he continues: 'Yet Toussaint's error sprang from the very qualities that made him what he was. If Dessalines could see so clearly and so simply, it was because the ties that bound this uneducated soldier to French civilisation were of the slenderest. He saw what was under his nose so well because he saw no further. Toussaint's failure was the failure of enlightenment, not of darkness.'

And the comment on those words that strike us as panic, 'All France is come to overwhelm us,' commits James finally to a judgment which may be perfectly true, and which, one feels, also tells us something about him, too. 'It was not fear,' writes James, 'he was never afraid. But certain traits of character run deep in great men. Despite all that he had done he was at bottom the same Toussaint who had hesitated to join the revolution in 1791, and for one whole month had protected his master's plantation from destruction. Only this time it was not a plantation and a few score slaves but a colony and hundreds and thousands of people.'

It was going to be war. While Toussaint was watching the fleet, and wondering whether France would overwhelm them, Dessalines was talking a different language elsewhere: 'If France wishes to try any nonsense here,' he told his army, 'everybody must rise together, men and women.' And when the war began, a new Toussaint had emerged. The autocrat again, but with a difference. He sent the same note to each of his commanders: 'Leave nothing white behind you.'

The result was a long experience of incredible barbarity with Dessalines more than a match for LeClerc in massacre. San Domingo was under fire again. Toussaint's crops turned to a furnace; his vision of peace in a free atmosphere was now in flames. One French supporter of the slave-trade—Lemmonier-Delafoisse—left this eyewitness account of Dessalines' men:

'The more they fell the greater seemed to be the courage of the rest. . . . They advanced singing, for the Negro sings everywhere, makes songs on everything. Their song was a song of brave men and went as follows:

'To the attack, grenadier,
Who gets killed, that's his affair.
Forget your ma,
Forget your pa,
To the attack, grenadier,
Who gets killed that's his affair.'

'This song was worth all our republican songs. Three times these brave men, arms in hand, advanced without firing a shot, and each time repulsed, only retired after leaving the ground strewed with three-quarters of their troop. One must have seen this bravery to have any conception of it. Those songs shouted into the sky in unison by two thousand voices, to which the cannon formed the bass, produced a thrilling effect. French courage alone could resist it. Indeed large ditches, an excellent artillery, perfect soldiers, gave us a great advantage. But for many a day that massed square which marched singing to its death, lighted by a magnificent sun, remained in my thoughts, and even today after more than forty years, this majestic and glorious spectacle still lives as vividly in my imagination as in the moments when I saw it.'

Toussaint had been kidnapped and taken straight to France. This had always been Napoleon's ambition: to get this ex-slave off San Domingo. He was hurried across France like cargo to be dumped in the cell that would be his grave. Escape was impossible; yet they guarded him as though he were a whole army. When it was known in one town that his train was passing that way, the French officers who had fought beside him against Britain and Spain asked permission to 'salute their old commander.' It was his last experience of human contact.

Deprived of food he was left to the rigours of this new winter; an old man, in exile and alone, freezing to death in the Jura mountains. But his spirit now resided in the blade of Dessalines' sword carving its way to the Haitian freedom that has remained to this day; and with it the name Toussaint, unforgotten and unforgettable as the common wind.

And it is wonderful that this epic of Toussaint's glory and his dying should have been rendered by C. L. R. James, one of the most energetic minds of our time, a neighbour of Toussaint's island, a heart and desire entirely within the tradition of Toussaint himself, a spirit that came to life in the rich and humble soil of a British colony in the Caribbean.

# ISHMAEL AT HOME

•

When a skipper sails with a smack he usually knows his
whole crew beforehand; but a man-of-war only gets its
orders at sea—that is what happens to genius, he is out
on the deep before he gets his orders, we others know
more or less what we have to do . . .
the thing is to find a truth which is true *for me*, to find
*the idea for which I can live and die.*

KIERKEGAARD

COLUMBUS WENT in search of Ophir; but the result was a different
kind of grain. The gold grew tall green; and the Lady Sugar, seduc-
tive as Josephine, increased the dowry of the anonymous slave. It
sweetened, hot and black, the irretrievable cup of Prospero's wealth.
One corner of the Caribbean was a kitchen rich with hands that
could never again claim their original landscape. 'It was,' says James,
'. . . the greatest colony in the world, the pride of France, and the
envy of every other imperialist nation. The whole structure rested on
the labour of half a million slaves.'

James was writing in the nineteen thirties, a peasant by recent
origin, a colonial by education, a Victorian with the rebel seed.
What is the real connection between James who knows Thackeray
by heart and James who wrote the history of Caliban's resurrection
from the natural prison of Prospero's regard? What is the connection
between these two Jameses and the James who analysed the political
implications, the historic meanings of Melville's American ship,
*The Pequod*? I can't see Ahab through James' eyes, although I know
what he means in that ingenious critical narrative, 'Mariners,
Renegades and Cast-aways.' I can see the sense in which Ahab is the
archetype of a dangerous master-builder, a man colonised by his own
obsession with a master plan. If one sees Prospero in the role of
emigrant, a new man intent on being a new master, I can see the
sense in which the ship's crew are Calibans alive and buried by a plan
that floats on the endless sea of commerce. For the target of their
pursuit is Moby Dick; and Moby Dick is worth his weight in gold.
And I understand Starbuck, a man gone weak with obedience, the
bureaucrat on the verge of lackey. James more than any man I know

aroused me to a responsibility which I can only describe as paying attention; but this relation was not an encounter between innocence which held a world of promises and a wisdom which sought to colonise the sky.

There was neither master nor slave, but two West Indians sprung from two different islands of the Caribbean, separated by some twenty-five years, talking from two different generations, talking always about their world, and talking, therefore, about a world infinitely wider than the islands; for the new world of the Caribbean is, in the time sense of world, the Twentieth Century.

But James's way of seeing is not mine although our perspectives may be the same; and that is as it should be. I can't therefore see why Ishmael should be relegated to the category of the neurotic intellectual. Vagrant and in exile, yes, but not for reasons of a false romanticism. Consider how that American Bible ends: 'And I alone am left to tell the story.' Alone does not here mean, I on my own, rudderless and without human aid. For that 'I' is Herman Melville himself, the man who chose the ocean for his enterprise. That 'I' is the unconscious authorship behind the Duke and mage from Milan. That 'I' is the name of a creature who serves or is served by an instinct, a need, and an absence which demands that significant experience be transmuted in a form other than what it appears to be. It is the illusion which returns the audience right back to the reality of this moment. We agree that Melville 'is the finest mind that has ever functioned in the New World and the greatest since Shakespeare's that has ever concerned itself with literature.' But we do not share the inhibition which James imposes upon himself in evaluating the purpose of the Whale. Lawrence says somewhere that his only regret was that the Whale didn't swallow Ahab's other leg. Lawrence of all people whose whole journey was devoted to the discovery of a whale which he, alone, would be able to swallow.

The West Indies are lucky to be where they are: next door to America, not the America of the Mason Dixon line or the colonising policies in the guise of freedom and self-defence, not the America that is afraid of the possibilities of its own strength. It's a different America that the West Indies can explore. It's the America that started in a womb of promise, the America that started as an alternative to the old and privileged Prospero, too old and too privileged to pay attention to the needs of his own native Calibans. In the Caribbean we are no more than island peaks; but our human content bears a striking parallel with that expectation upon which America was launched in the result, if not the method, of its early settlement.

'There is something in the contemplation of the mode in which

America has been settled that, in a noble breast, should for ever extinguish the prejudices of national dislikes. Settled by the people of all nations, all nations may claim her for their own. You cannot spill a drop of American blood without spilling the blood of the whole world. . . . Our blood is as the flood of the Amazon, made up of a thousand noble currents all pouring into one. . . . We are not a nation so much as a world. . . . Our ancestry is lost in the universal pageantry. . . . We are the heirs of all time, and with all nations we divide our inheritance.'

It is Melville again. Now we can understand why James—once the child of a Victorian classroom—can quote Thackeray for pages. We can also see why James, the adult, should have been driven, partly by his education and partly by his own subjective needs, to identify his future with the historic and unsurpassable enterprise of that great slave and revolutionary genius: Toussaint L'Ouverture.

The continuity of growth from these to Melville is almost natural. For James has been a Caribbean Columbus in reverse; and even though he may now be safely anchored in his original harbour he is none the less a living example of Ishmael. He didn't go whaling it's true, but he has always gone in search of those whose labour is a consistent rebuke to the monolithic authority of Moby Dick on land. He is Ishmael for the simple reason that he has never been, either by work or education, a renegade and a castaway. His heart has always been with those; but it is one of the paradoxes of desire that he never started there. Nor is it likely that he will ever end there.

It is precisely because he is this type of Ishmael that the American Government confined him, in spite of serious illness, to the mental torture of Ellis Island. His book, *Mariners, Renegades and Castaways*, is the most agonising plea I have ever read from a man asking the simple, human favour to go on living in a particular place.

Nearly ten years later, we can recognise the signature of his greatness by the utter lack of bitterness in any judgment he makes on the United States. It is not the gift of forgiveness which impedes such bitterness. It is rather the original resources of his humour which serves to transcend the immediate obstacle. It is the stature and example of this great West Indian which urges me to explain that if my generation ask America to leave us alone, we do not mean to refuse America's gifts. We are not afraid to accept those necessary tools which America can offer, but we would like to build our own Pequod. Our desire for dialogue through the sole process of honest talking must not be interpreted as anti-American. It is rather because we are pro-American that we speak in this way. We are pro-Whitman and pro-Melville and pro-Mark Twain. We don't mind worshipping in that kind of cathedral; for there is a possibility—indeed, more than a possibility—that we will introduce some new psalms.

But we are not too happy about standards of living if they are going to be an obstacle to a way of life. And Caliban, like Prospero, can always repeat his mistakes. We can be colonised by the pleasures that enter with foreign aid. America's most difficult task is no easier than ours; for America must learn to give, just as we must learn to receive. The gift of money is not the beginning for a relationship; for money is merely the name of a relation, and its fruits are only one part of the general atmosphere. We don't want the weather to change without our own choosing, for we don't want to lose sight of our season.

America is very much with us now: from Puerto Rico right down to Trinidad. But America is one island only; and we are used to living with many islands. From the very beginning we were part of the island of China, and the island of Africa and the island of India. The less money and the more islands, the better it may be for America herself. For there is every reason why America should be in our midst. A large chunk of Africa, that is also a part of us, has always been the conscience of America. And America can learn, by her presence in the Caribbean, how we have lived with that dilemma. We have not solved any racial questions; for prejudice is with us in one form or another; but we have been for a very long time a good example of the evolution of human relations in the future. That's not the only reason America should be in the Caribbean. We owe it to America. For we have always been mixed up in America's business. America has rescued the unemployed from time to time. From Barbados and Jamaica, Trinidad and elsewhere, West Indians have sought a future in America. They asked to enter America for the simplest and most acceptable reasons, a request that should never be refused. It was Caliban's request: 'I must eat my dinner.' And many hungry West Indians could have had their dinner if MacCarran could have based the emigration act on our example of living a way through the world's different races.

A vast number of the West Indians who flock to Britain might have sailed next door if America were confident enough to risk that entry; for it is still within America's power to do so. Moreover, we have a big stake in the building of America. Alexander Hamilton, the federal guy who contributed so richly to their constitutional literature, was a West Indian. C. L. R. James lectured in the universities of America, both north and south of civilisation. For eight years Eric Williams gave his services as a professor of Howard University where George Padmore received some of his education;

and Padmore, until his recent death, was adviser on African affairs
to the Prime Minister of Ghana. Nkrumah's judgment is authoritative on the affairs of that continent, and it was Nkrumah who told
the Ghanian nation on the occasion of Padmore's death that Africa,
not Ghana, but all Africa had lost one of her wisest counsellors. I
think America played some part in the wisdom which Nkrumah
acknowledged as Padmore's gift to the most tempestuous continent
at sea.

For Africa like the Caribbean is now very much at sea, and even
though we—like them—may not be able to tell which port we shall
harbour in, we would like the chance to reverse Prospero's magic
with the waves.

Which brings me back to Columbus and Columbus in reverse. For
Columbus number two is a very different kind of sailor. He travels
a different road of intentions. Today, there are West Indians, and
among them the very best of their generation, who have returned the
journey originally made by the slaves. But they haven't travelled
through the purgatory of the Middle Passage. However present the
echoes of slavery, these West Indians have lost the chains which held
their ancestors, ankle by ankle, mile after mile, through that night
of exile, from the African coast to the Caribbean cradle. These West
Indians have travelled from the Caribbean, sojourned by the demands of Prospero's language in the universities of Great Britain,
and then risked a wholly new adventure to the West African landscape. They are there as teachers. Not as masters, and there is a
magnificent Oxford Jamaican product who, as a teacher, spends
much of his time learning from the Africans in Accra and Kumasi
how to teach the music which Shakespeare made.

West Indians of Chinese and Indian ancestry need not be scared
of going. They will be welcome, provided they have arrived to work,
and are equipped for the work they have chosen. And Ghana and
Guinea should be made to feel that this welcome holds equally good
in Port-of-Spain and Kingston.

We need an Institute of African and Oriental Studies right in the
heart of Port-of-Spain.

In this Institute we will ask for some light on what has been discovered of the African civilisations before the European arrival. For
West Indians, on the whole, still have to learn that Africa existed—
not simply as desert, river and malaria—but as a home where men
were alive and engaged in a human struggle with nature. The presence of some Africans in the Caribbean will help to dislodge that
image of Africa as bush and artless nature, an image which Prospero
planted most successfully in the West Indian consciousness.

But where there is soil, there must be change, provided man is not condemned to the state of a dumb plant. And if Caliban, articulate and alive with promises, does not come to Prospero's aid, there may be awful trouble ahead for both of them. For deep down, Prospero may want to change. Prospero's reluctance is but a part of his fear, and that fear is only the measure of his own self-colonisation.

For colonisation is a reciprocal process. To be colonial is to be a man in a certain relation; and this relation is an example of exile.

It is here I must attempt to show how I see that reciprocity.

The colonising agent may begin with suggestions for improvement, and improvement is always welcome; for it's another word for change, with a promise of change for the better as you see better. It may start as a suggestion. Then the suggestion fails, and the colonised are alive with complaint. But the colonising agent has already chosen the future of this enterprise, the end of which is to get the colonised securely into his power. This power will almost certainly be used towards an end that may have nothing to do with the landscape where they both experience this encounter.

The Caribbean sugar was intended for the French Prosperos, to give one example. But failure is not an obstacle for a colonising power. The coloniser's business is to make failure look like the first stage of what really underlies his intention. He has earned the right to agree with the other's complaint. He can explain why it failed, and he is unanswerable, for it is his 'Game' which he is explaining.

If I am teaching an American cricket, he will have to take my word for it. If he gets hit on the head, I can explain the reason. He was using the baseball bat which is simply no good for my purposes.

Similarly, a district commissioner can explain why a method of irrigation has failed, and what Northern Nigerian peasant can argue the question of modern agricultural methods with him. It is not a failure of intelligence in the Nigerian. The method simply isn't his game. If he needs the result of the game, he must take the risk of having his apparent failure explained. The explanation is simple. From the start they should both have agreed on a common language of communication. I use language here in its widest sense. Even the Nigerian can see the logic of that; and victim as he is of the creative need for change, he enters, by a pure act of faith, a wholly new set of references.

Now Prospero is getting ready to use that weapon of language, interpreting language as his exclusive arrangement in these matters. And the district commissioner—let's imagine he was the very first— has scored a temporary triumph. But language is more than writing and talking. It has a history of meanings that relate to things other than agriculture. It can relate to Law; and Law is more than a collection of rules for day-to-day conduct. Law is the expression of a particular spirit in a particular historic time and circumstances. It is language in this sense which enables Prospero to climb to his throne. He is now crowned with privileges, and all Prosperos who succeed him must and will follow the original example. A history of examples percolating from level to level and generation to generation is what we mean by a tradition. And colonisation in this sense is simply a tradition of habits that become the normal way of seeing.

But Prospero has not won. For there is no victory, and even if there were, this kind of victory would not be possible when the entire enterprise was founded on a Lie. That district commissioner knows that the Nigerian's relation to him is not very different from any district commissioner's relation to the supreme agents of power who commissioned him to Calibanise the African village. He knows always —hence his deliberate social withdrawal—that the success of his enterprise depends entirely on his capacity for camouflage.

Camouflage is the devil's game, and it can be perfected to a point where God Himself is doubtful of His future. Didn't Jesus, with all that foreknowledge of His destiny—appear to waver when Satan invented an alternative no less rich in possibilities? It is because Jesus wavered that the whole episode is called a Temptation. It was a perfected camouflage at work. It was this perfected camouflage which made colonisation possible, and temporarily triumphant.

But colonisation has one certain psychological result. The colonised is slowly and ultimately separated from the original ground where the coloniser found him. Distance has been created between that Nigerian peasant and the total attributes which we could once regard as wholly Nigerian. It is this awareness of distance between what is his and what he has learnt to do, it is precisely this awareness which undermines his confidence in what he really was and what he could really be. For with time, that same camouflage, exploiting the pleasures which go with standards of living, have obscured from him his original understanding of a way of life. He contributes to this exploitation; for the pleasures implied and realised by those standards are an irresistible temptation.

Pleasures do not mean simply better housing and more amenities. They mean also greater privileges. These privileges must be learnt by the colonised, if he is going to prove that he deserved them. For there is always someone else waiting. If I don't want my child to go to Oxford—as Prospero has promised—I can be sure that my neighbour will accept. I must prove my right to this new privilege; and the best way of doing it is by colonising my neighbour on my master's behalf. To be a small master is better than not being a master at all.

From a state of enslavement, this brand new master has grown into a petty coloniser himself. But his luck can't last as long as Prospero's. For the language by which he colonises is not his invention. If he confuses his new Caliban, he will have to explain; and the easiest way would be to summon their original tongues. And camouflage won't work where each sees and is being seen. For Prospero's advantage was his alliance with the gods who helped him to be absent while his presence worked wonders.

No modern Prospero, whatever his Cabinet rank, can summon this magic. Today, the traditional Prospero has been seen. Moreover he has been seen by the help of the very methods which he introduced, the very language of motive and intentions which were once his most guarded secret. The old blackmail of Language simply won't work any longer. For the language of modern politics is no longer Prospero's exclusive vocabulary. It is Caliban's as well; and since there is no absolute from which a moral prescription may come, Caliban is at liberty to choose the meaning of this moment.

The blackmail that Language, meaning now Parliamentary Democracy, may be in danger in the new Independent African States, will not work. For Caliban has learnt that democracy is a way of being together, most desirable as an arrangement for peaceful living —but he knows that the Form will be betrayed if he ignores the specific human elements which are the substance of that Form. For democracy is an enterprise whose future must be worked out by those who know best the particular landscape and the particular nature of priorities. Freedom is an evil experiment if it means, among other things, the freedom to betray freedom by a gratuitous exploitation of freedom.

Freedom, in a political sense, is the recognition of the demand to be collectively responsible; and responsibility involves definite priorities. On any list of priorities, the health of a people must always supersede the theoretical perfection of a Form. It is only by paying attention to the particularity of this man, and demanding his attention as well, that the Form—which is a dialogue of conflicting methods about a commonly felt need—will be realised. Democracy should not be conceived by the graduates from colonialism as a background to which they are condemned to refer. That is cricket with a fixed history of rules. Democracy is an atmosphere and a future towards which you work.

Prospero is a shameless hypocrite whenever he raises his voice on this subject, for colonies have often had long phases of peaceful administration; but a Colonial Administration, as I have known it by experience and reading, is certainly not democratic. When the laws of a country give a man, foreign to that country, those reserve powers with which he may, at his own discretion, punish according to his conception of crime, a whole body of people whom he does not know and, in the circumstance, cannot afford to share ordinary human experience with—the foundation of such laws is the very reverse of what Prospero himself demanded of Caliban to understand by democracy.

If Prospero wants to demolish his own meaning, then he must find a new word, or alter his relation to the original lesson. If Caliban once contributed to his own colonisation; he has no intention, at this stage of his awareness, of conspiring against himself. The century is at once too old and too young to fear this kind of camouflage, to spend its energy arguing against this kind of blackmail.

For a similar method of blackmail is attempted through the language of Science and Technology. Science is no one's secret; and the modern Caliban is a greedy learner. He can learn methods of investigation as thoroughly as any Prospero with similar facilities. Moreover, he comes to these disciplines with a freshness of eye, a sharpness of curiosity; for their results still have the fascination of magic for his own landscape. And what a man can learn he can also teach. The Science and Technology blackmail is the very betrayal of the spirit of discovery which earned Europe those great achievements in working out the possible laws of natural phenomena.

Caliban can contribute to widening that same horizon which belongs equally to him and his contemporary Prospero; for it is only when they work together in the context of that horizon that the psychological legacy of their original contract will have been annulled. Caliban's 'Yes' will then acquire its human validity of reason; and Prospero's 'No' will have achieved the genuine privilege of being free to offer an alternative.

That level of No and Yes is masterless, and slaveless. It is a conflict which reaches its most creative form not between Prospero and Caliban, but rather between Prospero and Prospero: as well as between Caliban and Caliban. Each can return to the Skin without any inhibitions imposed by the exterior attributes of the Castle.

# THE AFRICAN PRESENCE

•

I shall no longer graze the donkey
Now my camel is full grown

*Jolof folk poem*

I

GHANA

AN AMERICAN tourist in Europe is often in search of monuments:
cathedrals and palaces, important graves, the whole kingdom of
names and faces that are kept alive by the architecture of history.
He rummages through his reading to pay homage, in person, to
those streets, and rooms and restaurants that have survived the men
who made them famous. He claims some share in this heritage, and
long before he arrives, his responses are, in some way, determined by
this sense of expectation. He is a descendant of men whose migration
from this continent was a freely chosen act, and whose memory is
kept alive today by his own way of looking at the world. Europe does
not add to his problem of identifying himself.

The West Indian Negro who sets out on a similar journey to
Africa is less secure. His relation to that continent is more personal
and more problematic. It is more personal because the conditions of
his life today, his status as a man, are a clear indication of the reasons which led to the departure of his ancestors from that continent.
That migration was not a freely chosen act; it was a commercial
deportation which has left its consequences heavily marked on every
level of his life in the West Indies. Consequences which are most
deeply felt in his personal life and relations with his environment:
the politics of colour and colonialism that are the very foundation
as well as the landmarks of his voyage from childhood to adolescence.
His relation to Africa is more problematic because he has not, like the
American, been introduced to it through history. His education did
not provide him with any reading to rummage through as a guide to
the lost kingdoms of names and places which give geography a
human significance. He knows it through rumour and myth which
is made sinister by a foreign tutelage, and he becomes, through the
gradual conditioning of his education, identified with fear: fear of
that continent as a world beyond human intervention. Part product

of that world, and living still under the shadow of its past disfigurement, he appears reluctant to acknowledge his share of the legacy which is part of his heritage.

So throughout that flight from London to Accra I was trying to put together the fragments of my early education; trying to recall when I had first heard the word Africa, what emotions it had registered. I recalled that at the age of eight or nine I had heard the headmaster of my primary school making some noise about Ethiopia. He seemed angry; for it was the 24th of May, and the English inspector of schools had come to distribute prizes. No one really told us what Ethiopia was. There were no maps in that room to indicate its position in the world. Some of us thought it might have been the Christian name of a lion whose surname was Judah. The name Judah made more sense since the Bible was a part of our alphabet.

Such were the fragments of rumour and fantasy which I was trying to put together during that flight. But planes leave little time for this kind of reflection, and when the land appeared, flat, scorched and empty, I found that I was even without any preconceptions. Nor was I prepared, on leaving the airport, for my first shock of familiarity.

At midday, indifferent to the stupefying heat of Accra, a loyal procession of Boy Scouts had arrived to welcome some dignitary from England. Incredibly correct in their stance, they went through the role of welcome. It was exactly like a West Indian village migrating its children in order to celebrate some important occasion. Neither waiters nor my friends could now distract my attention from the efficient soldiery of those little boys. Their limbs were tight as wire, now supple as water, according to the orders which their training had taught them to follow. Their faces split wide with laughter when a voice allowed them to stand at ease. But in a matter of seconds their muscles were like stone, the smiles rubbed out, and their eyes turned still and sinister as knives. The sun could set no mark on their complexion. When the wind came, the green and yellow scarves ran like flames around their necks, raving like a prisoner to be released.

They were completely identified with the role which they had rehearsed for today. It was a profound experience, for I was seeing myself in every detail which they lived. So I remembered again the old primary school headmaster reminding the English inspector about the name of the lion which was somewhere on this land mass. This experience was deeper and more resonant than the impression left by the phrase: 'we used to be like that.' It was not just a question of me and my village when I was the age of these boys. Like the funeral ceremony of the King, it was an example of habits and history

F

reincarnated in this moment. It was as though the Haitian ceremony of the Souls had come real: a resurrection of voices at once familiar and unknown had taken place.

The English Scoutmaster was a fragile man, lean, amiable, and full of wonder. I hadn't noticed him on the 'plane; for in that roaring kennel we were all anonymous cargo. But it was impossible to avoid him now. He tried to support a smile; but always the sun closed his teeth, reminding him that this heat was no laughing matter. He looked quite startled; and one wondered whether it was his recognition of the boys' imperviousness to the weather, or the stupendous shock of his own importance in their presence.

Soon it was all over: a brief speech of welcome and reply, a final salute, and the ceremony was dead. The boys forgot their uniform and turned the whole place into their own jamboree. They ran in all directions towards the buses where the village spectators, aunts and cousins, presumably, had watched them perform. They were all talking at the same time. The voices clashed like steel; and their hands were like batons conducting the wild cacophony of their argument. It was impossible to understand how so harmless a ritual as meeting that English Scoutmaster could now lead to such a terrifying chorus of discord.

What were they quarrelling about? Or what were they rejoicing about? For it was difficult to distinguish which noise was war and which was peace. I turned to ask my West Indian friend what it was all about. He smiled; and suddenly I realised the meaning of that smile and the fact about that invading noise. Neither of us could understand a word of what those boys were saying. Nor could the English Scoutmaster. It was at this point that the difference between my childhood and theirs broke wide open. They owed Prospero no debt of vocabulary. English was a way of thinking which they would achieve when the situation required it. But their passions were poured through another rhythm of speed.

'They are speaking Fanti and Ga,' said N.

'And if you know Fanti, does it mean that you also know Ga?'

I was getting my first lesson in speech magic.

'Not necessarily,' said N., 'but what often happens is this: when I speak to you in Fanti you will reply in Ga, and although I can't speak Ga and you can't speak Fanti, somewhere in between the meaning is clear.'

Sitting on the terrace of the airport hotel I had lived through again, and forgotten as quickly, all the trouble I had had with school uniforms. I found that I was soon talking, unheard, to myself; and instinctively the same delight kept revealing itself: 'But Ghana is free,' I was thinking, 'a free independent State.' And the implication of that silence was an acute awareness that the West Indies were not. And as we had our first drink, both N. and I agreed that it was Ghana which helped to reduce our feeling of disgrace.

The afternoon was, in its way, a kind of emergency. Accra had the look of a place unfinished: there was scaffolding everywhere, the open spaces where demolition had recently taken place, roads under repair, the brand-new building on the eve of opening. You could not detect the precise form of the town; you could not guess its centre, because the town itself was in the process of going up. It was a workshop whose centre was activity. You had the impression that it would change face every day. A year from now you would not know it. Ghana was in a fever of building: roads, schools, harbours and hospitals. It was, I felt, part of the freedom feeling.

And the names, not a day older than the present Government, were still fresh with the echo of an historic moment: Nkrumah Circle, Independence Avenue. And the life-size bust of the Prime Minister dominating the entrance to the House of Assembly with its urgent inscription: 'Seek Ye first the political Kingdom.'

But behind all this, there is the Ghana of mud-hut villages and an ancient communal living, impenetrable vegetation, the declining magic of chieftancy. As you come, so to speak, to the heart of the soil, the traditional belly and life-blood of the country, you realise that this is not only a country in a state of peaceful emergency; it is a country in a state of transition. The splendour of African dress comes first as a shock; but the shock is too frequent, and soon you are beyond surprise. Green and gold, orange and purple, night blue and lily white. Natural as grass, they are simply there, at once an ordinary and intoxicating part of the street, crowded with cars, pavement traders, cattle, and an occasional madman. Or a Hausa is seen making ready to meet his God. He unfolds his mat, squats and worships with his brow in the dust, unnoticed, as though he were an inanimate part of the pavement.

It is this amalgamation of the various styles of living, this feeling of ambiguity towards the future that gives the country its special quality of excitement. But what is even more striking is the overwhelming sense of confidence.

Some weeks later I witnessed an example of this confidence. I was sitting with a group of Ashantis in one of the popular hotels of Kumasi. We were talking about various aspects of Ashanti culture, and in particular the custom whereby the nephew and not the son is regarded as the heir. I had now grown used to the kind of variety in this place: a few Europeans, meaning white, jawing away over beer, the Ashanti girls looking magnificent in their cloth. One will never forget the rhythm of their bodies moving with an almost insolent casualness across the floor; some of the men in shirt and pants, others in N.T. smocks.

Suddenly A. left the table and walked up to two old women who were standing at the door. They were, one felt, the embodiment of all that is meant by Ashanti. The expression of the faces was male with the hair cropped close to the skull, and the fine, razor line making a complete circle round the base and brow of the skull. A. was also Ashanti, but the old women belonged to another world of intercourse. He sat them at a table, ordered their drinks, and returned to us.

'They came in from the village for a funeral,' he said, 'and felt like a drink before going back.'

Funerals, I should say, are an expensive business in this part of the world. Until you get to know the continuity of relations between the living and the dead, you can't help thinking of funerals as a kind of expensive bacchanal. The occasion surpasses Christmas for drinking; and once when my friend Kufuor suggested that I should get a lift into Accra with a driver who was thought very erratic, I had the distinct suspicion that it was some funeral drinking he was getting at.

A. was looking to see that all was well with the old women. We talked about their dress, the purple cloth drawn easily round the body, and tucked under the arm: the grave, silent concentration of the faces as though they were trying to read the meaning of this place, the intentions of the young, or the motives of those who were obviously foreign. When they finished their beer, they walked over to our table. Instinctively, everyone stood, and we shook hands all round, each man bowing to the brief curtsy of the old women. They were leaving. And what one was struck by was the formality of it all; as though each Ashanti understood by instinct his relation to those women within the context of a single and unified culture. They did not know each other; but they knew the meaning of age in their world of morality.

Then A. said: 'Five years ago they wouldn't have come in here.'

'But of course they could have come?' I suggested.

'They could have come,' said A., 'but they would not have had any desire to do so. It was not their sort of place.' And then he continued: 'And five years ago I might not have made it my business to remind them that it belongs to them.'

This is not just a change which denotes increase of privileges. It is a fundamental change of attitude even to privileges which could have been claimed five years before. It permeates everything that

Ghanians do or say. And here one saw the psychological significance of freedom. It does something to a man's way of seeing the world. It is an experience which is not gained by education or money, but by an instinctive re-evaluation of your place in the world, an attitude that is the logical by-product of political action. And again one felt the full meaning, the full desecration of human personality which is contained in the word: colonial. One felt that the West Indian of my generation was truly backward, in this sense. For he was not only without this experience of freedom won; it was not even a vital force or need in his way of seeing himself and the world which imprisoned him.

2

Now and again we see Africans make an appearance in films. They are arranged like nature in scenes which are to suggest the authenticity of a native crowd in the background. In moments of tension, they may be asked to stand still: black statues of mourning which help us to predict the tragedy that will befall some theft of sex which is now taking place between the virgin heroine and her handsome bandit on one night's shore leave.

Sometimes these Africans are asked to shout at a retreating white pirate who argues that he didn't mean to shoot the elephant. It was his idea of a Christmas toy for his little boy who keeps pets back home in Hampstead. These are not very interesting scenes, although one would like to know what words the Africans actually shout; since they have no script, and the producer hasn't yet learned their language.

But there are those films in which the African appears as a butler. Like a privileged slave who shows signs of learning, he has been promoted to a job on the inside. His uniform fits like white armour. He is an expert at balancing trays. He anticipates every need. He predicts every complaint. So he is always there, on the dot of time, and with every detail of the neighbours' greed. For this dinner party is for the Cocksures who live down the street, and the Parsons who have not long arrived.

This African servant speaks only with his hands. He hears his name take the form of salt, butter, or bread; and he answers with some receptacle containing food. And as though by magic, he knows exactly when to be absent. It is always during those character-evaluations of the native servants. The Cocksures are briefing the

Parsons on the kind of thing they must look out for. Soon the host rings a bell to have the table cleared; and the African returns with a few cousins. These are called 'small' Boys. Like Miranda towards Prospero, these small Boys have learnt from their Big Boy every duty that is expected of them. They move around the table exactly as they have seen him do. The white talk continues with elaborate examples from Mrs Cocksure's repertoire of ex-servants. She wants Mrs Parson to get it all straight. One example has to do with stealing; and another with telling lies—for these Africans, we are told, are born liars—and all these examples add up to a tremendous statement about degrees of civilisation, the absolute madness of expecting Big Boy and his cousins to run the country.

Mr Parsons, fresh from Chiswick, is astonished that this should have been said in the servants' presence. At least, the Cocksure lady could have waited until the Boys had left the room. But the Parsons are still strange. They will learn.

The table is cleared. It is time for coffee and the latest report on certain brunette wives whom the heat has led astray. But a minute before they settle into rumour, the hostess says: 'Good night. Remember tomorrow . . . and don't forget . . . about ten o'clock down at the Kingsway Stores.' And Big Boy answering to each order and request ends with his cousins in the chorus: 'Good night madam, good night massa . . . Good night everybody and all, good night!'

For the first time we realise that Big Boy does not only speak English, he understands it perfectly. Not a word was said around that table but it sank into his attention. And yet by some magic or self-control, some strange concealment of emotion; Big Boy had arranged a face which deceived us into thinking that it wasn't his; that his cousins were ignorant of English, and he himself was born deaf.

There is a camouflage of inflation which results in the role of Duke, Prince, God in person. And there is a camouflage of self-evaporation, which results in the role of Thing, excluded, devoid of language. The first can be easily detected; but the second contains an incalculable secret whose meaning stays absent until time and its own needs order an emergence.

Kingsway and Ricardo are holy names to the common man in Kumasi. They are hotels, night clubs, and points of reference for finding your way. An enquiry may take this form.

'How do you get to Suame?'

And the girl replies: 'You know Hotel de Kingsway?'

'Yes.'

'Good. You keep straight, straight down, then turn left and right like you dancing round. Then you see where the women making market there. Keep left and turn straight till you don't stop at all. One side is the race course and opposite you see a hospital on top where Lawyer Reindorph live. You pass where they sell petrol near the cinema house, and you keep straight till you turn again. If nobody present in the street, just wait till you can ask once more. Or maybe you take taxi from there. Is Suame you say you going?'

'Yes.'

'Suame, Suame. That's right. Same place what I say.'

'Thanks.'

'You from Accra?'

'No.'

'Kumasi?'

I hesitate; for Kumasi has offered its heart so thoroughly to my stay; that a negative reply strikes the air as a lie.

'I'm living in Kumasi with some friends.'

'With Lawyer Reindorph?'

'No. I live with a friend who works at Technology.'

'Mr Dawes?'

'That's right.'

'I wish you well, my brother.'

'Bye-bye.'

It is not easy, except within the context of a sustained narrative to capture the flavour of this dialogue. But a number of things are worth noticing. First of all the girl has given directions in a most circuitous way. Indeed, she could have misled you with the truth; for if you do what she says, you will find that she is right. The difficulty is to carry the details in your head. But it is worth it; for this outline is an example of how she sees the lay-out of the streets. It is also an example of the way personalities are seen and used. You say Lawyer Reindorph in the way you might say Post Office; for she knows Lawyer Reindorph's house is a house where strangers to Kumasi are always welcome. The garage is important because it is where the taxis feed. And the cinema is a kind of fundamental magic.

The African's reaction to films—I'm not speaking of the African intellectual—is an interesting example of the complete suspension of doubt. He reacts as a poet would like a reader to react to the illusion which the image at first creates. The echoes of the film remain.

Opposite Hotel de Kingsway where the taxis wait for hire, you will hear the young men speaking about the films they saw last night. They do not discuss it—for discussion is a kind of dismissal of the thing you are discussing—they dramatise the contents of their memory. They will go through, stage by stage, the development of the story, assuming the gestures and intentions of the actors. The boys will imitate the action of the horse, meaning the cowboy's horse. They will show how the great saviour man came riding into town; what happened when the 'bad men' noticed this stranger, never seen before.

The Western is completely re-lived; and since authenticity is demanded, more than one must be involved. The man who relates the film may ask another to stand opposite, and put his hand on his hip as though he were about to draw his pistol. So we have the Stranger-Man—who is dramatising—and the 'Bad Man' who didn't see the film, but who gets an even better version of the problem. What happens next?

You need a sheriff, a bar, some horses. Above all, you need a girl. In the Western, this girl turns out to be the fruit and reward of the Stranger-Man's virtue. But the African knows that she is really what the shooting is going to be about. So he continues his impersonation, pointing to a lady who is sitting, proud as the sky and equally alone, in the Hotel de Kingsway veranda some fifty feet above his head. If she happens to be a European—European in Africa simply means white without distinction of geography or nationality: Canadian, German, Frenchman and Irishman are all called European—there, sipping a whisky and ginger is the Sacred White Cow, waiting and wondering whether and how she will be ridden.

Stranger-Man continues this Western drama. Hotel de Kingsway is the bar. Barclays Bank right opposite is the Colorado money-house which the 'bad men' want to visit when everybody is asleep. The taxis parked for hire are a good substitute for horses; all the more convincing since they drive away from time to time with their drunken or exhausted cargo. This is pure theatre taking place under the sky, watched by the punishing eye of the sun. It's an example of the African's capacity to entertain himself; for neither 'Bad Man' nor Stranger-Man will be in the least interested in who are watching them, or whether they are being watched at all.

They are not acting. They are living out a memory of last night's magnificent triumph of the Stranger-Man riding his big horse into town, restoring law and order, and finally—which was the original intention—conquering his Sacred Cow who is the Sheriff's virgin Miranda.

It is happening at ten o'clock in the morning, and we shouldn't ask whether these boys ever go to work. Such an enquiry is as heretical and foolish as questioning the magic which made *The Tempest*. The point is they are there, living a moment by restoring the contents of memory back to a reality. And something very unfortunate is going to happen very soon, as I will show.

'What happen next?' asks the Boy in the role of Mr Bad Man.

'Step back, take a next step back,' says the Boy in the role of Mr Stranger-Man.

'Like so?' Mr Bad Man asks. He wants to be sure, since he didn't see the film.

'Proper correct you standing now,' says Mr Stranger-Man.

Mr Stranger-Man walks around the cars, selects the taxi which is going to be his ever so faithful horse, pats its backside, moves forward and leans on the bonnet which is a most reliable neck in spite of the absence of bridle and bit. So the action has begun.

Mr Stranger-Man is pretending that he is not paying attention to Mr Bad Man. He isn't here to make any trouble. In fact, he is here precisely because he wants to avoid trouble; for the last time trouble caught up with him in his home town, he killed a man. He is not at all sure whether he did it on purpose, or whether it's the accident the town refused to call self-defence. So he ran. And he wants to rest here, just rest peacefully.

He doesn't even want to look at the Sheriff's virgin Miranda; for he knows if he sees her, particularly if she walks out waving her magic wand, offering her gifts not for sale but for the love of Nature, Mr Stranger-Man knows there will be trouble; for he cannot resist the sputnik leap towards that beautiful and dangerous precipice of bust and bottom. He simply can't. Nature will not allow his desire to go on strike. It is Mr Stranger-Man's guilty task to conquer his vices. And the swiftest and easiest way is often to commit them. That's why he will 'get' the Sheriff's virgin Miranda. And having got her, he will 'take' her away. They have to set up a new little place all on their own; for the simple reason that no man wants to repeat his mistakes in the same place and in the same circumstances. For in spite of the four children—two big boys and two beautiful girls— Miranda will remain a virgin. And virginity, like Caliban's original nature, is an awful restriction. The existence within demands to get out.

That Sacred White Cow who now sits on the leisurely veranda of Hotel de Kingsway is not so sacred or so white, meaning pure. Above all, she is certainly no cow. And when her waiting is over, her capture accomplished by her own strategy of resistance and surren- der—when the whole marriage of love and fulfilment has been sanctioned by that legitimate increase in the country's population— when stability is a fact, Miranda, the mother, will become Caliban, the demand. And neither horse nor pistol will help Mr Stranger-Man.

For Miranda's tongue is swifter than any hoof; and her knowledge, the knowledge in her way of seeing, is more fatal than the flight of bullets.

What is it she demands? What is it the Stranger-Man cannot give? She does not know; but in order to give her demand some substance she has to baptise it with a name which has no visible correlative in nature. She calls it fulfilment. And all her life becomes a heart-breaking search for this monster.

Mr Bad Man is waiting; for he notices that Stranger-Man is idle. He notices that Stranger-Man says nothing, does nothing, appears, in fact, to be nothing. Stranger-Man treats him as though he is not there. And that can't be true; for it is Stranger-Man who put him there. It was Stranger-Man's arrival which pulled him up sharp, confronted him with a fact no one can deny: he was always there.

What is Stranger-Man thinking? Is it about the Sacred White Cow above their heads? Is it about the bank next door? For farming can be an expensive pleasure? What is it? The best way to find out is to ask. Mr Bad Man decides to ask; and here he has entered his role with complete accuracy.

He wasn't at the cinema last night, and it is not just a question of remembering similar situations. His decision is the logical outcome of Stranger-Man's presence. So he moves towards Stranger-Man who notices, but does not stir. He moves closer, yet Stranger-Man doesn't stir. Mr Bad Man stops, raises his hands from his hips; folds them across his chest, a gesture both of strength and peace. He watches Stranger-Man as though he were a tree, or an extension of the horse. Less than a horse, for at least the horse has given signs of strain. Nervousness made it neigh a few minutes ago. But Stranger-Man didn't seem to hear.

Silence is no good. Mr Bad Man decides to speak; but speech requires protection, so he returns his hands to his hips. He moves near. He is now breath reach from Stranger-Man. And it is at this point that Stranger-Man is alive to the possibilities of degradation. It is really his body which orders action. For the body is extremely sensitive to any form of invasion. It can tell the difference between a blow on the head—painful but an accident—and a slight elbowing of the ribs, painless, barely felt, but a warning tangible and remembered as a signal for danger.

If Mr Bad Man had sneezed, and the mucus sprayed over Stranger-Man's face, no harm would have been done. But it is the peculiar assault of that breath; a challenge, a mockery of Stranger-Man's dignity which is human dignity. For Stranger-Man believes that since he is strange to this town, he is therefore like everybody who doesn't live here. It is the absence of another, in our moments of specific victimisation, which is our guarantee that there is a right and a wrong. Justice must be done, and the best way not to betray it is to begin with a correction of this concrete example of injustice. So Stranger-Man has spoken for the first time.

'No, thank you,' he says.

It's his reply given once and for all to Mr Bad Man's thrice offered generosity: 'Have a drink?'

The answer is: 'No.' And Stranger-Man's silence makes that certain. Mr Bad Man turns to go; he takes a step away as Stranger-Man seems to distract his glance. Suddenly Mr Bad Man turns round and startles Stranger-Man by this gratuitous return. Stranger-Man can't tell whether he means to shoot or not, but life hangs on a second's mistake. Doubt is the first stage of defeat. Intentions can only be revealed by action. And one cannot wait for the future of an action. You are its future, whatever the state of your body. And that's what happened now.

Face set towards face, alert and eager, Mr Bad Man's shoulder seemed to climb towards his chin. Perhaps a drop of whisky had fallen on his mouth from the careless glass of the Sacred White Cow. Mr Bad Man was only trying to console the itch of skin, but how is Stranger-Man to know the details of that movement of shoulder? That movement was an action which gave an order to Stranger-Man; and in that moment, less than a moment, order and action were identified, and contained in a single act. In self-defence! This act is always honoured and forgiven by the term self-defence. In pure self-defence Stranger-Man drew his pistols. The result is a part of average knowledge.

But there are two different kinds of result, two different kinds of future to this drama; for the film is an arrangement which begins with a bribe. We are cheated of life, since we know that there is no event in spite of all the incidents which we follow. We watch the cowboys, we hear the horses' hooves, we thrill to the music of the vagrant guitar stringed with whisky and smoke in a hole populated by tarts. We observe the efficiency of the rifles; the bullets and the cannibal wail of the Red Indians tear up the roots of our ears with a sound of terror. The cowboy has 'got' his girl; and their first kiss is like the clap of volcanoes. Love has won its way through death; for many, many enemies and Indians have been shot. We thrill to the killing because it is safe to do so. It is clear to us that all but a few have been killed; and yet no one has died.

There will be a wedding and the corpses will come. Whatever our doubts, we dare not question that Love; for it would be a blasphemy against life, against the magic which served Prospero in turning the sea upside down; it would be a denial of the fact of mystery: the mystery which ruled Shakespeare, ordering him to function at the highest possible level of intensity as well as concreteness of observation. We cannot deny these things; hence the reality of the film which is an illusion. Soon is it night. The cinema is closed. Nothing can happen until tomorrow, nothing except a drink, some sex, or another night's lesson in how to occupy the bed that is no wider than an ordinary grave.

But the Boys under the Hotel de Kingsway have resurrected last night's film; they have returned it to this moment which is the actual stage for their drama. They were not discussing it, which is perfectly safe. These Boys were not imitating those heroes in celluloid. They were not pretending to be like the Stranger-Man and the Bad Man. They had become such men. This moment was alive and therefore different from the film itself. And this is what happened to make it so different.

When Stranger-Man noticed that Bad Man was getting near; that Bad Man was probably going to shoot, he heard his order for defence, and he acted upon that order. But neither Stranger-Man nor Bad Man, aroused to a shooting war outside Hotel de Kingsway, could predict the future. Outside the peaceful and noisy reach of Hotel de Kingsway, these cowboys are summoned to a shooting war; but neither has a gun. The situation made no allowance for it; but the drama had to go on. And if a taxi can be a horse, then a pistol can be a fist. That was the difference in the two futures. Nobody got hurt in the Western; but Stranger-Man broke Bad Man's nose; made a bloody mess of his own shirt; and for the first time they found themselves surrounded by an audience. The police had arrived.

And they did their duty. But how could the Law recapture the truth of each moment which those Boys had lived, once from memory and later as a fact? When the easy-going magistrate asks what happened, they are dumb. He interprets their silence as stupidity which is an example of his own blindness. For it is not stupidity. That silence is evidence of those Boys' speechlessness in their whole predicament. They don't know where to begin the explanation. The easiest way out is to say guilty, and hope that the magistrate's liver is not in bad order. Heaven and Prospero's magic will have to be on their side this morning; for the Law is exceedingly literate; but it cannot see. It has no sight.

A mother will weep; a cousin will take some fufu, kenke and

salted nuts to the cell; but society will not notice their absence from this corner.

Vagrant, free and defenceless as the birds, they are learning to travel from moment to moment, from accident to accident. Their desires may grow lawless as the celluloid gangsters they dramatise; for their energy is great, but their hands are idle.

NIGERIA

Each place acquires its own priorities in your memory; so Nigeria remains so far my first experience of travelling great tracks of country by road. Distance had become purely a matter of time: another hour has passed; it was five hours when we last paused; it will be two days before we arrive. One felt the double sense of time when one reflected that men had travelled the distance from Lagos to London, on to Peking and back three or four times before my friend and I would arrive at Zaria.

I was determined to drive all the way. From Kumasi to Accra had become a simple interval between Budweiser beer and White Horse whisky. The road from Accra to Lome was in repair; and after Lome it was always a question of guessing what would happen from here to the next village. Would they have finished that road since Abdul last saw it? Would they have ripped up a new one during his holiday in Ghana? Would the next be finished as his engineering friend had promised on his way to Accra? We had to wait and see; and as we approached the threat of Harmattan, we had to make our peace with waiting; for it was often difficult to see.

From night we passed into dust which flew like rain on to the windscreen. I read the map, looking for a landmark whenever a new village occurred; then tried to memorise the order of the names: From Kumasi to Accra; from Accra to Lome; through Dahomey and on to Lagos. We will stop at Lagos; next move may be Ibadan; and then, said Abdul, we shall just have begun. From Ibadan to Bida, Oyo and Illorin. We will sleep at Illorin where Abdul's sister lives. And then, says Abdul, we shall just have begun. From dawn at Ilorin into dust at daybreak, and afterwards we get thirsty and decide to stop at Tegina. All afternoon with Harmattan and then a hospital reminded me that I had friends at Kaduna. So we would pause at Kaduna. It would soon be night, and Abdul, responsible as his surgeon hands, reminded everyone that the dark was bad for driving, and we still had a little way before we finally parked at Zaria. So now we were at the promised Zaria.

The household was waiting for their resident surgeon who had been gone for a month. While they cleared the car, we walked into the house, on to a terrace with a view of the hospital. Abdul said 'Well, what next? Tomorrow I can get someone to take you to Kano.' I had forgotten tomorrow's name, so I said with some reluctance: 'Not tomorrow. Next day perhaps, but not tomorrow.' But I knew, in some way, that it couldn't be Kano next day. I am reluctant to write, and since I didn't want to lose the landmarks my memory had made, I decided that next day would be set aside for a brief summary of the landscape. It's these notes which return, more vividly than the phrases, my image of each place.

### Lagos

Border. Vegetation. Outskirts. Poor drainage. Dirt, dead water, flies and confusion. Always and everywhere noise and children. A monster of a house leaps up beside the derelict compound. Freedom can mean cleaning places up. Across the lagoon and into the 'residential' area, largely expatriate. English suburban with a mixture of the new Nigerian professional classes. At the Lido night club Nigerian young women have surrendered cloth and taken to skirts that fit the trade. At the bar a small regiment of English P.W.D. men waiting. In front of the Nigerian House of Representatives there is a new and very tall statue of the Queen. She must certainly disapprove of her countrymen's habits in foreign places.

### Tuesday, January 20th.

Near disaster between Ibadan and Illorin. A. driving, cautious as usual. Taking about the proportion of doctors to the population in the north. Four hundred to seventeen million, to be precise. A few hundred yards away we saw a man walking dead centre of the road. A. pressed the horn, it seemed rather soon. Caution, I thought. A. hooted again, louder and longer; and now we were too near to stop without crushing the man. The car swerved inches from a precipice. Speechless we stopped and watched each other. The man was still walking dead centre of the road. It was difficult to tell how old he was; but he was blind; and since he never seemed to hear, I assumed he must also have been deaf. There wasn't another village in sight for miles.

### Tegina

Can't believe it. Never seen a policeman take such liberties before. Uniform in order. Cap, stripes, the lot. Thick brown putties like bandages strapped tight from knees to ankles. But no boots? I asked Abdul where he had left his boots. 'Not unusual,' said A. Perfectly civilised, meaning sensible. The lack of boots makes for greater speed if the prisoner escapes. Would be a serious disadvantage those boots, since the prisoner wears none. Agreed!

## Kaduna

Returning via the East. Train leaves at six thirty. Will reach Enugu at seven thirty the next night. A. will telephone S. What a tedious journey. Scene at station unforgettable. The leper. The crippled woman with child on her back. Like the visit to pagan village last week where woman with growth the size of a melon hung from her waist, dragging her forward. In the course of my visit to north, kept hearing the professional complaint: 'You can't get them to come for treatment.' Therefore, I conclude, a way must be found of getting to them; for it is criminal to wait until they decide.

\* \* \* \*

I had left Kaduna at six thirty that evening and I reached my destination shortly after seven the following night. I knew no one here; but my host in Zaria had telephoned a friend of his and asked that he help. I came to learn in West Africa—Ghana is no different—that his help means: Please find room and some food for my friend. This is the quality of spontaneity which got poor Caliban into such trouble. For S. had not only got the message from Zaria. He was actually at the railway station an hour before the train arrived. For once unpunctuality was not my fault. The old train was late.

Who was this S.? Why did he put himself out to find me, host me, tell me about the country, its politics, its personalities who are inseparable from its politics? Was it because he was married to a West Indian girl? Partly. But it is my conviction that he would have done the same if he were married to an African woman. He was simply concerned about the future of the African continent, and in particular Nigeria. He had a stake, I mean a moral stake, in the future of colonial territories. The West Indies was his concern, and Nigeria was mine. Hence the spontaneity.

Moreover, he was an expert in his field. He was not exposed to the demands of a degraded silence, or a necessary camouflage in the interest of maintaining his position. He knew his job; for everyone accepted that he was one of the most brilliant of his profession in the whole country. This is really the first thing which has to be got right. When a colonial knows his job; when he knows his relation to what he is doing, and the validity of that work for the community in which he lives, he is spared a great deal of shame and humiliation. He may

be punished in one way or another, but what he *is*, in the specific
context of his work, cannot really be undermined.

A Minister of the same region was giving a party that night, and S.
offered to take me along. I was eager to go, for one interesting thing
about such a party is that you can see people whose judgments are
public property. They give orders which you have to obey. They
make speeches on the radio. Now you can say: There is the man
whom you heard last night. He was saying so and so. You wished
then that you could see him, for it would have been interesting to
watch how his face was behaving when his tongue was carrying him
away. Did he have a moustache? Did he keep pulling at it in order
to occupy his hands? Did he scratch the back of his neck every
seventeen seconds. Contemplate the shape of his thumb as he pretended that the audience was really absent?

These considerations did not apply to anyone at that party, but I
offer them as a way of showing the value of such parties. The human
presence has its own laws of vibration, and vibrations communicate.
Sometimes you can feel the meaning of that girl's refusal to speak.
She is afraid she will reveal her curiosity; she does not want to betray
the precise order of her passions. At least not here, at least not now.
To let him see is to be regarded as *easy*. What is worth having is
worth postponing. It is better, in the circumstances, to summon the
assistance of hay fever, achieve the face of an exhausted beauty, and
ask your sister's husband to drop you home. There is a diplomacy in
the arrangements for Love and its future.

But the Nigerian Minister's under-secretary, who is an Englishman, can't go home whether he wants to or not. He can't summon
hay fever or any other kind of fever; for it is his business to stay. He
needs to see what's going on, and he hopes to hear if there is something in the offing which has been kept hidden from his scrutiny.
There are certain questions he cannot ask his Minister in office;
and since they are not friends—neither he nor the Minister is in any
doubt about that—he dare not take certain liberties. His behaviour
is in the nature of an organised intimacy, a strategic servility. For
that man has been working in that country for nearly twenty years.
He never dreamt that this night would come about; that these roles
would be so completely reversed; that Prospero, while retaining his
magic, would enter a castle with a new complexion.

Decades of absolute authority over servants—of whom the Minister's father was one—made it absolutely impossible for him to
conceive of himself as an African's subordinate. For that is precisely
what he was. A civil servant whose boss was the Minister now hosting
the topbrass of the new régime. This Englishman has come alive to

a most terrifying awareness of his predicament. A principle of camouflage has frozen up his moral imagination; and now he finds himself colonised by the very system upon which his era of privilege has given the appearance of an absolute. In this situation, my sympathy is with this man. For the first time in his life, perhaps, he has been confronted by the meaning and possibility of his existence as man in a particular situation at a particular historic time. If his bosses in England have foxed him, it is too late for him to fool himself. The game is up. There is a new master, and there will have to be new men. Can he become a new man? Or will he become a different kind of lackey?

Remember: he has children who may be at an expensive boarding school in England; and there is simply no other country in the world—including England—where he can find an income that will keep those children there. They are being trained to sit on his throne without the slightest warning that Daddy has lost his crown. They are telling their friends at school about a daddy who simply does not exist; and if Daddy is not to lose the power and influence which Prospero held over Miranda, then Daddy has got to postpone telling them the truth.

His children have actually started their education, I mean their education in human relations—with a lie. Who is to tell those children the truth? Are we content to watch them crawl through the degrading legacy of a lie that doesn't even work any longer. How are they going to deal with the Nigerian Minister's grandson? Hasn't it occurred to the Labour Party that they have come near to betraying a whole generation of children in England? I am not concerned with the speculations that suggest why Labour lost the last election. I would like to understand the psychology which allowed them to treat the schools as institutions where nothing of great urgency is happening.

It is a matter of no importance what legislation they passed in 1945 about education. The fact remains that they made no attempt to confront the task of protecting a whole generation of children from the Lie that the English Daddy in Nigeria must go on telling his children back home. I mention all this in connection with a remark of Mr Kingsley Martin at a Fabian dinner. Addressing his compatriots he said that things had got too easy in England. They had solved their problems, but it was their duty to widen their horizons. They must think of Africa; for Africa was 'our' proletariat.

This is a fallacy. The problem for England is bigger than it has ever been. It is the problem of that English father's return; for he may not be a big enough man, a new enough man, to live with the transformation which his situation demands. Can he change over from master—not to slave—but rather to an ordinary citizen who serves a community by his gifts of experience and skill? Can he do it against the background of his accumulated experience as a master? For it is the only condition on which he can remain in that country. Africans are not anti-English or anti-European. They ask simply that Prospero must be transformed, rejuvenated, and ultimately restored to his original condition of a man among men.

I have great sympathy and respect for the English Nonconformist conscience. Men like Kingsley Martin and the dead though very much alive Noel Brailsford, and Fenner Brockway and Basil Davidson have done great service, not only to Africa, but to their own country by their particular concern for Africa. Davidson is an example of an Englishman who approaches African problems, not merely in the service of Africa—which is inevitable anyway—but also as a starting ground for examining his own premises as a man, for exploring the basis of his conscience as a Left Wing intellectual. Africans are bound to benefit from this kind of self-examination. But we must not confuse the perspectives by a false notion of universality.

The Africans are no foreign country's proletariat. In certain parts of that continent, the Africans are still the Queen's colonials; and if the reports which invade us from the popular press—even the popular and hostile press—are correct, then it seems that the Africans have decided to speak to the Queen about these matters. Her Majesty's servants, meaning any British Cabinet, must not do anything to frustrate or pollute the true meaning of that dialogue which the Queen will understand when her colonials are allowed to speak. Queens understand peasants; for both, in their different ways, are aristocrats.

Let us transfer this to the actual situation from which it was drawn: the circumstances of the party in Nigeria. Consider the position of the Nigerian Minister. The political revolution, with its consequent revolution in sensibility, has been so swift that the Minister hasn't had any time to put distance between himself and the people whose vote gave him his office. He can't play at being Prospero for the simple reason that he was Caliban only yesterday; and there are a few hundred thousand Calibans waiting to unfrock him if he gets into the wrong pulpit. His family, including a formidable regiment of cousins scattered throughout the length and breadth of the land, have not changed their habits, or their style of living. He may drink as much champagne as he likes with the Governor-General, or any visiting European diplomat; but when he returns to his village, or when his village comes to speak with him, he is right back where he started. They discuss their business over some fufu and a little palm wine, if you can find the tapster near-by.

Position has not really cut him off from that organic relation to his own way of life which is also the life of his people. One tremendous advantage for West Africa is the absence of a watch-dog middle class, the kind of middle class which have been used to kennel West Indian aspirations in every direction. The Minister's barber is likely to be the same as the watchman's. (Just imagine Mr Macmillan having his whiskers clipped somewhere in the East End, and you'll see what I mean.)

At the party I noticed something which struck me as very healthy. One was not aware of any group being in a minority. It was not the kind of atmosphere which would suggest counting heads. Not at all. The whole thing seemed right. Even the English wives were there. I say 'even,' because it is the English colonial wife who makes the most trouble in this kind of situation. The English wife resents her loss of status. It is the Minister's wife who is the first lady in the kingdom of cocktails and potato crisps. It is a fascinating situation; for the African wife enters this new role as though nothing had changed. She is pleased to welcome Mrs So-and-So. That is not a diplomatic welcome, although it is a diplomatic occasion. To that African wife, welcome has always meant welcome, and if Mrs So-and-So had visited her ten years ago, the architectural circumstances would have been different, but the welcome would have been the same.

What happens to the English wife? Her dilemma takes the form of extreme behaviour. In the corner with another English wife, she is secretive, contemplative, caught, but determined to endure. In the next corner with the Minister's wife, she is gracious as any wife might be to the wife of her husband's boss. One new element in this situation is that this wife is not likely to ask any favours of the Minister's wife; favours, I mean, on her husband's behalf. For the first time the English wife risks genuine human contact.

The Minister's wife is no intellectual. She knows that something is going on in her native land, but she hasn't investigated it through books and the current literature dealing with colonial problems. In a sense she doesn't need to. For she is the thing itself, the very history which the English wife must cope with. What then do they talk about? What is the safest subject? What is the one subject about which any two mothers are deeply and genuinely interested? They talk about their children. It is the children, the instinctive experience of being mother, which will now bridge that enormous and unspeakable distance between one woman and another.

The English wife is at a serious disadvantage. She notices that the

Minister's wife, in spite of her status, talks like a woman who has nothing to hide. For what is there to hide? After all, the English wife doesn't know the details of African family life; but she knows the former circumstances of this African wife. The Minister and his wife lived in that compound not so long ago. The English wife's stupefaction does not in the least disturb the Minister's wife. She is, indeed, the lady. But how can the English wife speak of her children without censoring a thousand and one things?

'Will you send your boy to England?' the English wife asks.

The Minister's wife smiles. 'Yes, I would like it very much. That he goes to England for his studies.'

The English wife is delighted. All is not lost. Status or no status, *they*, meaning the Africans, will still need *our* thing. What is this thing? It is precisely that *language* with which Prospero tried to annihilate the concrete existence of Caliban. But the dichotomy expressed by *they* and *our thing*—is no more than a postponement. It's like getting blind drunk on your way home. You require an alcholic amnesia to cope with the charges which that vigilant wife is waiting to confront you with. But tomorrow, the liquor will have lost its rule; and the wife will make sure that you listen before you have time to summon your mask again. She assaults you with your situation at the very break of the dawn. 'If not now, when?' she insists. 'It will be now or never. If never, say so; since I may have other arrangements.'

For what happens to the English wife when her hostess asks: 'The children, will they come to see us this Christmas?' The answer is bound to be an evasion or a lie. Why? Then re-read the foregoing sentence, and notice whom the English children are coming to see. Not Nigeria in general, not this region in particular, but *us*. And that *us* includes the English wife and her husband.

It is extremely risky for everyone if the English children visit *them*. For children are traitors by instinct; or so they seem to their parents. Their treachery is directed against all forms of concealment; and their questions lead swiftly and brutally to all sorts of sinister cupboards.

It is the English wife who is in crisis. She has shared her husband's camouflage from start to finish. She treated it like Christmas, wholly forgetful that Santa Claus is no one's husband.

I studied this drama until the rain decided to wash the lawn away. It was time to return to my friend's house. Perhaps he would tell me how he felt about all this. How did his wife, whose orientation was mine, really see this? What would be the likely future of the Minister and his wife, meaning all wives and Ministers in their situation? We went home and we talked far into the night.

A common acceptance of noise makes life a straight-forward and enlightening experience for a West Indian and a West African who share similar concerns about the future of Prospero in the light of Caliban's resurrection. For the world in which we live is no longer Prospero's, and it will never be again. The party went on. We could hear it while we talked, only a laugh's throw away. The English were the loudest. How strange that this should be so. They were drinking and singing far into the night. And I wondered about the nature of that enjoyment. It is not unlike 'the false laugh which the West Indian summons as he watches the film brutalisation of the African's personality in the role of a mooncow.' It would require a different kind of book to say how I see this approval of mockery in the West Indian's grin; it would require a different kind of drama—a work of serious fiction—to show the meaning of that English voice laughing its enjoyment throughout the night. It is sufficient to say that their laugh—both English and West Indian—at once expresses and conceals a fact which they are terrified of bringing into the light.

\* \* \* \*

On the following morning I travelled with my friends to see another part of Nigeria. The West Indian wife is a lawyer, and I have a great interest in the theatre of the courtroom. She is a most striking presence, not unfamiliar to anyone who has lived in Trinidad. Olive-soft complexion, smooth with the mixture of more than one race at work in her features. But the result was an accomplished fact, a thing in itself. It was a West Indian face. She was unusual for a West Indian woman of her generation. She was determined to take her place, the place of any other Nigerian wife, in her husband's community. Its language of custom and habit was new to her; but it was what she had chosen, and she seemed determined to live by the laws of her choice. She was unusual for a Trinidadian, because she seemed to me like a Barbadian. That is, she struck me as being a little more 'civilised' than the average Trinidadian woman. She was more aware of the world she lived in for one thing. She seemed more discreet and selective in her choice of conversation. It was her general stance, the feminine softness of manner, the completeness of line and bone which made up the landscape of her face: it was this harmony which made me react with surprise when she arranged the wig on her head, and started to cross-examine the witness. And here was the problem of language with a new dimension.

The Counsel for the Crown was a West Indian, the Judge was an Irishman, the accused was a Nigerian who spoke no other language but Ibo. Neither the Irishman nor the West Indian had a working knowledge of Ibo. The future of the accused, the particular kind of house he would have to reside in for the next five, ten, maybe fifteen years—for the charge was a grave one—the future of this man's sentence depended on the accuracy of a translation.

The young clerk who enlightened us about the English meanings was always trying to restrain his laughter, for the accused seemed to be a man of great wit when Ibo was his weapon. But subtlety is not easily passed from one language to another. I shall give an example. During his long cross-examination of the constable, the accused asked a question which aroused a temporary merriment among all the Ibos in court. Were there no Judge, were they in the open air, I felt that the court would have turned to carnival. Therefore, I was curious to hear the clerk's translation. It was simply this:

Clerk (addressing the constable): He wants to know if you ever see or set eyes on him ever before the time of the arrest?

Constable (glancing to West Indian Counsel): No!

Clerk (relaying constable's reply to accused and waits for further difficulties): He wants to know if it was the first time you ever sign the same kind of paper you say you see him sign?

Constable (after a long pause): No!

The atmosphere was rich with suggestion, under-statement, and actual implication. The point is: delivered in Ibo, the question was informing the constable, 'I dare you to say, No.' The constable's reply was also 'No,' which meant that 'Yes had been betrayed.' On whose side was the truth?

I can't say. For the key witness was still missing (and would probably not be found). Moreover, I had to leave that afternoon for Benin where a German would be waiting for me. Our destination was another hundred miles away where they were having an extra-mural conference. But communications are a nightmare, and there is no point using the magic of civil aviation. When time is short and you are greedy to see the whole landscape of face and place, it is an exhausting experience. I had to arrive to meet the German on Tuesday, so that I could leave in time to connect with my friend Alex who had come all the way to Benin.

From Benin, which was simply a station in transit, Alex and I were going south to Sapele, which is Alex's home-town, one hundred miles away from Benin. Why was Alex taking me there? He wanted me to meet his mother who is one of his father's senior wives in a collection of eight. He wanted me to see how a polygamous family lived: who were his brothers and what they did. Who were his cousins and how they thought! He wanted me to see this in spite of—

I use 'in spite of' for the benefit of West Indians—he wanted me to see his world, the world of his childhood, in spite of the other world that could make some claim to his achievements. For Alex went to Dulwich at the age of fourteen and then to Oxford. He is now a medical research Fellow at University College, Ibadan, where the mysteries of the blood are his business. He doesn't doctor for money. He goes all over the place 'collecting blood' which he studies as though he were Columbus in search of gold.

When last I heard from him, he was back at New College, writing down the results of what he had found. He will compare that with what Oxford taught him. He will work along with his colleagues at Oxford who are equipped to follow what he is saying, and who may not know the concrete circumstances of children's lives in Nigeria; for Alex works, almost exclusively, on the blood of the children. He is waging a war against that enemy which cuts down the lives of Nigerian children like leaves between the ages of six months and two years.

Oxford helps, and he in turn helps Oxford. Who can say what will be the result? We don't know, but the project is sound. The science which teaches Alex to analyse the blood, write theses about it, and pass on the result to the Nigerian and Oxford doctors in the Nigerian bush: that science does not belong to Oxford any more than it belongs to Alex. It is an example and an enterprise in human effort on behalf of human beings.

But notice the change in sensibility between one generation and another. Alex's father had long talks with me about his son's future. The old man was wise when he chose to give his son this kind of education. But now he is worried. He sees all sorts of little people spring up in politics and private practice; and he wonders why his son should earn so much less than these men who never experience a week's difficulties from their native village. It seems a strange providence which allows such things to happen. But the old man is a case of age acting with wisdom at one time, and innocent of arrangements at another. Wisdom remains on the old man's side; youth and a more varied experience are the son's new advantages. Yet their enterprise is the same although the father's traditional way of life has given way to the son's adventure. The adventure is safe if Nigeria can learn one basic fact; learn it, apply it, turn it into Gospel for the schools. Let the first commandment announce that there is absolutely no connection between value and price. Alex can sell his services at any price; but no man can buy the meaning of the old Chief's decision.

\* \* \* \*

AMERICA

I don't know what regulations ships follow in arranging friendships among their passengers, but my journey from Southampton to New York was an interval of restful paradox. I was travelling tourist class on the *Queen Mary*. It was the end of summer, and the passengers were largely exiles who were returning home; Scots, English girls and a few Irish. I don't remember now who was my cabin mate, but my meal-time neighbours are unforgettable. There were about seven or eight women between the ages of fifty-nine and sixty-three, a prosperous Venezuelan business man in his late sixties, and myself.

I was seated at one end of the table and opposite the Venezuelan. This was a happy coincidence, for my first real job was teaching English to Venezuelan boarding students in Trinidad. The Venezuelan and I talked a great deal about his country and his holiday. He was returning from Barcelona which he swore he would never visit again. Six months of leisure had filled him with nausea for the attractions of modern Spain. If that is what all those places are like, he kept saying, then I had better stay in Caracas, try Buenos Aires; but Spain never again.

It struck me that the reflections of the women were not unlike this man's. They were comparing experiences of their native towns and villages in England and Scotland; and they always spoke with great nostalgia for their childhood. These were wonderful days; but one experience always seemed to spoil the wonder of the past. This was the experience of meeting their old friends: people whom they had known at school and who had remained in work, marriage and retirement where they were born.

This return to the past, now measured by their different orientation in a new country, a new civilisation, created a certain duality in their desires. Somehow they would have liked to remain with their root; and yet they would not have changed their new life for anything in the world. They were Americans by adoption, and they had raised families which were American by birth. Their children would have found the towns and villages of the Old World very tiresome. But these mothers had a greater variety of experience than the children, and so they were caught somewhere between loyalty to the Old and gratitude for the New. As a result, they would speak of England and the Old World in very much the same way a child might speak of an ageing grandmother who was turning dotish. There was no loss of affection; but it was sad and a pity that granny was not the woman she used to be. They couldn't argue with the young about it, because it was one of those facts of experience removed from any logical discourse.

It took a few days before talk circulated with ease.

Young people can afford to be garrulous about anything; for there is plenty of time to redeem their folly. But it seems that elderly people are very careful among themselves not to let down the virtues which age has gratuitously promised them. But something of a revolt occurred one morning.

My Venezuelan friend had shown a great passion for a certain type of sausage. It was a fat sausage which, as far as I remember, was always served for breakfast. He had arrived late this morning, and when the waiter came up, no less solicitous than before, the Venezuelan noticed that his sausage was different. It was a thin sausage. He said he wanted the other kind of sausage, and he pointed to my plate to make sure that the waiter had understood.

The waiter said that the fat sausages were all finished. The Venezuelan thought he was lying, for there were still two days before we arrived, and it wasn't likely or even appropriate for the *Queen Mary* to run short of anything it had introduced its passengers to. The waiter was adamant, which spoke well for his dignity. But the Venezuelan grew furious at the thought that this waiter might have taken him for a sucker. Perhaps he thought that the difference of language was a source of discrimination. He rose from the table, waving a huge white napkin as he summoned the waiter's superior.

The purser came and made enquiries. He was servile as a slave who feared that his master might make some trouble. To be at sea is to be trapped. Surveying all the plates on the table, the Venezuelan stated his case with his fingers. The whole dining hall was now involved, some wondering what was wrong, others waiting to see how wrong it would be. The waiter went on with his work. The purser begged his guest to sit while he checked with the kitchen staff.

Some minutes later, a different waiter arrived with a different sausage. It was a medium-sized sausage. The Venezuelan had partly won, but I don't know if he realised how distressed the women were. They thought it so undignified that a travelling gentleman should want to wage war at sea on an issue so common as a tube stuffed with minced pig meat. Now he was not only *watched*; he had proved that he was a man *to be watched*. The discovery of fatter sausages must have convinced him that if you pay your money for service, you were entitled to be served as you demanded.

He'd decided, therefore, to participate fully in the privileges of his spending. Two evenings before we arrived, the purser had collected all willing tourist class passengers for a game of Bingo. We had all forgotten the Venezuelan until we heard his voice announcing the first victory. Hardly three minutes had passed when the triumphant voice howled: Bingo! The purser looked regretful; but when they checked with the Venezuelan, they discovered that he had called too soon. The Venezuelan seemed a little bewildered that he could have been wrong; but he showed no sign of trepidation.

As though recalling the sausage encounter, it occurred to the purser that there should be punishment for this kind of error. The passengers were all agreed; but the Venezuelan was saved since it was decided that the punishment would not be applied this time. It seemed fair that a warning should be given. The English can be extraordinarily expert at deciding the moment to be fair. And now the purser was fair.

Bingo started again. Now and again someone showed signs of victory, but was in doubt about speaking too soon. An atmosphere of excessive caution had been imposed by one error. And so it proceeded until a voice, very cautious and very firm, said: BINGO. It was the Venezuelan. And I regret to say that he was wrong again.

The crew demanded punishment. Every man thought and ordered that the rules must be obeyed. Justice had to be done. The Venezuelan looked as though he too were on the side of Justice. The method of punishment was announced. The passengers were unanimous about the purser's choice. It is worth studying why certain requests should be seen as punishment. The Venezuelan had been ordered to sing. They all wanted to enjoy his failure. With infinite patience and dignity, he rose from his chair. He surveyed the faces. He confided in his handkerchief, walked calmly towards the centre of the floor past the chairs that led to the door on the left. He was gone; and he never returned. I saw him for the last time in the Customs.

## 3

There is probably no country in the world which contributes more freely to exaggerated rumour about itself. I had been already warned that I should be careful about what I said. After all, I was colonial and a Negro, and any emphasis I made about the history and implications of this status could be given a convenient political interpretation. I never paid much attention to such warnings, for my colonial status in England, and the habitual superciliousness of the English towards anything American had always urged me towards passionate defence of the New World. Moreover, I had never been a

member of any political party at any time of my life, and I had come
to believe that this lack of communal allegiance would be sufficient
proof of my innocence.

It was not until I visited the American Consul in London that I
felt the need to watch my step. The Guggenheim Foundation had
supplied me with all the documents which would facilitate my getting
a visa. There was only the question of a physical examination which
no document could exempt me from. It took a week before I could
learn whether this machine of mine would satisfy the standards of
American health; for the examination was rigorous in its thorough-
ness.

They took tests of my blood, they examined my ears and my teeth,
the suppleness of my knees, and the reliability of my spine. I was
X-rayed. I had been thoroughly done. When the results came back,
I felt not only free from all illness, but absolutely above and beyond
any disease medical science could predict. My diet hadn't changed
much in the last four years; I had eaten and lived like any ordinary
West Indian emigrant in London; but the American O.K. had given
me a new and formidable power of physical well-being. When I was
told that my visa would be ready on the following day, I felt that I
was on my way to the moon. I walked along Oxford Street like a
boy fresh from his keep-fit class. I went into a pub, swallowed a pint
of bitter and smiled like a sailor just home from sea.

But I didn't realise that my confidence would be in danger on
the other side of the Atlantic. The delay in the Customs seemed so
unnecessary; for I had never even been to court as a witness. My
record was clean; and in my innocence I thought the name Guggenheim was a large enough shield from this excessive cross-examination.
When this American asked me where I was going to live, I said quite
honestly that I didn't know. But I had been given various addresses.
I gave the address of my American publishers whose name had the
same weight as Guggenheim. Then the Customs asked with perfect
but irrelevant logic, whether I was going to live there. I started to
feel that he didn't believe what I had said about the publishers and
the Guggenheim Foundation. Yet he had all the papers in front of
him. The signatures corresponded to the name in my passport; and
suddenly I had the acute feeling that he must have thought I had
forged all these papers. I saw myself in a new light, a possible expert
in devious arrangements. This went on for some time, and when I
thought it was all over I was suddenly shocked by the size of my
importance. He had given me a document to read and consider
before making my reply. Innocent as grass, as remote from crime as
I was now from the cradle, I heard myself promising that it was not

and would never be my intention to overthrow the Government of the United States.

Citizenship had assumed new and terrifying responsibilities; and with this reminder I was set free to breathe the air which had often haunted my childhood. For America had always existed as a dream in my imagination, a place where everything was possible, a kingdom next door to the sky.

For a whole week I travelled through Manhattan like a boy scout on holiday. Literature seemed irrelevant beside the eloquence of those sky-scrapers. I had no time to think who or what civilisation had built them. It was the work of human hands, man's energy, a collective enterprise. I thought simply that some of them were too tall. Buildings made and inhabited by men shouldn't, for some reason, be so tall. Perhaps they symbolised a short cut to heaven. You could climb them, and they never seemed to end.

What was redeeming about this attitude was the speed with which Americans would pull them down, as though the imagination did not only supply short cuts, but could actually change the whole perspective of paradise. The wickedness of politics and prices I would discover later; but my attention had been captured by this relation to nature, this example of human power and energy which could transform simple stone into such formidable monuments. This architecture was not only new, it was an essential ingredient of a wholly New World; and since the Caribbean was only next door, this World was, in a sense, mine.

I would walk all evening, sometimes in rain, through the acrobatic illumination of Broadway. It emerged in a magnificent nightmare of flames; and it was here, at night, when the lights raced up and across these steep stone palaces that one saw the American face to advantage. There was a correct, obvious, and inevitable uniformity in all this variety of stone, face and sky. The rhythm of speech and movement was right. Everything was indigenous and yet without root; and this suggested the irrelevance and, on occasions, the rumoured harshness of the American manner in Europe. For there is a certain tribal resonance associated with the term 'American abroad,' and one felt that the American, in any place but America, was like a native song and dance removed from the context of its ritual and landscape. Its power and expansiveness will not permit anonymity. Its echoes, however innocent, are in the nature of an intrusion.

These American nights were pure magic: the repetition of small bars, the sound of jazz, near and endless as the kitchen odours which drifted from closed doors and open-air spit. Food seemed a part of the nation's Constitution. There was a rhythm of impermanence which seemed to impose a surface of energy on everything. It didn't seem to anyone that death was a fact; yet every face had negotiated some compromise with mortality. Everything was invention: food, relaxation, noise, crisis, silence. The city had taken every precaution against the possibility of solitude. Loneliness, like liquor, was a commodity.

I would walk until my back ached, often returning to the same street several times. An interval in the bars, and sometimes a brief sojourn in the cinema. Spontaneity was everywhere. Like the tide of lights overhead, each welcome contained a warning against taking risks. Some faces gave a clue that the owners had a row of teeth in reserve. Daggers might have been concealed, but the blunt exposure of the cop's pistol and club told that death could be a simple and legal event.

My hotel was ten minutes' walk from Radio City; and in the morning I could watch from the fifth floor window this unfamiliar triumph of energy over objects: the temporary conquest of nature for some convenient arrangement with living. Here at a glance, one saw how the landscape had been ordered by hands. There was no more servile performance than the march of those lights over Times Square at night. The air seemed to obey human orders. Comfort was an absolute justice. It was the American way of pushing nature around.

On my return to the hotel one night, I decided for the first time that I would listen to the radio. The box was real; the voice was human; but the method of announcing news seemed to me a most extraordinary departure from Old World neutrality. The B.B.C. became as remote as the Middle Ages, and no less secure. One had to learn how to take these items of news seriously. For example: the announcer, his voice brisk and full of comfort, invited attention with these words, 'And now this is XRX telling you what's happening in this crazy-mixed-up world of ours.' This would be the equivalent of the B.B.C. refrain: 'This is the B.B.C. Home Service.' At the end of every two or three items, the 'crazy-mixed-up refrain' filled the pause. And some equally strange things were being said.

On his way from receiving an honorary degree, Mr Eisenhower was reported to have said to some seven thousand assembled to greet him: 'Give me a chance and I'll be down there with the crowd waving to the sucker in my place.' There is something quite aristocratic in that risk of intimacy. And whether it was intended or not, a film advertisement soon followed. After some preamble about the names and diversions of the stars, our reasons for going to this cinema were quite firmly stated: 'You'll enjoy this film for it deals with a healthy subject: the assassination of a president.' A most unorthodox juxtaposition of events, I thought, and it occurred to me that the Customs man was not altogether at fault for punishing me with questions about overthrowing the American Government. Either it was too secure to meddle with strangers, or it was much too insecure to take any risks.

Every day was stranger, more fascinating, and more like the next. It was just over a week when I decided that it was now time to stop looking and pay attention. I had gone into a drugstore and asked: 'Do you sell stationery?' The waiter looked at me as though I had said dynamite.

I realised how ignorant foreigners can be!

It was white America who had invited me; it was white America who had received me. And it was white America who was going to support my stay. But I could have no illusions about my situation in the general context of American culture. If America was a dream in my imagination, then Harlem was the source of a most consuming curiosity. I wanted to see what was happening 'up there.'

R. is a Trinidadian who had been living in America for a long time. I had known her sister in London, and some letters of introduction brought R. and myself together. A week or so after my arrival, she wrote to say that she would be moving back to town, and could we arrange a meeting. She knew the upper crust of Harlem, and it was from this summit that I was invited to view the dark mysteries of that world. For Harlem is a world which is part of and other than America. Harlem is simply Harlem, a stupendous wonder in the heart of a city which is, in itself, a fascinating nightmare. She came to the hotel a few days later. This hotel was white, not by legislation, but by actual practice. Unlike the English, the Americans are very frank about the facts of race. For I had telephoned the evening I arrived; and I knew that between the interval of my telephoning my American publishers and my meeting with one of the editors, a list of hotels had already been drawn up, the most appropriate—noting my profession, my visiting status and my colour—and Scott had given me a letter when I was leaving the publisher's office. When I passed the letter to the receptionist, she passed it to a man who read it and he pointed to a slot where the actual room key was waiting. No questions, not even questions of signature were raised until my luggage was delivered, and I came back down to enquire about a meal.

It was the first time I was meeting R.; so I realised why those white heads, both male and female, had turned to follow her stride all the way down the corridor. It was not simply because they were curious to detect whom this Negro girl had come to date. It was part of a more natural impulse. They had turned because R. was what is called in American compliments, a gasser. Her figure was at once the prescription and the cure for any American male. You knew without measurements that it had met the statistics of the day.

She was a beautiful mixture of Negro and Amerindian: nutmeg brown with a huge, black harvest of hair rolling over her shoulders. The dress was hand-knitted, white wool with wide grains running parallel from neck to knees. The waist was severely belted, and when she sat, the naked dark landscape of legs was there for anyone to see. The upward curved nose and the black sparkle of the eyes reminded me of her sister; but it didn't take long to realise that there was an enormous difference in the influence which England and America had wrought on two sisters, born in the same town and, until their departure, educated by the same parents.

R. was much more sophisticated than J. Equally fastidious in taste, R. was more assured. America had obviously taught her not to care too much if she was wrong. Questions could be asked, and things would be put right. Why not? So she had plunged me into conversation as though this was our first reunion in ten years of a friendship whose origin neither of us could remember. She said she was writing a book; and I had a feeling that she might have brought the manuscript in her bag. Why not?

She was eloquent, curious and astonishingly energetic. From time to time she would interrupt the flow of questions with a formal apology: 'I hope you don't mind me asking you . . .!' And it was clear to me that if I had raised any objections, she would have apologised, fixed her hair in that brief pause, and then gone straight ahead with a similar kind of question. Her sister would have been formal from start to finish, concealing with exquisite graciousness her desire to be seen in the very best possible light. But America had taught R. that it did not matter where you were, the best way to find out was simply to ask. The quickest way to let a stranger know what you thought was simply to talk. This was, in a way, the directness of a Caliban who had combined the patient indifference of the donkey with the formidable might of the elephant. We finished our Manhattans, and went in search of the richest food Fifth Avenue could offer. It was my introduction to American sea food.

Towards the end of the meal, I thought it was time to ask R. a question. I had talked about people whom we both knew; but I had not yet tried to find out how R. ticked. So I asked her what she did when she wasn't writing her book. She had taken a degree in social and domestic science at Howard University. She was a teacher, but recently she had left Manhattan and gone to live way out in White Plains because a couple had asked her to take care of their dog. This was her present occupation; and it didn't sound plausible until R. explained.

It would appear that this couple were on the verge of separation, but they were uncertain about the wisdom of divorce at this stage of their conflict. They were professional Negro middle class, and obviously comfortable; for each had agreed to take the marriage to a psychiatrist. If the couch reported unfavourably on their sexual union, and the psychiatrist advised divorce, then it would be divorce.

The psychiatrist, with characteristic cunning, warned against divorce. Their problem was to face up to the Problem which involved seeing a lot of him in the future. He had heard their confessions for some time; and he advised that they should take a holiday in separate places. The husband named his resort, and the psychiatrist chose the wife's, since he wanted to make sure that neither husband nor wife could get in touch with each other during this extra-marital convalescence. But there was one problem remaining. An expensive white poodle was the joint property of the couple. The wife wanted to take the poodle with her. The husband, in a fit of malice, maintained that he had bought it. The psychiatrist wasn't going to let a poodle wreck his plans, and promptly suggested that neither should have it. He argued with some logic that the presence of the dog would be an unfortunate reminder to each that the other was still there. The poodle would be a source of memories which would not help. They couldn't leave the pet alone; and so it was at this point that my friend R. was summoned to housemaid the animal.

During this long and very detailed analysis of marital difficulties in contemporary American life, I realised that the word, problem, was acquiring a new meaning for me. In the past I had used this word to generalise a condition; it was no more than a convenient name. But R. used it in such a way that it became an element, indeed the very source of every private perplexity.

In other words, it was not the result of living together. It was the original force, the total atmosphere which sealed the fate of every relationship. And I was again struck by the difference in the ways of thinking between R. and her sister. If you had suggested to the sister in London that she had a problem, she would have interpreted it as an invitation to come to bed; and you would have been promptly asked to take leave of the lady. Any such discussion would have been out of the question.

Our lunch was late and very long. But we both enjoyed it. There was still an hour or so left before it turned dark; and we walked along Fifth Avenue, looking at shop windows, and talking about Trinidad. Then we went into the subway; and the pilgrimage to Harlem had begun. This was my first excursion to the African presence in America. There were lots of West Indians living there, and I was hoping I would meet some of them.

R. took me to a bar on 127th Street. It was also a restaurant. The atmosphere warned that it was no ordinary nigger joint, although it was impossible to detect any signs of exclusiveness. In the West Indies I would have known at a glance, by the very feel and sound of the place, whether it was Civil Service, miscellaneous by reason of cricket, or exclusively professional. But you couldn't tell here, because clothes were no sign of status. Six blocks away, in any dubious dive, the clientele would have been as well dressed. And there was no difference of accent to trace the possible background of education. In the West Indies I would have known whether the vernacular was really that man's sole rhythm of speech, or whether he had slipped into it for reasons of banter; or whether it was a moment's excitement which had brought about his temporary lapse from standard English. These attributes did not exist here.

The element of American superiority was in the efficiency of the service. There was a short barman who moved like a squirrel from end to end of the bar. His hands were magnet where half a dozen small glasses were stuck between his fingers. He would rest them on the bar, swivel round to collect the drink, and suddenly he was facing you again: four large bottles, balanced two to each hand, while he served four different drinks in those six glasses. And he never stopped talking. Now it was comment on the drink, reply to a distant whisper, advice on what buttons to press on the jukebox in the far corner. He was the perfect juggler with bottle and glass. And he had been doing this for several years with hardly an error to his name.

He came over to our table and took an order for drinks. Now I could see him better. The face was soft charcoal black, high cheekbone, and hair the colour of red brick, iron-combed, and brilliantly plastered against his skull. The hair kept changing colour according to the shade of the bulb which threw shadow on his head.

Three tables away, a woman was sitting alone. Cutlery had been arranged. She read until the waitress arrived with the tray-load of food in one hand and a bottle of beer in the next. There was the same grace and speed in the girl's movement. Plates were put down, drink poured, napkins delivered and toothpicks indicated: all at one go as

G

though these actions were an equal part of the same unbroken movement. The waitress had gone, and R. saw me staring at the woman who sat alone. She had begun to eat.

'Do you know her?' R. asked me.

'Is she alone?'

My reply was something of a mystery to R. since she knew that my courtesy would not allow this kind of distraction.

'Is she going to eat alone?' I asked.

And R. promptly replied that American women were not like West Indian women. They were independent. They worked and they spent as they pleased. But it wasn't the independence which amazed me. It was the size of the steak. It was enough meat for a family of seven in England: that huge flank of grilled carcass with a solitary shaft of bone shaped like a T. I tried to explain to R. that her sister in London would be horrified to be associated with such open-air gluttony.

'What time is it now?' R. asked.

'Seven o'clock.'

R. smiled as though she were teaching her poodle a few useful tricks; then glanced towards the woman and said: 'She will probably have a snack about ten.'

English language or no English language, Negro or no Negro, I was definitely in foreign territory.

Some time during the next few weeks I left the down-town hotel and moved into Harlem. I would sojourn in Greenwich Village before I left America, but there was plenty of time. I wanted to do Harlem on my own. R. had got me a share in an apartment on 135th Street and Riverside Drive. The house was actually on the Drive, a stone's throw from the Hudson river. In the evenings I would cross the street, and there was the bridge joining me to New Jersey. It was a marvellous corner; but it imposed strange responsibilities on me. For I was often being reminded that I did not really live in Harlem. I lived on Riverside Drive.

The distinction is important, for the fact of Harlem is an eternity away from the meaning of Riverside Drive. But I ate all my meals in the heart of Harlem which was two minutes' walk from my door. My actual address was Riverside Drive; but if it were possible to swing the building around, its backside would face the Drive and my window would look right down on Broadway. Same number, same block with the front door opening to Broadway and there could be no question that my address was Harlem. So I used two addresses. Sometimes I said Harlem, and sometimes I said Riverside Drive.

It was during this period that I met that group of American

Negroes who come within the category of the black élite. I often went to my first 'up town' bar on 127th Street. And it became my refuge during the heat wave. It was from that bar that I went to meet a public relations lady from one of the largest Negro magazines in the world. Our destination was Long Island where a social celebrity was giving a party on the occasion of her departure from a fabulous white mansion where she had lived for some seven or eight years. Since it was near Christmas, she had decided to combine the two memories: Christmas and Farewell.

There were five of us in the car: three women, myself and the driver who was the husband of one of the women. One woman had come in from Chicago that morning. The party was her sole reason for flying into New York, and she told me that she would probably return on the following day according to how she felt. I had read about our hostess in current social news; but it was the flight from Chicago which reminded me that I was from a village. I understood what R. meant by the independence of the American woman; for the lady from Chicago hadn't brought her husband with her.

The women talked for the whole length of the way; and what struck me after two hours of driving was their stamina and their authority. They talked about the domesticities of entertainment. They exchanged news about friends whom they had retired. They exchanged addresses about new friends, and kept each other up to date with the latest events. The journalist was obviously in search of rumour. Now and again the lady from Chicago would ask me how I liked America. It was as though she wanted to remind me that I had not been forgotten. I couldn't think of anything to say: and in any case my attention would soon be distracted by the other male voice asking his wife not to interfere. He was sure he was still on the right road to Long Island. Now the journalist would use the same interval to assure me that she wanted me specially to experience this evening; for it didn't happen every day.

But I would have preferred not to be spoken to since I was always so slow in answering. Also, I found their talk more interesting than they would have found my conversational responses. For their commentaries on old and, in some cases, forgotten friends, gave me some idea of the sources of income among prosperous Negroes.

'When did Judas sell his place?' someone would ask.

And in the course of contradictory replies, I would learn that 'sell' did not necessarily imply buy. It could mean swap. Judas might even have sold his place to Judas although it was not Judas who appeared to own it. And 'place' had a wide variety of meanings. It could mean liquor store, life insurance or funeral parlour. It could also mean an 'operation' which had no specific physical residence. But Judas, whoever he might be, was a barometer for measuring expense.

Judas was a man who spent large sums of money. For this type of American Negro whom I met—I don't know whether it's equally true of American Whites—always placed the emphasis on how much something had cost. Perhaps it was a party, a house, an experiment of some dubious nature. But it was the cost which emerged as the criterion. The price of a thing was an indication of his past; so that if he were poor now, you were left in no doubt that he was once a man of some substance. And the reminder was only a way of convincing himself that it would happen again. Similarly, if he were rich, he would use some phase of poverty as his introduction to a past which was inseparable from his present stature; for the greater the poverty he had conquered, the greater was the achievement which his circumstances now illustrated. This confident switch to the past is not difficult to maintain, for the past is never far away. Moreover, it is not unlikely that it might return.

Judas had passed through several stages during these exchanges. Now it seemed we had arrived. I saw lots of cars parked ahead, and I was getting ready for the occasion when the Chicago lady told me that we still had some distance to go.

'Lots of parties out here tonight,' I said.

'It's the same party,' she said, 'but there are lots of people, and lots of people mean lots of cars.'

She was being friendly, but I realised that I would have to be on my guard; for I suddenly felt again that I was in a strange country. This party was being given by an American Negro, but the bond of Negro wouldn't necessarily help me through my mistakes. For however indifferent one might be to money, it establishes an atmosphere which demands attention. Moreover, I was a writer; and ordinarily that wouldn't help at all.

To give one example of the strength which the white world had won in the black imagination, I had noticed during my early visits to the 27 Bar that I was a source of curiosity partly because I was Negro and not American, partly because I had arrived in New York from London where I lived. Had I arrived from the West Indies in much the same role, I would have been less important in their eyes. For that bar was the sanctuary of professional men, and I was not *seen* as a professional man. I was a writer which could mean almost anything, and which, in their experience of American Negro journalist often meant: poor. Ambitious and bright, perhaps, but poor.

There was the other Negro journalist—I recall with regret one conspicuous female expert—whose prosperity grew with every increasing disaster inflicted upon the Negro. I have often wondered what would be the justification for such an existence, how would it apply itself, if America woke up tomorrow and found that there was no Negro problem. But there was one thing which gave me, as a writer, some status. I was in the United States on the invitation of white money. The temperature of the air would change whenever it was said that He (he was the aura in which the name George would find its royal assent) was here on a Guggenheim. That name became the magic carpet on which I could float. They had not read any books of mine; they had not read James Baldwin, one of the finest of American writers; but Guggenheim was synonymous with millionaire; and millionaires don't go wasting money on niggers, especially non-American niggers. The Guggenheims were on to something worthwhile, profitable; and this man was somehow or other linked up with it.

This attitude caused me great confusion and pain one night in Harlem where I had gone with some friends to the opening of a new bar. I was having a good time in a rather quiet way. Some speechmaking was taking place, and I was glad that it didn't have anything to do with literature. I felt safe. Nobody was going to ask me to speak on the future of the liquor trade. But to my astonishment, I heard the Master of Ceremonies announce—the way he would if Nat King Cole had arrived—that a celebrity from afar had come to honour the opening of this Bar. No one warned me this would happen; but I was utterly speechless when the Master of Ceremonies repeated that 'we were honoured to have here, I can't see him at the moment, but he'll come up soon—we have here the world's greatest living author.' A blinding shaft of light was now searching the room, spreading everywhere to detect the victim of this stupendous camouflage. There were no white faces in the bar, so the world's greatest must have been Negro. The place was an uproar of applause. Neither heaven nor hell was going to get me to speak there or anywhere else in that role. So I refused to come out of hiding.

To be seen is bad enough. But to be looked for can be a most disconcerting experience. I was way out of sight, in a far corner. But the Master of Ceremonies refused to proceed until he had thoroughly hooked his fish. With a marvellous gesture of kindness, he told the 'house' that there would be no speech. It was in fact in the great tradition of great men that they were modest and shy. But would our friend who had come from England—the West Indies would have been too small an arena for the illusion he needed to create—just show his face, take a bow and leave it at that.

The light had found me; and suddenly I remembered that look of exhausted gratitude which often came on Joe Louis' face at the end of a fight; so I got up and briefly raised my right arm in a natural show of victory, our victory.

I didn't think anything of the kind would happen tonight; for this party was in another dimension of dollar notes. We had arrived. The hostess met us at the door where a beautiful girl of about eighteen was waiting with small brochures in a wicker-basket. The maid waited until we had been formally greeted; then she distributed the brochures.

The ladies launched into welcome and reminiscence with the hostess; and I waited, wondering whether it was altogether in good taste to be seen in conversation with the little nutmeg maid. She was easily the youngest and most beautiful woman within sight. Soon the hostess greeted me, and we all went up a flight of stairs. I was shown a room on the left which had been reserved for the men's coats; and the ladies followed the corridor towards one of the rooms on the right which was for the ladies' 'things.'

It was an atmosphere of extravagant spending. I don't know how much the place would be worth, but a hell of a lot of money had changed hands over this huge white myth. When we met again in the corridor, the hostess took me on a conducted tour from floor to floor, explaining the use of the rooms. There was the Blue room; and there was the Pink room; and there were others, all christened like animal pets: given the name of its particular colour.

If I seem very objective about all this now; it is because much time has passed. For I took no liberties with that atmosphere. I behaved with a discreetness, a certain austerity and rectitude which my colonial education had prepared me for. I may have forgotten some of the lessons, but I went to a colonial High School where the chief purpose was the creation of a boy who, at any time and in any part of the world, would be recognised for what his school had made him: A Gentleman.

But I was now a gentleman with a difference. I was in doubt about the appropriateness of my presence in this temple. It was clear to me, after some months in America, that my whole conception of gentleman was not only obsolete, but absolutely suicidal if you were going to survive as a citizen in this competitive arena. I had no money except the monthly allowance from the Fellowship. It was chicken feed compared with what most of these people could afford to lose in an afternoon. But I had Guggenheim on my side; and Guggenheim was synonymous with millionaire; and millionaire is syllables which these people understand and might one day pronounce with a feeling of pride. If these American Negroes didn't want to deal with me, a West Indian, a writer, and a visitor interested in the great experiment of the New World, then they would have to dealt with the Great White God, Guggenheim.

So I asked the hostess at this point (we were on our way to the great hall where the guests were being shepherded into new friendships), I asked, please, could I have a little drink before meeting my American friends? By this time I had heard who were present: among them a judge, an officer of important rank in the American armed forces; an ex-wife of the leading American hit parade singer. At another level, there were professional classes. Entertainers who have conquered Hollywood came rather high in this hierarchy, not merely because they were worth a lot of money, but also because they had earned it in competition with the white world.

We went down to the bar which was really a large *salon* with a whole liquor store built in. I mean that it looked exactly like any ordinary hotel bar, and almost as adequately stocked. The walls were crowded with photographs, mainly of Negroes in the entertainment world. There were a few white faces; and it is very interesting to study these.

'I would like a whisky,' I said, and the hostess told me to go over and ask so-and-so for whatever I wanted. There was a smartly dressed man behind the bar. He wore an evening suit, black from head to foot, with a white shirt and black bow-tie. He moved in his clothes with extraordinary briskness.

'Whisky,' I said.

'Bourbon or Scotch?'

'Bourbon.'

'Say when?' he said, and I decided not to be in any hurry about that 'when.' He glanced at me with some apprehension and repeated 'when.' I smiled, thanked him, and repeated that I was sure it was all right; I wouldn't need any water, any milk, any soda. I wouldn't need anything except two dissolving precipices of ice. I was determined to loosen up with a Bourbon on the rocks.

I lingered at the bar for some time, looking around exchanging smiles and preliminary greetings with unknown people, people whom I might get to know during the course of the early next morning. I didn't want to encourage any talk about the West Indies, because you couldn't be sure what feeling was. The American Negro and West Indian relation struck me as a very delicate one. I limited my comments to our hostess, remarking on her popularity, and her attractiveness. Her charm was one of the most strikingly genuine things in the whole place. This woman carried herself with great accomplishment, and with a highly perfected ease.

Then a white American came up, and he started bullying me into talk about myself. The white American has an unerring instinct for spotting a Negro who is not an American; and this man was obviously trying to find out what I felt about 'these people.' I have a profound objection to being regarded as an exception by people whose circumstances are, in fact, highly exceptional. I don't like being a party to restricted virtue. So I was brief and accurate. Place of birth, residence in London, and to the question: What do you do? (which always means income) I said that I made my living as a writer.

'What do you write?'

'Books.'

'About what?'

'Us.'

'In what style?'

'Mine.'

'Have you had anything published?'

'Everything that is worth publishing.'

He paused; and fraternity certainly didn't reside in the irritated firmness of his jaw.

'You seem very confident.'

'I am simply telling the truth.'

Then he relaxed again and asked: 'Have you met many of "these people"?' It was the category 'these people' which I found irrelevant to the total circumstances of this room. And I thought it was time for some more Bourbon. I asked him to join me in this drink. He refused. I regretted, and turned to my friend behind the bar. I wanted another little chipped volcano of ice and half as much Bourbon again. The Bourbon had done its work. My head was not screwed on or off. It was simply there. I wouldn't get into any argument about anything; but if I were asked questions, I would answer to the best of my knowledge; and if those questions had to do with me and my work, then I was, perhaps, the most reliable authority in the field. I felt completely at home. My only limitation was dancing, which I liked; but I couldn't dance well. But what with the crowd, the atmosphere of approaching nirvanas, sooner or later my legs would have to betray their illiteracy. Like Caliban, I would ask, at some time, for my supper, meaning strictly: a dancing partner.

My white prosecutor had gone about his business. And soon I was feeling like an ambassador; for my eye caught an old friend from the Village. He was a playwright and a painter; and his first play, with Eartha Kitt in the leading role, had just appeared on Broadway. That's precisely why he had been invited. He was a poor man, an artist and a Negro—which are three cataclysmic disqualifications for sympathy—but Broadway was on his side. And the kind of Christmas paper on which Broadway is built is no joke. It is a dream-boat to a haven where greed invites you, a place where you can feel securely exiled from the common needs of common men who, throughout the world, argue not with kings or politicians, but with life, begging God's breath of wind not to disgrace their knees which hunger had made weak and defenceless as infancy itself.

The playwright came over, we shook hands and grinned as though some divinity had given us licence to make any face we liked. He was an exception among the Americans I had met. When I asked him whether I could pour him a Bourbon, he said, 'Take it easy,' meaning that he didn't drink. I was reminded of a Haitian who, in reply to my question, 'Do you smoke?' replied: 'I sing.' Then it took me a little time to realise the Haitian meant that a jealous watch had to be kept over the conservation of his voice.

I asked my artist friend how the play was doing. He seemed a little apprehensive about its future (in spite of an excellent press) for there was a warning that Miss Eartha Kitt would be offering her services elsewhere. Since the cast was nearly all Negro; and many Negroes had been waiting for this kind of 'break,' they were now at the mercy of Miss Kitt's decisions.

I had the impression that Miss Kitt would not be very popular among those who had lost their jobs; but it should be borne in mind that the power which her decision represented, the implications of it for a number of actors who had hoped for this day; this kind of power should never be within any one person's reach. It doesn't help to judge Miss Kitt unfavourably until we face the fact that something is dreadfully wrong with the organisation of the art in which Miss Kitt has displayed her gifts.

My playwright friend and I talked a lot about this, and the people who were at the party. He wanted to know how I had got invited; and I told him about the journalist from the Negro maga-zine. This is how I learnt that the Chicago lady had recently bought some Chinese print for ten thousand dollars. I asked him whether it was really worth all that spending; and he replied with a chuckle that it didn't matter. In Chicago, one or two Negroes with money had decided to give their wealth a certain tone; and they were agreed that culture should come to their aid. Since Chinese art, like the Chinese language, gave the most resistance to any authoritative knowledge, since no one in the particular circumstances would be able to argue the relative worth of the Chinese print, then the Chinese print was the safest investment. That made sense to me; for in Trinidad some of us had taken to writing modern poetry, because 'modern' meant exemption from any charge of meaningless distortion.

I learnt now that I was in the midst of Negro society at its very highest level of colonial achievement. Some of these people had not only won top places in the nation's important systems of national defence and cultural expansion. Many of them had challenged the supremacy of the white standard in a white arena; in Hollywood, on Broadway, in the National as distinct from the Negro press.

I had a good little investment here; for a book of mine had not long appeared in America and was reviewed at great length, photograph and all, in the *New York Times*. To be accepted on merit as a worshipper in that great Cathedral where taste is supposed to be no respecter of complexions is not unlike the West Indian's delight with the prim-lipped approval of the *London Times*.

It is the psychology of a type of exile who has found a temporary harbour of friendship; a colonial reprieve from the doubt that one may not be up to standard: To have made the grade, not simply among people of one's own roots, education and expectations, but to have done it precisely where the doing had always been regarded as impossibility, an understandable improbability, or at most a remarkable event in a territory where new frontiers of judgment will have to be marked.

Prospero doesn't mind re-marking these frontiers provided Caliban doesn't play the ass with further intrusion; provided, in other words, he doesn't ask for a new map altogether. The 'rudeness' of a colonial politician can sometimes be child's play compared with the 'rudeness' of a colonial artist who refuses to argue because he insists that his work is evidence that this kind of argument is a waste of time. Caliban may say: I don't deny your importance, for all work may have some importance. You and I are descendants of Shakespeare. We can't choose our heritage. But it has happened that Shakespeare and I have more in common than you and I or you and Shakespeare. It isn't his fault or mine or yours, for that matter. I raise the point simply to draw your attention to the origin of your error. For I am not interested in looking back except as a way of leaping elsewhere and anger, therefore, is the wrong name for that look. Nor am I lucky in the sense that Jim or whatever his name likes to think he is not. I have a room where some work gets done; but its function is in no way connected with altitude. It is neither at the top, the bottom or even the left wing of the old kingdom. Roots would be a more likely landscape for its construction. There is no hurry whether it's hurrying up or down. I'm not Outside anything except death; for to be alive is to be irretrievably on the inside, whatever the geography of that side. I am here because I am here, and I am only emphasising these obvious facts because it has occurred to me that your way of seeing has to do with a childish notion that you are not here, but elsewhere. Your ruminations claim the strength of a privileged despair, but that's a dubious strength; for it is unlikely that any man can speak with conviction about important matters unless he sees himself related to an important occasion.

The dialogue which Caliban now offers Prospero is an important occasion; for it is based upon and derives from a very great drama. I would describe that drama as the release of two-thirds of the world's population from the long and painful purgatory of unawareness. We cannot predict the shape of this explosive resurrection of new needs and new energies, but it is here, your new landscape as well as mine. The world from which our reciprocal ways of seeing have sprung was once Prospero's world. It is no longer his. Moreover, it will never be his again. It is ours, the legacy of many centuries, demanding of us a new kind of effort, a new kind of sight for viewing the possible horizons of our own century. Let the future make whatever judgments the errors of the future will allow. But accept the fact that we are here, seeing and being seen in a certain way.

I had seen that party in my way. I felt no ill will towards the people; but Negro or not, my blood rebelled against the colossal myth which, in rewarding their ambitions, had fatally impoverished their spirit.

\* \* \* \*

Not long after this party I went to spend a week with an Anglo-American couple. The husband was from the Southern States. As a young man, he had deserted the white supremacy of Georgia for the more civilised atmosphere of Harvard. He had been a teacher at Sarah Lawrence, and was now well known in the publishing world. It is to this man that I owe my experience of white America at a certain domestic level.

He was, I would say, a healthy example of the puritan conscience in revolt. In our several conversations during that week, he would respond with the greatest frankness to my questions about those aspects of American life which involved me personally as a visitor: Race, Literature, Politics, Violence. For during my stay in America, there was a good deal of teen-age hooliganism in the Puerto Rican section of New York. It was also the time when a twelve-year-old boy, Tull, had been taken from his home by four white men who battered him to death, then dumped the barely recognisable corpse in the river. The boy had gone to a shop to buy sweets, and raped a white woman by looking at her longer than she thought necessary and appropriate to his presence in the shop. It is difficult to conceive the calculated brutality which could urge men to find that boy's home some hours later, drag him away from his grandmother and finish him off mercilessly with iron and fists.

It is against this background of events that my American host who was a white Southerner was discussing his country. He worked on 42nd Street and came home every evening by train and car. We ate around seven thirty; talked until about ten when he would retire to study his mail, and plot his next day in the office. He was up at six and off by seven thirty to meet the rigours of the American executive. Heaven knows when he rested. He was certainly incapable of being idle. I became very fond of him; and I think my admiration had little to do with his interest in my personal comfort. It was his energy that I admired, as well as his capacity to survive the responsibilities of a life that must have been, both in its personal and official spheres, extremely rigorous.

They lived in a village which had retained its Indian name and was reputed to be part of the richest county in the world. Suburbia is the kingdom of those who have just arrived at comfort; but this hive surpassed the suburbs and was known as Exurbia. It is in connection with the Negro party on Long Island that I want to refer to my stay with this family; and since I do not want to interpret or schematise my recollections, I shall refer to the notes which I made as a way of keeping my writing hand at work.

Tuesday, December 16th

The house is full of animals breeding or convalescing. A French poodle has just given birth to two black babies; and somewhere in another room a cat is expected to offer a litter of six in a day or so. I'm to accompany Mrs A. to the vet's this morning with two more cats. One with a torn leg and the other with a savaged tail. No one can tell whether these got stuck in a rat-trap, or a dog's mouth, but that's the situation. Mrs A. is Welsh, an elderly woman with a slight stoop, short, narrow, and utterly domestic. The voice is off-key most of the time, excessively and incongruously English. There is a sweet little girl, fourteen to fifteen, who has just gone off to school, so Mrs A. and I are left to each other's mercies. . . .

Tonight the lecturer in creative writing and one of her colleagues will come to dinner. Tomorrow I am to be taken over by Dr M. who is the principal; and on Thursday the Director of Education (I think it is) will have us all to dinner. . . . Everything here (America) seems so rarefied: the order and the tidiness of things; and the lavatories are positively terrifying in their contradictory spotlessness. You've got to remind yourself why you are there. The cats had to be left with the vet for a day or so; and there is going to be some kind of operation on the tail of one and the leg of the other. Mrs A. got terribly scratched on both hands, but bore it all with that overwhelming sense of 'never mind.' She was quite tickled by the vet's suggestion that one cat probably needed, or deserved castration. The male principle, I observe, doesn't thrive well in this country. It is certainly the kingdom of women; not so much a matriarchy as a feminine conspiracy. . . . It's they who invented the dotted line, and turned every signature into a warrant. . . .

(Film star seen at close quarters.) A blond slab of ice in an obscene endeavour to give off steam. . . .

Friday

Took the morning off to look around the local library. Mrs A. had driven me down in the car, and promised to leave me alone for half an hour. Of course I had to be put directly in the care of the librarian and an assistant. . . .

Try to describe Mrs A. a little. Devoted and attentive. Yesterday we went into the drugstore looking for Players; found some and she promptly insisted that these be put on the house bill; and when I said this morning that I wanted to go out to the village to get some more cigarettes, she announced with a triumphant smile that she had already seen to that. She made it my birthday; and I haven't yet got over the paper bag with five packages of giant size Winstons which she said I must keep in my room. I thought she was joking until it occurred to me that they never smoke anything but Chesterfield; and it was she who had heard me ask for Winstons one morning in the same drugstore. I'm trying to find an animal whose face and expression would give me a clue to Mrs A. Animals are very helpful in this way; quite often it is through some recollection of a bird or beast that I hit upon a more or less exact description. Have got the animal equivalent for Mrs A. hidden somewhere at the back of my skull, but it won't surface. . . .

That stoop of hers is peculiarly disturbing, not just some deformity (nothing really seems deformed) which you can regard without considering. It's a kind of professional stance, a tendency like wearing one's hat at a certain angle, not by chance but with purpose and insistence. So that stoop. I watch her from the side sometimes, and I'm struck by the face, baked and powdered and hanging like a leg of mutton from the roots of her hair. A good deal of whisky has travelled around that face which nourishes an ingrown sadness

which returns to the face again in a surface of soreness that is all
flowery and pink. The mouth is small and thin, a deficiency of lips
which tremble like the face of an agitated rat. Sometimes I feel
acutely distressed when she is about to say something. You get a
feeling of something tremendous about to happen. A declaration, a
surrender, some sad and whimpering recognition of final disaster, I
look away trying to avoid her glance and to conceal my own awareness of that aching anxiety which seems to throttle the engine or put
out the fire. And then Mrs A. would say with great tenderness and
care, 'I am very fond of people.'

The hair is combed right back and two fat plaits reach from ear to
ear across the centre of her skull. A thin white ridge runs from the
skin of the forehead down the middle of the head. It is the expression
of an English settler who has been tethered by a quiet, complacent
suffering in some very remote corner of a vast and impossible empire.
You've never seen weed shrink and make ready to die in a soil of
rock, but fluttering with every rush of wind in an impressive role of
being merrily alive. There is that quality of victorious ruin about
Mrs A. We make an odd couple together, evidence, I suppose, of a
certain harmonious incongruity. I fear sometimes that my speech
might betray me, but there are moments when I would like to tell
her, 'I am very fond of people too.'

Saturday

An evening at B.F.'s who is a managing editor on one of the chain
magazines which include *Time*, *Life*, *Fortune*, etc. This was an unusual experience: the first time I had heard this level of American
citizens talk about American politics and interview me on the European reaction to Americans at home and abroad. F. has a son at
Oxford; and he read a letter from the boy who had just attended his
first meeting of the Oxford Union. . . . Americans don't appreciate
how tired the English are. Earnestness is a luxury which the nerves
can't cope with on that island. Americans get very disappointed to
hear that people (academic in England) refuse to be serious; in fact,
they think it bad manners. . . .

There was a Quaker among us; seemed astonished to learn that I
didn't play games, had no hobbies. 'What I mean,' he said, 'is, well,
how do you relax when you aren't writing?' I was going to say that
I drink; but the relationship was too green for that. I didn't remember how I relaxed.

Later that night a ferocious argument developed between the
Americans on the relative danger of McCarthy. I said nothing.

All this had followed soon after the Long Island party; and I quote it here because it has occurred to me five years later that I did not at any time draw any parallels between the two occasions. There was no attempt to compare the Negro hostess with the Anglo-American couple although their earning capacity might have been the same or even in favour of the Negro lady on Long Island. I know that this absence of a comparative judgment was not deliberate; and it is that omission which I find interesting. I believe that the same would be true of many another West Indian; for it is our tendency to deal with each situation as though it were distinct, separate, and all on its own. We tend not to see or live situations according to the continuity of events; and it is only when circumstances victimise us that we start making necessary connections.

When I returned to Manhattan—I had now gone to live in Greenwich Village—a West Indian took me to see an old friend of his. This man was an American Negro who was born in Tennessee. He had worked in one of the Southern Big Houses. He spoke with the greatest affection about his former employers, and offered some elaborate and very fantastic examples of Negro-White relations which he had witnessed. He enquired about my stay with the American from Georgia. I talked about the village, the school where I had given a talk, and my general impression of people I had met. This seemed irrelevant to his purpose. Then he asked with an emphasis that made all my previous talk irrelevant, 'Where did you sleep?' At first I smiled; for he couldn't have thought that in the circumstances I would have been offered or accepted quarters which were detached from the house. I described the house; gave him some picture of the rooms on the first floor where we all had slept. There were three bedrooms. Mrs A. and her husband slept in the large room at the far end; the daughter slept in her own room, and I was put in the room next to hers. When I had given all these details, my American friend looked at me as though he were grateful for the clue to this mysterious invitation to spend a week with that family.

'You know why he put the daughter next to you?' he asked.

'But that was her room anyway,' I suggested.

'Makes no difference,' he said, 'I've seen it before. You were put there to see whether the daughter had a taste for niggers.' This was said with such authority (the man had spent most of his life in a white house in Tennessee) and it struck me as being so fantastic that I wondered who was going off his head: me, the American Negro, or my Southern host? I do not want to discredit the Negro's experiences; but I found it impossible to think that in the circumstances, as I knew them, any such calculation could have been at work. I still find it impossible to believe this of a man who valued my work, that was the basis of our meeting, and had therefore made it his business to show me some aspects of American life which, ordinarily, I might have missed. But I visited the South before I left America; and it was during my stay in Georgia among Negroes both rich and poor, that I saw something of the soil which had produced such a weight of suspicion and hatred in the consciousness of the American Negro.

On my way back from Georgia, I decided to stop off in Washington. There was a large number of West Indians at Howard University and I knew that we would all be glad to meet after all these years. We had gone to the same High School in Barbados; or we had met during our school days as rival cricketers and athletes. I selected Blair whose brother I had seen a lot of in London; wrote him a letter long before I got to Georgia, and promised that I wouldn't leave America before seeing the boys in Washington.

I stayed a week or more with Blair and his wife. We hunted down every West Indian whom we had known in the past. There were parties, long nights full of anecdote and nostalgia for the old days. But no one really wanted to return to the old island which had made those days. Blair had come from an eminently respectable middle-class family in Barbados. His father was a distinguished name in the Civil Service. His brother, now a lawyer in England, would probably finish his career as a judge. Though different in degrees of privilege, the others had come from much the same background. Our early education was identical. Our interests had remained very much the same; but our anxieties were entirely different.

Night and day Blair and I would talk about England, America, the West Indies, his family, Americans; and it added up to a thorough account of his stay in America. It was eight years since he arrived; and each year was crowded with incidents; and each incident contained a similar distress. Race was dominant in his talk. Eight years had not yet embittered him; but the seeds of a young bitterness were there. I got the impression that when you lived in this part of America, every morning was a preparation for some emergency. Nothing might happen; but the worst had always been anticipated. The most memorable of his stories described his first experience of the absolute barrier between white and black in the American South, 'You remember Piggy?' Blair asked. 'Fat white boy. Was at school with me.'

In a matter of minutes I had remembered Piggy. Our schools were not the same; but they were near. We often met, and those who lived out of town used the same buses. You couldn't miss Piggy walking towards the bus stand in the afternoon. He was too fat for anyone to forget him.

So Piggy having been fixed once and for all, the story proceeded. Blair and Piggy had known each other quite well at school; but it is a chameleon-like democracy which at once binds and separates these boys. For they probably never met after they had left school. But the morning Blair was leaving for America he saw Piggy at the airport. They greeted each other, and to their mutual delight Piggy was going to America too. It was like being back at school. Moreover they both had a passion for chess, and Piggy had brought along his board.

Forgetful of distance or time they had arranged their own entertainment. America did not exist; for this flight had become a slow journey back to their original classroom. They boarded the plane; and from the moment the seat belts could be relaxed, it was chess all the way. The school had come alive: opinions on the defects of certain masters; who made how many runs in nineteen whatever it was? was it really worth all that trouble and punishment learning irregular verbs? And between them, like a duty neither dare betray, was the game of chess. It seemed that they had paid no one any attention until a voice said that they should fasten seat belts. The plane was about to land at Miami. They hadn't finished the game; each felt certain of victory; and each knew what the other would suggest; for they had often done it at school. They left the board exactly as it was and went out to see where they were.

The word Miami meant nothing but Don Ameche, Betty Grable, and a host of popular films which had reached Barbados from this wealth of scenery. They entered the restaurant, took a seat, and went on talking about the school. Then the waitress arrived; and Piggy started to make a choice of food for himself and Blair.

'You can't sit here,' the woman said.

But neither Blair nor Piggy had caught her meaning. They both stood and apologised, believing that the table had been reserved. It was as natural a violation as shooting paper darts when their headmaster, who was English, had turned his back. To the woman's astonishment, both boys moved together in search of another table. Now she looked at Piggy and explained: 'You can stay, but your friend will have to go over there.' And she left them standing, silent and bewildered as any old, blind couple who had lost their way.

These boys were intelligent; they had known colour prejudice, for the democracy of their school was never allowed to prolong itself into their social life; but they had never imagined this aspect of racism. They had never thought of colour as a kind of wall, a distance which could not be closed by individual choice in personal relationships. The democracy that worked at school and cricket was a useless memory as they walked back to the plane, living a nightmare of silence. They returned to their seats. The plane took off again; but this journey was the same and different.

The plane roared and went away; the American passengers were probably unaware of what was happening here. The pieces had remained as those boys left them; but neither hand moved to suggest a start. Neither Piggy nor Blair looked at each other; and heaven knows what was happening in their heads. For the chess board was still there; but their school had died. From Miami to New York, and not a word passed between those two boys. To be deposited and discharged at Idlewild! That was their greatest relief. For the first time they spoke. Piggy said: 'Good-bye.' And Blair replied: 'Good-bye Piggy.' It was all they could manage. Each would have liked to wish the other good luck; but they couldn't talk, speech had lost its power. Nothing could be said after that ominous noise: Good-bye.

# JOURNEY TO AN EXPECTATION

•

Word over all, beautiful as the sky,
Beautiful that war and all its deeds of carnage
    must in time be utterly lost,
That the hands of the sisters of Death and Night
    wash again, and ever again this soil'd world.
                                        WALT WHITMAN

    Do not go gentle into that good night.
    Rage, rage against the dying of the light.
                                        DYLAN THOMAS

IT IS now ten years since that morning in mid-March when Sam
Selvon and I left for England. I have tried to chart, through my
own experience, some of the events of that period, for it is also the
decade in which the West Indian acquired recognition as a writer,
first outside and later within his own society. This order of acceptance was logical since a native commodity of any kind must always
achieve imperial sanction before it is received back in its own soil.
This is equally true of Calypso and the Steel Band. But there has
been a slight modification in colonial anxieties. The middle classes
have actually taken to mixing with the peasants and longshore men
who attend the lectures in the University of Woodford Square. After
twenty-five years of pilgrimage and pursuit both in the New World
and the Old, C. L. R. James, the greatest of all Caribbean teachers,
is now back home. He will probably become the Dean of Woodford
Square.

    In other words, the generation between fifteen and twenty-five
will have started with advantages which were denied myself and
Sam. All that I have said so far is rich and painful epilogue to an era
whose light has both obscured and sharpened our vision. In one of
his serious warnings, St Paul told the Corinthians for whom it was a
moment of great paradox: 'Let each man be sure on what he builds.'
For the West Indian of all classes, work is the only sure rescue from
that long sleep which followed the emancipation of the slaves. It is
not inappropriate, therefore, that I should reverse one or two of
Prospero's meanings, and make this last chapter the prologue to my

book. The voyage was over. The captain would soon turn the stow-
away over to the police. England lay before us, not a place, or a
people but as a promise and an expectation. Sam and I had left
home for the same reasons. We had come to England to be writers.
And now we were about to be anchored at Southampton, we
realised that we had no return ticket. We had no experience in
crime. Moreover, our colonial status condemned us fortunately to
the rights of full citizenship. In no circumstances could we qualify for
deportation. There was no going back. All the gaiety of reprieve
which we felt on our departure had now turned to apprehension.
Like one of the many characters which he has since created, Sam said
on the deck: 'Is who send we up in this place?' For it was a punishing
wind which drove us from looking at the landscape. An English voice
said that it was the worst spring he had known in fifty years. We
believed him, but it seemed very cold comfort for people in our
circumstances.

The emigrants were largely men in search of work. During the
voyage we had got to know each other very well. The theme of all
talk was the same. It had to do with some conception of a better
break. We lived between the deck—which was a kind of camping
ground—and the communal dormitory where we slept, wrote letters,
or simply wondered what would happen.

Selvon and I, like members of some secret society, were always
together. But this comradeship turned to a strange reticence during
the last few days of the journey. Sam had taken to walking alone in
the more remote parts of the ship. Sometimes he would be seen working in odd corners: a small grey typewriter on his knees and long
black locks of hair fallen forward, almost screening him from view.
He would go up on the deck if no one was there. He would take
refuge in the dormitory whenever it was empty.

He had already written a large part of his first novel, *A Brighter
Sun*; and he was probably wondering what would happen to the rest.
He was nervous; and he was, in a way, more equipped than I to
deal with the future. Fiction was not my ally, and I had left my
poems behind. I had absolutely nothing to offer. Now this March
wind had started terrible fears; for it didn't just slap you round the
throat. It went right through your collar bone. All my village concerns had come alive. To be cold meant for me as a child, to have a
cold; and when you had a cold a mother's warning was intended,
exclusively, for the protection of the chest. If your chest was exposed,
the result would be pneumonia; and since few villagers had ever
survived pneumonia; an exposed chest was a cold-free invitation
to the grave. But pneumonia had given way to another fear. Two or

three days before we arrived, the ship had started to make us uncomfortable. It pitched; it rolled; it did everything except go under. It was at breakfast one morning that the seas got more truculent. No one could eat with the plates sliding all over the table; so I gobbled down some tomatoes and decided to feel my way towards the bunks. Suddenly my stomach revolted; and I rushed into the washroom.

When I opened my eyes, I noticed with a shock that my vomit was predominantly red. This was the colour of an awful malady; and the letters T.B. tolled like a chapel bell in my head. I had caught it; and that *it* was one of the most malignant defects my village could imagine. For this illness did not only mean an erosion of the body; it meant a complete leprosy of character as well. For when I was a boy in Barbados, tubercular cases were sent to the Alms House which should not have been used as a hospital at all. The Alms House was the place where the old waited until it was time for the State to bury them. It was a tomb from which no man or woman could return to dignity in the judgment of his community.

My fear was so intense as I watched this vomit, that my memory had failed to remind me what I had eaten for breakfast. Dying was terrifying enough; but it seemed such a waste of money and time if one were going to die within six months of arrival in this place which had been chosen for the specific purpose of staying alive. And to be buried in foreign dirt! To be spaded by anonymous hands!

Now I remembered the breakfast. I told myself: 'Of course it's the tomato juice.' And some other part of me replied: 'You're too old to fool yourself.' To be or not to be tomato: that was the question; and the only way I could transcend its meaning was by postponing the answer. I had to put all this right out of my mind; and the easiest way to achieve this denial of a personal difficulty is to identify oneself with a general situation. You translate *me* into *we* and take refuge in *it*. This shift of personality in its actual manifestations can be most interesting.

Our luggage had been transferred to the Customs, I started to behave as though the English landscape were familiar territory; as though I had been here. Berkeley Gaskin, a name I had always revered as a cricketer, was with me; and he was the first cricketer I had met whose conversation would define him as an intellectual. Berkeley called for a pint of bitter. We drank first to the victory of the West Indies Test team; for it was the 1950 Test series which had brought him here. I had no doubt that Worrell—since we went to the same school—would beat the hell out of Trevor Bailey and that lot. We had learnt our cricket in the road, on the beach and over any ploughed up grass piece. What with dirt, sand and dust

flying at the same speed as the ball, any good batsman from Barbados
had a sound education in seeing what was coming at him. Berkeley
and I were sure West Indies would win; for in matters of cricket,
we are always confident although we may be often wrong.

I had forgotten my tomato question until Berkeley raised his glass
and said with a gravity which I thought meant more than goodwill:
'I want to drink specially to your future in this country.' I wondered
whether Berkeley had noticed anything. We had talked a lot about
writing but I had nothing to show; and the name Poet is synonymous
with Fool, if there are no verses available. Again I dismissed all this,
and assumed an ease of manner which you would expect from a
veteran exile. Since the situation was in no position to question my
confidence, I saw the situation as not understanding what was really
happening. In other words, I would have to be accepted on my own
terms which were, of course, an example of camouflage.

But the atmosphere returned to normal when the Boys were getting
ready to board the train. We were on our way to London; and everyone felt fine. The old emigrants, men who were returning from
holiday, were putting the amateurs through their paces. There were
strange stories about white women who misbehaved on boats. All
this was perplexing, however true. But it was that instinctive return
to our respective roots which made for a different kind of confidence.
The Boys had now turned the coach into a West Indian occasion.
They joked; some sang; and the experiences of childhood were
always on the agenda.

It is here that one sees a discovery actually taking shape. No
Barbadian, no Trinidadian, no St Lucian, no islander from the West
Indies sees himself as a West Indian until he encounters another
islander in foreign territory. It was only when the Barbadian childhood corresponded with the Grenadian or the Guianese childhood
in important details of folk-lore, that the wider identification was
arrived at. In this sense, most West Indians of my generation were
born in England. The category West Indian, formerly understood
as a geographical term, now assumes cultural significance. All this
became much clearer to me when, years later, I would hear West
Indians arguing about being *West Indians*. The argument would
usually grow from the charge that X was not a good West Indian.
To be a bad West Indian means to give priority of interest and
ambition to the particular island where you were born. It is bad
because your development has taught you that the water which
separates us can make no difference to the basic fact that we are
West Indians; that we have a similar history behind us. I know
Barbadians, Trinidadians and Jamaicans who go to great trouble

in order to establish that they are first of all a West Indian. This category undergoes interesting changes. Today, ten years after that March morning, and five years since America, I find that I refrain from saying that I am from the West Indies, for it implies a British colonial limitation. I say rather, I am from the Caribbean, hoping the picture of French and Spanish West Indies will be taken for granted. So the discovery had taken place, partly due to the folklore, and partly to the singing, and especially to the kind of banter which goes between islander and islander.

The Barbadian is proud, for reasons that have an exact parallel in England. It is not correct to say that the Barbadian is very English; for that is to make English a criterion of what, in the case of the Barbadian, is a universal quality. I would say that the Barbadian has much the same relation to Barbados which the Englishman has to England. They both have an inordinate pride in the feel and look of the land they call theirs. In the case of the Barbadian I think I know the reason. The size of the island, and the incredible density of population has created his relation to the soil. To a Barbadian every square inch of land should be planted up. It is a criminal waste to let land just lie there, doing nothing. Agriculture is his glory. With a small plot of an acre the Barbadian will boast six crops although the whole acre is already covered with sugar cane. You wonder what he is talking about if you are a stranger; but he will invite you to see.

First he has a fence growing on every side. This fence is not dead wood or corrugated iron. It is a natural cucumber vine which breeds like rabbits; and rising high above the vine are leaves and pods swollen fat with green peas. On every side of this acre there is a fence which grows two solid crops.

Now we enter a gateway in the fence. The sugar cane is thick. You can see nothing until he tells you where to look; for you are standing on another vine that rambles like green snakes all through the roots of the sugar cane. It's a pumpkin vine which will feed the children in a whole street for weeks on end until the harvest is over. That's crop number four. The fifth is not too difficult to detect if you find your way through the canes. There are two or three rows of fragile trees with prickly red pods which are plucked, dried and boiled once every year. These pods are the basis of a rich scarlet brew which is called 'Sorrel'; it is inseparable from the birth of Christ. No sorrel, no Christmas; and 'Christmas ain't no Christmas if it ain't have a little drop o' Sorrel.' The fifth crop is, perhaps, the most important; for it is highly questionable whether the islands of the British Caribbean would be inhabited today were it not for the irreplaceable bread fruit. This little tenant farmer has two of these trees with an annual produce of three suppers a week for a family of five. The bread fruit is a very weighty dish. It looks like a ton of paste on the plate. It is not posh; but it has most precious memories for every peasant.

And finally, you will be introduced to the sixth crop as though it were an apology for all that has gone before. At a respectable distance from the ripening bread fruit, there is a small family of pear trees, purple and green; and it is this delectable fruit which may be the farmer's pride.

You can beg him for a bread fruit; you may pocket a cucumber without arousing his wrath; but any raid on the pear tree is an unforgivable blasphemy against the land.

Some Barbadians are known to keep a hive in the bread fruit tree; and although honey can fetch a good price, he would never consider bee-produce a legitimate crop. But he may have another function for the hive. If bees are in residence, their reputation is a stinging reminder to any thief who may have a passion for pears. It is, therefore, the size of his plot, this almost human coalition between a man's hands and the earth he ploughs which creates a wholly new set of feelings towards the land.

This contact with the land as a source of life from day to day is not evident in the Trinidadian. Trinidadians don't have that kind of land pride at all. The Jamaicans have it, but in a different way from the Barbadians.

A number of small farmers actually own the land. It is theirs. They do not only see it as a partner in the enterprise of staying alive, it is a refuge, a source of independence. If the boss in town gets fresh, then you can tell him to haul his arse and you can go straight back to your little yard, meaning that piece of land behind the house. Many of the emigrants who come to Britain from Jamaica are, I feel, examples of this type of small farmer. What is sad about this aspect of migration is that they paid their passages through the sale or mortgage of the little piece of land behind the house.

But the Barbadian and the Jamaicans are very different types by social experience. The Jamaican has a certain natural aggressiveness which the Barbadian simply regards as uncouth. The Barbadian will think that it is not enough to say that Jamaicans don't know how to behave. It is more than that. The Jamaicans are simply 'Wild hogs.' Of course, the Jamaicans have a simple explanation of the Barbadian. The Barbadian has a complex about being civilised because the general standard of literacy is and has always been higher in Barbados than in any other British West Indian island. In one way or another, the Barbadian sees all this as giving him the right to speak in the name of civilisation. Moreover, there is hardly a West Indian territory where Barbadians do not hold important positions in education; either as headmasters, senior assistants, or directors of education. All this massive preparation he has over the Jamaican. So how can the Jamaican cope in argument on matters of education? Very simply, he replies. The English didn't only teach you, but he actually taught you how not to learn. 'Like when we had some trouble in the R.A.F. instead of you standing up like a man, and say, listen limey sergeant, watch your step—not so you, you sit down like a child and beg: excuse me, please.' To which the Trinidadian would reply: 'Case in bag,' meaning there is nothing more to be said.

This kind of quarrel can reach such furious proportions that it will only stop when a voice makes the colonial charge; and then all you call yourself West Indians, trying to play you is West Indians when you can't even sit in harmony and reason out—like how those wicked English people can sit—and reason out how to crucify the enemy. As a result one of the most wounding attacks you can make on a West Indian is to accuse him of being a little colonial stooge.

This journey from Southampton to Waterloo is an important lesson in colonial history. Many of these Boys had never before been asked the question: 'Will you be having lunch, sir?' But it is exactly the question which they had often asked an employer who looked like an English waiter. They had entered a wholly new role; and they would reply to the waiter as though he had been serving them for a lifetime. At least, one aspect of the old myth was in serious danger. For they realised—not read or heard but realised that white hands did nigger work in this country. They would not yet begin to rationalise this astonishing reversal of roles, but one of its meanings had sunk in their consciousness. It had gone home, so to speak, and it would stay there; in the soil of their thinking.

I emphasise this point because I have often raised it with some of my English friends. Seldom, if ever, do I discuss these matters with people who are not my friends, but those friends of mine who have come to London from the provinces with similar illusions of London as the Golden Chance would tell me that their isolation, and their whole situation was very much the same as the West Indian's.

There are also among my friends people who have worked in the colonies; and they too will argue that they, as strangers, felt the same hostility from the new environment; that they were very much in the position of the West Indian on his arrival in England. You can draw parallels for anything under the sun; but this is an example of misused parallels.

The English Civil Servant going to the colonies leaves with the knowledge—imparted by history, political fact and myth—that his privileges are already established. This privilege is proved almost in the moment of his arrival; for he discovers—at first to his astonishment—that Frank whom he knew at university in Scotland is earning a hundred pounds less for doing the same job. What starts his guilt is the bitter recollection that he was never a match for Frank in problems of gynaecology. It is painful for him to accept the actual fact of this privilege; and it doesn't help very much when he has to meet Frank. So the easiest way out is to avoid any such meeting beyond their actual hours of work.

On the other hand, the West Indian arrives here as a man reprieved from the humiliation of this arrangement which he has known all his life. He sees this new place as an alternative: open, free with an equal chance for any British citizen; and since the white hands do nigger work, it certainly looks as though the colour screen has been removed once and for all. The students, in particular, are victims of this way of thinking. Moreover, their relative comfort in Oxford or Cambridge will help to reinforce the illusion. They notice a cold stare, an enigmatic sneer, the built-in compliment which is used to praise, and at the same time remind them who and what they are. But education has trained them in duplicity; their whole life becomes an experiment in double-think. The factory boy's anger expressed on bus or in the Tube, strikes them as uncouth; for in the remote sanatorium of Oxford they exist as a kind of an expensive casualty. And Oxford wakes up one morning to an appalling scandal. It is England's scandal. For the bells have tolled over Notting Hill Gate; and student or not, Oxford knows that the bell has tolled for all who suffer from a defect of colour.

It is amazing what effort a certain type of West Indian will make in order to assure white friends that nothing has ever happened to him; that all his life in England has been a memorable participation in civilised pleasures.

2

At Waterloo the Boys started to get nervous again. The train had encouraged amnesia; but at last we were on solid ground. Most of us had no idea where we would be going from here; but the question remained: 'Where will John sleep?' Like a staff of indomitable midwives, representatives from the British Council were waiting at the station to receive those who qualified as students. At that time, their exclusive concern was for the students. The rest had to hope that

Fox, Goliath Number Two, or Bat Ears—all Boys from back home—
might have come to Waterloo. During this interval of waiting,
another lesson is learnt. They realise that some islands are really very
small; for this London doesn't sound like a place at all.

'Where Jo Jo living?' one of the amateurs will ask.

'In a place call High Gate,' the veteran says.

'And where Bat Ears 'cause he always writing to say how he see
Jo Jo every Saturday night?'

'Bat Ears was living in Camden Town,' the veteran explains, 'but
I hear some o' the Boys say he collect some trouble and had to move
down Wimbledon.'

It is all names to the amateur; and he is not afraid of names. He
wants to make a move; for he must see Bat Ears and Jo Jo before he
settles down. In fact, the whole problem of shelter hasn't crossed his
mind; for Jo Jo, Bat Ears and Goliath Number Two are all in
England, and come rain or hurricane, he must find somewhere to
sleep.

'Let us walk by Camden Town first,' he says, 'then perhaps we
can track back 'pon the place where you say the Gate High. 'Cause
Jo Jo will be vexed blue murder if I don't go see him first.'

The veteran tries to explain that these distances are not quite like
the gulley hill tracks back home, a brief quarrel ensues; for the
amateur has made a damaging accusation.

'But is what wrong with you, Sphinx?' he asks. 'Only two years
you leave home, and now you are talking tourist talk 'bout how it
don't have no walking in this town. Tell me, Sphinx, is how come
you drop your ol' walking habits?'

It is the amateur's lesson in size.

But Selvon and I were duly recommended for a place in a London
students' hostel; and it is here that we met Mate. There were three
of us to a room the size of a successful publisher's office. The Ghanaian
was a medical student and, since I hadn't quite got over my fear of
T.B., I had a very special relation to him. I thought that he would
see something which I didn't want anyone to know at the time. So I
spoke to him in a way which suggested the need to learn. For
example: 'Do you think it would be all right to go out without a coat
today?' But one morning he scared the hell out of me. I had forgotten that he was in the room, or rather that I might have been seen
from his end of the mirror. I was cleaning my teeth; I had paused to
check the exact colour of that gargle. He must have been watching
me, for I was almost speechless when I heard the voice say: 'Are you
sure it is all right?' There I was again, confronted by the menace
of that *It*. Now I did something which reminded me of the arrival at

Southampton. I said, in a tone of measured caution: 'You can never be sure, can you?'

I had entered the role of the doctor warning a patient against carelessness; and in that role I was now accepted as a man who could be trusted not to play about with his health; in other words, the worst kind of patient for a colonial doctor whose prestige depends entirely on money and whose money is got either through the carelessness of the natives or his own indifference to the health of his country. Selvon exposes this most brilliantly in his first novel: *A Brighter Sun.*

The Ghanaian felt more assured; and we became friends. But I wonder whether he knew what was happening. Ten years later, in 1958, I met him in Ghana; but our greeting was so warm and so utterly happy in its welcome that we just talked about 'the old days' without any special reference to any item which made up those days. He had changed enormously. From the austere, rigid, and defensive young student to a relaxed, gracious, and truly authoritative young doctor. The third lodger was a Nigerian whom we called Mate. I'm not sure whether this was the name he gave, or whether Selvon had chosen it. For Selvon is a master at this kind of invention. The contracted phrase, nigger-gram, meaning the circulation of rumour at top speed—is his discovery. There can hardly be another writer who has contributed in this way to the vocabulary of West Indian conversation.

Mate was a student whose monthly allowance had been temporarily suspended. Since Sam and I were not students, and knew with certainty when our money would come to an end, we formed some moral allegiance to Mate.

He was a man of average height; but the bulge of his shoulders gave the impression that he was short. His glance was deceptive, for his eyes were dull, almost idle; and yet he saw everything. His stride reminded one of a bear in slow motion although his head was kept level with the surrounding view. He had been deprived of his monthly allowance, but it would be restored when he wrote a letter of apology to his father who had quarrelled with him on matters of conduct. But Mate would not write, nor would he make any concession to style. He always wore a suit, arranged in every pleat and seam with impeccable neatness. He brushed everything before he dressed, and he repeated the same chore before he went to bed. He might not regain his allowance; but he would never betray his clothes. They expected a certain standard from him. His whole gait was soft, leisurely, assured.

Both Selvon and I became very fond of Mate; and although I

haven't seen him for some seven years I still hear of him; for Sam, who has an unerring instinct for keeping in touch with the right people, is always running into Mate.

The second evening after we arrived, Mate suggested that he and I should go for a walk. We went along Gloucester Place towards the High Street and into Kensington Gardens. What strikes me as interesting now is that I don't think I asked Mate anything about Africa. We talked about England, and in particular about those people, meaning an active regiment of women who were either introducing their dogs to one another, or plotting the direction their journey should take. There was something strangely business-like about them; and there was a look of obvious comprehension on the dogs' faces. Like that Trinidadian on the boat, I made a typical colonial discovery that evening. On first appearance the women reminded me of the expatriate English who live it up in colonies like Barbados and Trinidad; and it crossed my mind then that one or two might have been Governor's wives back home on long leave. So I stopped walking when Mate said in the most casual tone of voice: 'Want one?' I knew there were prostitutes the world over; but I couldn't relate these ladies to the Trade. For in the West Indies whores didn't dress in such magnificent finery, and they would never be seen with dogs.

They couldn't wear such clothes for very obvious reasons. They never made enough to buy them, what with rent and children. And they wouldn't be seen with dogs, because the West Indies is not, generally speaking, a dog country. For there are basically two kinds of dogs in the West Indies: Stray Dogs and Watch Dogs. Stray dogs are more or less public property whose owners refuse to make any claim. Moreover stray dogs live largely by theft, and that is a great source of hatred in a village where food is scarce. Very gentle men have been known to murder a stray dog for the loss of a flying fish. The death was not calculated, and the father didn't mind going hungry; but this theft deprived his son of breakfast on the very morning when the boy was going to take that examination which would earn him a place at Oxford. There were noble reasons behind that tragedy.

But stray dogs were not altogether outcast. I remember so vividly how the S.P.C.A. vans would come tearing through our urban village in pursuit of stray dogs. There had been an order to clean up the street so to speak, and the stray dogs, like all garbage, were to be carted away. The stray dogs would go into hiding; and some people, who couldn't make up their minds about keeping dogs, would actually help to hide them. They refused to give evidence to the

S.P.C.A. detective; for stray dogs had often rendered valuable service. If a stray dog had not forgotten how to bark there was always a chance that he might wake you before some intruder had made his way through the open door. Thief though he was, the dog hadn't forgotten his duty when he heard foreign steps arriving after midnight.

In these circumstances, it could be very difficult for the S.P.C.A. detective to distinguish between stray dogs and watch dogs. There was only one safe and legal way to settle the matter. Watch dogs were dogs which had been licensed. Dogs without a licence were stray dogs.

If one may draw a parallel without any suggestion that prostitutes anywhere are bitches, I would say that the difference between the ladies in Kensington finery and those in Barbados was not unlike the difference between stray dogs and watch dogs. Kensington was licensed and Barbados was not. Kensington did a lot of careful watching out; Barbados was restricted to a lot of patient waiting in.

But there it was: my discovery that a sort of economic democracy would soon be conducted under those skirts. It was really a discovery of what people call standards of living.

I didn't take up Mate's suggestion, partly because he had changed the subject and partly because I couldn't afford to add V.D. to T.B. For this is another thing to be understood. One of the basic fears planted in me as a little boy was that those 'women on the street' carried sickness. And as big boys, we were sometimes warned by schoolteachers and even doctors against any temptation to be seduced by 'those women'; not merely because we would contract the disease, but we might 'give it' to the girl we were going to marry. And you couldn't introduce that sort of pollution into a respectable family. It was a common superstition in my village that something must have been wrong with a man whose wife had had more than one miscarriage. Wrong meant the sickness or some form of it.

Sam and I saw Mate every day. He didn't come down to breakfast, but we would meet in the hall or the table tennis room. It was nearly a fortnight before Sam or I learnt that Mate should not have been living in that room at all. We were mystified. G. left shortly after this, and Sam moved in. He took a very special interest in Mate. So we learnt why Mate had been asked to leave the hostel some three months before we arrived in England. He left and moved back one dawn through the help of Buzz, a medical student down from Glasgow. But Buzz had gone back, and in a most extraordinary way Sam and I took over from Buzz. Since Mate couldn't go down to breakfast for fear he would be seen, we brought breakfast up to Mate. That wasn't difficult; for there was a rule that you could have one egg and a slip of bacon only, but no restriction whatsoever on bread and butter which were laid out on the table. Taking turns, Sam and I would butter about a dozen slices of bread, put them in a paper bag, and take them to the room when we had finished eating. Mate would still be asleep. He never woke until about ten or eleven in the morning before the maid came in to clean. By then he had made the bed afresh, and gone into the bathroom. One of us would put a coat or books on it, anything to suggest that it was not being slept in by a third person. An hour or so later, Mate would appear downstairs, immaculate and to order like any colonial barrister at the height of his career. No one could question his presence in the hostel, for he was now just another visitor who had come to see two old friends, Sam and George. And such a visit was perfectly in order.

It was about this time that I really got to know Selvon; for he is an extremely gentle man, and his modesty makes for misunderstanding what he really is. I learnt then—and nothing has ever happened to change it—that he had great generosity of heart. During the year or two which followed, when we met, he was always giving something. He would say as though it were a rebuke, 'But why you don't take that man?' Not meaning money which he could not afford, but something that was urgently needed like an overcoat, or a pullover, or a jacket which had grown too short.

He could part with the extra article of clothing because he had started to earn a few guineas from the B.B.C. with his short stories. I was still very much at scratch since prose was not my business! I might have written one or two atmospheric pieces with an episode to give the thing direction, but I wasn't having any serious truck with fiction. My ambition was to learn to use words in verse so that I might at some time be able to dramatise experience in the theatre. Poetic drama then seemed the highest and most intensely satisfying form of literary expression. I was a West Indian poet, and I wasn't deserting that. Sam had never spoken to me about this; but I believe he might have been wondering what I would do, for he never saw me as anything but a poet, and there was little chance of a poet holding his own where money was concerned. I wonder whether this is a typical sympathy felt by novelists towards poets? But I would take pullover and coat without any feeling of special gratitude; although I felt a little cramped in not being able to offer Sam anything by way of clothes. But after the publication of my first book, there was a change in my circumstances in relation to giving and taking—and it just happened, for happen is the only word that can suggest the lack of calculation in this giving and taking. It has gone on to this day. I don't see Selvon as often as I might, perhaps because I never leave his house without something; and Sam never visits me frequently, I imagine, for similar reasons.

But no break took place in that journey which started in Port-of-Spain to London, and which has brought us together by chance, in New York, and Barcelona. So when I was going to Ghana in 1958, I was persuading Sam to try and get to India, because I would have liked to see on paper what he, as a descendant of Indians, would make of India in the light of his experience as a West Indian. I had contemplated a book in which I would put beside his experience of India my own experience of West Africa. Sam hasn't yet got to India, but that book may still take place. It will be valuable for the West Indies; and for obvious reasons.

I have dwelt at some length on this, not to speak up in praise of Selvon. He doesn't need that kind of recommendation from me. In spite of the ignorant judgment of the *New Statesman* reviewer ('his talent may not be important, but it is precious'), Selvon is the greatest, and therefore the most important folk poet the British Caribbean has yet produced. I emphasise all this in order to draw attention to a fallacy which has threatened to ruin the political life of Trinidad. This fallacy assumes its most irresponsible sanctions in the following remarks of V. S. Naipaul:

'Mr Samuel Selvon, who has won a reputation for his stories of West Indians in London, is *an Indian*. In Trinidad, where he comes from, he would be called an East Indian. . . . Mr Lamming is a Barbadian Negro. . . . It is not fully realised how completely the West Indian Negro identifies himself with England. . . . Africa has been forgotten; films about African tribesmen excite derisive West Indian laughter. . . .'

It is precisely because Africa has not been forgotten that the West Indian embarrassment takes the form of derisive laughter. And how do we explain, in spite of this amnesia, the Calypso, which is the basic folk rhythm of the Caribbean. The difficulty is that Mr Naipaul's education is based entirely on the word, and his conception of intelligence is limited to answering examination questions.

Given this growing racial antagonism between Indians and Negroes both in Trinidad and British Guiana, you may say that the relationship between Lamming and Selvon is part of a similar community of interests. You are both writers. And that is precisely where my argument will not rest. For Naipaul is also Indian and a writer, and Selvon's reservations about him are no less than mine. What holds

Selvon and myself together is precisely what could hold Indians and Negroes together in Trinidad. It is their common background of social history which can be called West Indian: a background whose basic feature is the peasant sensibility. Neither Sam nor I could feel the slightest embarrassment about this; whereas Naipaul, with the diabolical help of Oxford University, has done a thorough job of wiping this out of his guts.

His books can't move beyond a castrated satire; and although satire may be a useful element in fiction, no important work, comparable to Selvon's, can rest safely on satire alone. When such a writer is a colonial, ashamed of his cultural background and striving like mad to prove himself through promotion to the peaks of a 'superior' culture whose values are gravely in doubt, then satire, like the charge of philistinism, is for me nothing more than a refuge. And it is too small a refuge for a writer who wishes to be taken seriously.

I speak bluntly because this book, in spite of the country of first publication, is directed to my generation throughout the Caribbean, irrespective of language, race or political status. Our situation is deeply lacking both in political unity and creative pride. We are not alone, but we are too small to encourage such a burden of chaos. And if something positive is not attempted very soon, we may find ourselves as a community isolated from all that really matters in the evolution of the twentieth century.

3

THE ROCK

We looked on your countenance and found nothing
That we could recognise, nothing to revive the memory,
You had lost your tears, offered them back to your lover,
Mended your prodigal ways and returned to your mother.

And now the past was forgotten, the present unheeded to,
Your love had melted within the blue waters that washed your shores,
And you had returned, penitent and morose, to your mother,
For you were a stalemate and could be accepted by no other.

Those fragile weeds that crept upon your shoulders didn't understand
There was nothing you could do for them,
Soon life would be denied them, and they would fall at your feet,
Innocent, motherless children whom you could not greet.

H

And so we wished that time and the age would change,
Your mother would unclasp her arms, grant you your will,
Perchance your lover should come back, take your hand
And make you what you were before, a little island.

This experience of the Rock took place after I had left Barbados in 1946 to work as a teacher in Trinidad. A year later I went back on holiday. I used to go swimming all over the island, but this was the first time I had ever visited Silver Beach. And it was in my original village that I wrote the poem. Now it seems clearer how the experience of the Rock had got identified with all Barbados.

When I was about twelve years old, I had had the shattering experience of seeing old Papa Grandison, my godfather, forced to move his small house from the site which generations of children had learnt to speak of as 'the corner where Papa who keep goats does live.' The house was really one large room partitioned into three separate quarters: an enormous box with a gabled roof. There was a yard about the length of a cricket pitch, and about the same distance in width. It was surrounded on three sides by a board fence; and Papa reared his goats within this enclosure.

Before I got promoted to the High School, I used to play at being foreman to a group of boys whose ambition was to take Papa's goats grazing. We would race them down the rail-tracks and look for any deserted grasspiece. But Papa never knew that it was also our intention to watch the young billy-goat mount its sister. These goats didn't seem to have any understanding at all of family relations, so we would encourage them to mate until it was time for the foreman to order the chase back to Papa's yard.

He also kept ducks and a large flock of pigeons which nested and slept under the house. At five o'clock, which was feeding time in the afternoon, you would see blue circles soaring above Papa's house; then Papa would appear in the yard and make some kind of throttled cry which meant: 'Come.' The pigeons would circle and stop until Papa's hands were covered with feathers. Soon they flew away, and Papa's hands once laden with corn were now empty. The pigeons were a priceless delicacy; but the goats are more memorable. It was a tradition whose origin no one could tell that I would eat with Papa on Sundays. That had nothing to do with my own meal at home that day. In other words, I ate twice every Sunday. But I had to eat the first meal with Papa. If I hadn't arrived by twelve midday —he would have just returned from church—Papa would shout from his window for everyone to hear. The exact words were: 'George?' (delivered as a question) 'Ready'—which was spoken as an order.

George?

Ready!

And I was there. But Papa hadn't called one Sunday, and it was long after twelve. I must have been aware of this in some way, for I went over to Papa's house expecting some kind of trouble. I entered without the slightest sound. No one was in the house, and soon I realised why Papa hadn't called. He and Gwen, the wife who shared his last days, were in the yard. I buckled myself in the corner, widened a crease in the half-door, and watched Papa helping a goat to deliver its young. It was my first conscious experience of what happened at birth, and what birth did actually look like. Had spies informed, my mother would have murdered the devil in me with her Victorian rod. But it was valuable; for there was something between Papa's hands and the goat's travail: the way he helped the young kid out of its tangle of night and blood into life; there was something between that life and Papa's hands which made you feel that the animal was human; for Papa certainly wasn't any goat.

Similarly, there was some terrible robbery at work the night Papa had to move his old house miles away in a village where no one knew him. For how could a man like Papa start learning new people: Papa who was the very meaning of greatness in the shop where he had worked, even then, as a cooper. There was no one in my village within word reach of that corner whom Papa had not earned the right to rebuke. His age was not just years, but a whole way of being together with generations of children whom he had seen mature into fathers, or stumble, one way and another, into disgrace. This was the same Papa whom a wicked arrangement of money had forced to move, making a cheap market of every pigeon and all but one goat. The land had been sold to a new syndicate who were black men; but Papa had to leave because he couldn't afford to pay cash for his tenancy, or risk instalments on behalf of a future which could not be very long. He was already over seventy.

The village carpenters dismantled the old house. Board by single board, they lifted partition and roof away; we laid every inch of his wooden refuge over the wide push cart, and the village carpenters carried that Rock which was Papa's Castle miles away at night and among people who would probably pass him on the street next morning: another foreign, old face, wrinkled and ready to die.

Such a man could have nothing left but the richness of his skin which clearly told his age, and the wisdom it concealed from those who were too Innocent to know. I was now a big boy, natural as any prince in High School uniform: a young tiger in sky-blue blazer with yellow braid the colour of ripe citrus. Papa had rejoiced the day news came that a scholarship had opened the doors of that school to one of his boys. Merit and charity had blessed his old age; for it was his ambition that all of his boys should, at least, go there. And his ambition for one boy was too large to let him see or care that this school had one intention: that it was training me to forget and be separate from the things that Papa was: peasant and alive.

The carpenters knew me as a gentleman by daylight; and I don't think I would have liked anyone from the school to see me that night; for I walked all the way—not me so much as the force within which binds me eternally to the root that was Papa—miles and each mile an eternity I walked, crying like an infant, every step of the way beside that push cart with Papa's watch dog on my left. And the meaning of Papa's departure is the story of *In the Castle of My Skin*.

I first came across the phrase, 'castle of my skin,' in a poem by the West Indian poet, Derek Walcott. In a great torrent of rage inseparable from hate, the poet is addressing some white presence, and the assault is stated: 'You in the castle of your skin, I among the swineherd.' This phrase had coincided with my search for a title, and I remembered that night and knew that in spite of his Age, meaning Skin, Papa could never possibly see himself among swine. Nor could the village. So I thought it was correct, and even necessary to appropriate that image in order to restore the castle where it belonged.

Papa's Rock had been taken, his Castle ignored; but Papa would always remain. That journey was a lesson in exile and permanence; that night was a colonial example of alienation. It must have been the origin of that farewell which Papa and I bade each other in the book which was built on his Rock.

*'I know it in my heart o' hearts I won't set foot here again,' he said. He had rested a hand on my shoulder. Then he took it away and as quickly put it back. I had an idea what had happened but I wasn't sure he would have liked me to talk about it. The Alms House wasn't the kind of residence one admitted. I know that. I wanted to find out what he thought about going, but it seemed silly to ask him. What could he feel? Moreover, I didn't want to arouse any unbearable emotions. I didn't know how long he had lived in the village, but I was sure it was longer than any of the villagers I knew. He had known the shoemaker as a boy.*

*'We both settin' forth tomorrow,' he said. 'I to my last restin'-place before the grave, an' you into the wide wide world.'*

*I stood for a moment waiting to see whether he might put on the light. The feeling had seized me again. You had seen the last of something.*

*''Twus a night like this nine years ago when those waters roll.' The village/my mother/a boy among the boys/a man who knew his people won't feel*

*alone/to be a different kind of creature. Words and voices falling like a full shower and the old man returning with the pebble under the grape leaf on the sand: You won't see me again, my son.*

*The earth where I walked was a marvel of blackness and I knew in a sense more deep than simple departure I had said farewell, farewell to the land.*

And we were both right. I would have liked to read him back his own dialogue; but I was already in exile here. Then my mother wrote to say that she had taken the book with the rumour of praise, for Papa to share. In the new village he had spent most of his time in bed. Papa recognised her voice; he could never forget my name; but the Castle and the Skin made no sense at all. He could follow nothing she said: for he was dying. An interval of days and he was dead! It was as though his Rock had returned in the shape of a wreath bound by hard covers and abundant with words which told his way of talking.

Papa was a colonial; so am I; so is our once absolute Prospero. For it is that mutual experience of separation from their original ground which makes both master and slave colonial. To be colonial is to be in a state of exile. And the exile is always colonial by circumstances: a man colonised by his incestuous love of a past whose glory is not worth our total human suicide; colonised by a popular whoredom of talents whose dividends he knows he does not deserve; colonised by an abstract conscience which must identify its need with another's distress through a process of affection called justice; colonised by the barely liveable acceptance of domestic complaint; colonised, if black in skin, by the agonising assault of the other's eye whose meanings are based on a way of seeing he vainly tries to alter; and ultimately colonised by some absent vision which, for want of another faith, he hopefully calls the Future.

But the mystery of the colonial is this: while he remains alive, his instinct, always and for ever creative, must choose a way to change the meaning and perspective of this ancient tyranny.

There is, for me, some deep bond between Papa's dead hands and Selvon's living generosity; the generosity that shapes every life in his books. For Selvon never sneers at his characters. He is always with them in what they are doing, the foolish things as well as the beautiful things. If Papa is a colonial symbol of traditional man; then the lives embodied in Selvon's prose are peasants preparing for a Season of Adventure.

And this is the theme of my work for Tomorrow!

LONDON:
15th December, 1959 – 5th February, 1960.

# INDEX

## Ann Arbor Paperbacks

Waddell, *The Desert Fathers*
Erasmus, *The Praise of Folly*
Donne, *Devotions*
Malthus, *Population: The First Essay*
Berdyaev, *The Origin of Russian Communism*
Einhard, *The Life of Charlemagne*
Edwards, *The Nature of True Virtue*
Gilson, *Héloïse and Abélard*
Aristotle, *Metaphysics*
Kant, *Education*
Boulding, *The Image*
Duckett, *The Gateway to the Middle Ages*
  (3 vols.): *Italy; France and Britain;
  Monasticism*
Bowditch and Ramsland, *Voices of the
  Industrial Revolution*
Luxemburg, *The Russian Revolution* and
  *Leninism or Marxism?*
Rexroth, *Poems from the Greek Anthology*
Zoshchenko, *Scenes from the Bathhouse*
Thrupp, *The Merchant Class of Medieval
  London*
Procopius, *Secret History*
Adcock, *Roman Political Ideas and Practice*
Swanson, *The Birth of the Gods*
Xenophon, *The March Up Country*
Buchanan and Tullock, *The Calculus of
  Consent*
Hobson, *Imperialism*
Kinietz, *The Indians of the Western Great
  Lakes 1615–1760*
Bromage, *Writing for Business*
Lurie, *Mountain Wolf Woman, Sister of
  Crashing Thunder*
Leonard, *Baroque Times in Old Mexico*
Meier, *Negro Thought in America,
  1880–1915*
Burke, *The Philosophy of Edmund Burke*
Michelet, *Joan of Arc*
Conze, *Buddhist Thought in India*
Arberry, *Aspects of Islamic Civilization*
Chesnutt, *The Wife of His Youth and
  Other Stories*
Gross, *Sound and Form in Modern Poetry*
Zola, *The Masterpiece*
Chesnutt, *The Marrow of Tradition*
Aristophanes, *Four Comedies*
Aristophanes, *Three Comedies*
Chesnutt, *The Conjure Woman*
Duckett, *Carolingian Portraits*
Rapoport and Chammah, *Prisoner's Dilemma*
Aristotle, *Poetics*
Peattie, *The View from the Barrio*

Duckett, *Death and Life in the Tenth Century*
Langford, *Galileo, Science and the Church*
McNaughton, *The Taoist Vision*
Anderson, *Matthew Arnold and the Classical
  Tradition*
Milio, *9226 Kercheval*
Breton, *Manifestoes of Surrealism*
Scholz, *Carolingian Chronicles*
Wik, *Henry Ford and Grass-roots America*
Sahlins and Service, *Evolution and Culture*
Wickham, *Early Medieval Italy*
Waddell, *The Wandering Scholars*
Mannoni, *Prospero and Caliban*
Aron, *Democracy and Totalitarianism*
Shy, *A People Numerous and Armed*
Taylor, *Roman Voting Assemblies*
Hesiod, *The Works and Days; Theogony; The
  Shield of Herakles*
Raverat, *Period Piece*
Lamming, *In the Castle of My Skin*
Fisher, *The Conjure-Man Dies*
Strayer, *The Albigensian Crusades*
Lamming, *The Pleasures of Exile*
Lamming, *Natives of My Person*
Glaspell, *Lifted Masks and Other Works*
Grand, *The Heavenly Twins*
Cornford, *The Origin of Attic Comedy*
Allen, *Wolves of Minong*
Fisher, *The Walls of Jericho*
Lamming, *The Emigrants*
Loudon, *The Mummy!*
Kemble and Butler Leigh, *Principles and
  Privilege*
Thomas, *Out of Time*
Flanagan, *You Alone Are Dancing*
Kotre and Hall, *Seasons of Life*
Shen, *Almost a Revolution*
Meckel, *Save the Babies*
Laver and Schofield, *Multiparty Government*
Rutt, *The Bamboo Grove*
Endelman, *The Jews of Georgian England,
  1714–1830*
Lamming, *Season of Adventure*
Radin, *Crashing Thunder*
Mirel, *The Rise and Fall of an Urban School
  System*
Brainard, *When the Rainbow Goddess Wept*
Brook, *Documents on the Rape of Nanking*
Mendel, *Vision and Violence*
Hymes, *Reinventing Anthropology*
Mulroy, *Early Greek Lyric Poetry*
Siegel, *The Rope of God*
Buss, *La Partera*